THE STORIES OLD TOWNS TELL

THE STORIES OLD TOWNS TELL

A JOURNEY THROUGH CITIES AT THE HEART OF EUROPE

MAREK KOHN

YALE UNIVERSITY PRESS
NEW HAVEN AND LONDON

For information about this and other Yale University Press publications, please contact:
U.S. Office: sales.press@yale.edu   yalebooks.com
Europe Office: sales@yaleup.co.uk   yalebooks.co.uk

Set in Adobe Caslon Pro by IDSUK (DataConnection) Ltd
Printed in Great Britain by TJ Books, Padstow, Cornwall

Library of Congress Control Number: 2022948967

ISBN 978-0-300-26784-6

A catalogue record for this book is available from the British Library.

10 9 8 7 6 5 4 3 2 1

For Sue and Teo

Contents

CONTENTS

VILNIUS

MIDDLE EUROPE

LUBLIN

PRAGUE

FRANKFURT AM MAIN

MIDDLE EUROPE

Illustrations

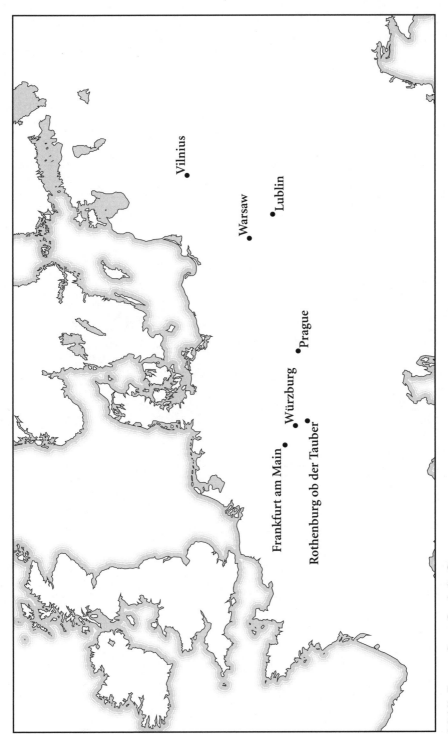

Middle Europe: Seven Symbolic Quarters

Introduction
Seven Symbolic Quarters

In the summer of 2017, I was invited to answer a questionnaire for 'Conversations with Europe', an online project created by Rebecca Buck, a pro-European blogger. One of the questions was 'Do you have a favourite place in Europe? If so, where is it and why do you love it?'

I only had to think about that for a moment before I saw the answer in my mind's eye. 'The Old Town,' I replied. 'It has a cobbled square, lots of Gothic overhangs, colourful heraldry featuring lions and boars' heads, narrow alleys and not many right angles. It is in my imagination, as well as in the middle of many European cities, and I love it because it is the heart of my Europe.'[1]

The idea for this book grew from that reply, but it had a lifetime behind it. When I was a young child, my first journey abroad took me from England to the heart of Europe. It crossed the two countries in which most of this book's action takes place, Germany and Poland, although in those days Germany itself was two countries. I was just old enough to be anxious about what would happen when we came to what was known as the Iron Curtain, and then to be a little disappointed that there was no great metal barrier across the railway lines running into East Berlin, just a guard in a sentry box at the side of the track. My anxieties were revived by the East German security officer who boarded the train, and I must have been relieved when he finally decided our papers were in order. Did he have a green uniform with a pistol in a holster? In my memory it seems that he did. A column of tanks had clattered past, borne on the wagons of a goods train, as we waited on a platform in West Germany. Deep inside Poland, a station's pre-war German name was visible through a fading coat of paint on its signal box.

These scenes of division and the shadows of war impressed Europe's history upon me. Time has passed; Europe's history has continued to unfold: while the images in my memory have become attenuated, their lessons have grown more profound. But they haven't diminished the appeal of the fantasy Old Town, definitely Middle European as far as I'm concerned, in which history is charming and harmless. If anything, they have enhanced it. A comfortingly half-timbered and cobbled historic European quarter is the ideal spot for a brief escape from European history repeating itself.

The journey's destination was the town of Toruń, where the Polish side of my family has had a home since before the war. Toruń's centre, proudly Gothic, was my first Old Town, and I still feel it to be part of my personal heritage – despite having previously failed to learn from its robust grid-plan that some of the finest Old Towns in Europe are built on right angles. When I visited it in 2018, to register my details after recovering the Polish citizenship that had been revoked before my childhood visit, I took the opportunity to orient myself for an exploration of Old Towns. I found a gazetteer laid out along the central street: a series of tablets bearing the heraldic shields of cities to which Toruń had been linked by trade networks, reaching westwards as far as Leiden and Cologne, during the Middle Ages and the Renaissance. With the Iron Curtain gone and borders within the European Union mostly not even a formality, the city had celebrated its historic place in Europe by selecting symbols from its past that claimed a place for it in Europe's future. The tablets form an

1. A town hall, a cathedral, city walls, tenement houses and the remains of a castle: Toruń boasts a full set of Old Town features.

elegant display, and a neat illustration of how Old Towns are made to work.[2]

Another Old Town occupied a special place in the stories about Poland's history and character that I was told as a child. It was at the heart of the story of Warsaw's destruction by Nazi German occupiers and the Polish capital's post-war reconstruction, in which Poles cleared the rubble by hand and then painstakingly recreated the Old Town in its historic form. The lesson was that despite the extraordinary barbarities visited upon Poland by its enemies, the nation's spirit could not be broken. It was a lesson not just for Poles but for the world at large, as President Biden affirmed when he spoke at Warsaw's Royal Castle, which forms an ensemble with the adjacent Old Town, a month after Russia launched its assault on Ukraine. 'We are gathered here at the Royal Castle in this city that holds a sacred place in the history not only of Europe, but humankind's unending search for freedom,' he declared. As Joe Biden and his team appreciated, the Castle was a setting of ideal symbolic aptness for the American president's history-defining message, that democracy faced 'years and decades' of struggle against the forces of autocracy.[3]

By using the Royal Castle as the stage for a rallying speech in response to Russia's invasion, Biden demonstrated that historic quarters are not just reserves for relics, but live sites with roles to play in current affairs and contemporary consciousness. A further demonstration followed in the summer, when the wrecks of Russian armoured vehicles knocked out by Ukrainian forces were put on display in the square between the Royal Castle and the Old Town. The oxidised armour, symbolising the possibility that Russia could be defeated, was thus posed against a background of buildings rebuilt after their destruction by the Nazi aggressors. Introducing the exhibit, the Polish prime minister's chief of staff declared that the square embodies 'the heroism of the Polish defenders during the Warsaw Uprising', while also standing as a witness to the devastation inflicted on the city by the occupiers. 'Today we are dealing with a similar situation in Ukraine,' he observed, 'Russian barbarians . . . are destroying villages and cities.' The story of Warsaw's Old Town in 1944 was summoned up to help tell the story of Ukrainian cities in 2022.[4]

On another front, a few months before Russia's onslaught initiated a new phase of Europe's history, Poland's justice minister welcomed the European Union's Commissioner for Justice to Warsaw with a framed photo of the Old Town laid waste after the Nazi occupation. Having previously accused the European Union of waging 'hybrid war' against Poland, in a dispute about Polish government actions that the EU regarded as threats to the rule of law, the minister explained that his passive-aggressive gift symbolised Poland's sensitivities about the equal treatment of nations. It certainly illustrated the indestructible symbolic authority of the Old Town's ruins, the moral foundation of the reconstructed quarter.[5]

As a child of Polish heritage, I was awed and filled with pride by Poland's great national stories. As a person of both British and Polish heritage, I've gone through life with a constant background awareness that one story is never the whole story, a belief that it is better to bring identities together than to keep them apart, and a sense that stories are enriched by informing each other. I found a text that spoke to those feelings in a third Old Town, that of Lublin in south-eastern Poland, where one of the old gatehouse buildings has been turned into a centre devoted to the memory of the city's Jewish population, exterminated in the Holocaust. A panel on the wall addresses a frequently asked question:

> Jews who come here ask us: Why do you do this? After all, you are not Jewish. You are Poles and the Jewish town is not your history.
>
> Poles ask us: Why do you do this? After all, you are Poles and the Jewish town is not our history. Or maybe you are Jewish?
>
> We explain patiently that it is our common, Polish-Jewish history.
>
> To remember the murdered Jews you do not have to be Jewish.

Like the mathematical models that scientists devise in order to clarify the complexities of life, this sequence demonstrates the power and the necessity of simplification. In most contexts, unqualified distinctions between 'Jews' and 'Poles' act to efface the possibility that people might be both Jewish and Polish. Here the binary acts in the opposite direction. It serves to heighten the rhetorical contrast, and thereby to sharpen the argument that the two groups are more closely intertwined than is widely assumed.

Those who read the Polish and Hebrew versions of the text will be aware of the fraught histories that lie behind it. But those who read the text in English may not appreciate the implications that underlie Polish questions about whether a person is Jewish, or the undermining effects that they can have upon both public and personal conversation. As it happened, I encountered the question myself at the end of the tour, in a gallery dedicated to 'Righteous' non-Jewish Poles who helped Jewish compatriots during the war. When I remarked that one of the Jews mentioned in a panel had the same name as me, the guide suggested that I might be a relative. I replied that from what I knew of my family tree, it was very unlikely. He gave me a sceptical look that made it plain he thought I was denying Jewish ancestry. I'm reluctant to answer the question because it is always loaded, one way or another, and also because the full answer remains mysterious. But I'm happy to imagine that my surname marks a time when Jewish and Christian Poles could be relatively relaxed about interlinking their family histories through marriage.

There is too much to say on these themes, and often the more that is said, the more difficult it becomes to resolve them. Sometimes divisive certainties are best countered not by nuance but by a simple and bold declaration of values. The assertion of a 'common, Polish-Jewish history' was like a revelation that I already knew, filling me with a sweet sense of recognition, gratitude and relief combined. I still feel heartened when I look at the photo I took of the panel, and reassured that better histories are possible.

A cobbled square in an old quarter of a European city, filled with people eating ice creams and chatting in their various languages, is a scene of triumph. Historic spaces in which people gather together freely and convivially, among strangers but at ease with them, represent how far the continent has succeeded in transcending its history. Turning the past into picturesque ambience, they convey a sense of safety and peace. Where the remnants of old defensive walls still stand, the obsolete masonry offers the reassuring suggestion that the age of conflicts was a long time ago. Old Towns affirm that the European condition need not be one of eternal conflict between endlessly arising and realigning adversaries. They are beacons of the redemptive European project.

The message is especially eloquent in cities that were devastated during the Second World War and then divided from each other for more than forty years of cold war by the Iron Curtain. In the heart of Europe – Germany and the lands to its east – the most catastrophic episodes in the Old Towns' long histories took place within living memory, during the Second World War: firestorms, massacres, ethnic cleansing, genocide. Those were the foundations upon which historic quarters were rebuilt into urban arcadias. When the Cold War and the twentieth century were finally behind them, the region's Old Towns completed their transformation from places in which war seemed inescapable to ones in which it seemed unimaginable – at least until Russia brought the fear of imperial aggression back to Europe once again.

The facades plastered over the fractures, though. Old Towns make harmonious compositions out of history by omitting, erasing or downplaying some of its storylines. Since the end of the Second World War, Old Towns have been painstakingly constructed to narrate their histories selectively, edited to highlight some strands while occluding others. To regard the work done on them as simply preservation, the respectful maintenance of a relic island while the rest of the city gets on with its dynamic urban life, is to miss the point of Old Towns. They are the central symbolic districts of cities, their role as fundamental as those of the central business districts or government quarters. Old Towns are foci of collective memory that make suggestions about collective character. They are nuclei of identity, representing nations and peoples as well as the cities in which they are embedded.[6]

That is inevitably a work in progress, for identities are always changing, and their supporting narratives need to be adjusted with them – either to acknowledge change or to pretend that it doesn't happen. Old Towns are always under construction. They are refurbished, restored, reframed, and sometimes rebuilt altogether. Frankfurt am Main opened its 'new Old Town' in 2018, against a backdrop of skyscrapers. It was the latest rethink for a German city still uncertain about what kind of relationship it should have with its past, more than seventy years after the end of the war.

By that point, Europeans seemed to have forgotten the lesson of the war, that they must build a new common history dating from 1945. Fewer and fewer of those who had learned it through personal experience were still alive, and as the last of those who had actually fought the war approached extinction, the mood changed. Perhaps it was not entirely coincidental that Europe and the wider world underwent a shift away from openness, amid loud demands to put nations first and to define them narrowly. Neighbours were to be begrudged and strangers to be regarded with suspicion. People wanted their borders back.

Two years after the opening of Frankfurt's new Old Town, they got them. Lines that had become visible only on maps became impassable barriers as European states sealed themselves off in response to the coronavirus pandemic. The eerie emptiness of public spaces provided a jarring illustration of why we should treasure the sight of people wandering through cobbled streets, eating ice creams and mingling with each other freely. And two years after that, as coronavirus restrictions were beginning to be lifted, Russia's attack on Ukraine showed that European cities could still be devastated by bombardment. The onslaught was brutal proof that however far Europe has come since 1945, it has not come far enough.

These developments have thrown the significance of Old Towns into relief. Zones that have been configured to promote singular historical narratives, rather than to interweave the plural histories that they could represent, form a constellation that documents the post-war history of European nationalism itself. If Europe is to hold together instead of pulling itself apart, it has to find ways of reconciling its histories. With their densely packed payloads of symbols, its Old Towns are key sites not just of its past, but also for its future. Their potential for telling inclusive stories has not yet been fully explored. As the American literary critic Van Wyck Brooks observed in 1918, the past 'is an inexhaustible storehouse of apt attitudes and adaptable ideals'. It can furnish a selection of attitudes and ideals to match those favoured in any subsequent period, enabling the compilation of what Brooks called a 'usable past'.[7]

Around the world, history is returning with a plethora of vengeances. People are turning to the past from different sides. Some want a reckoning with it; others want to live in it. For people of diverse backgrounds to live well together, they need to develop narratives that integrate their histories, or at least to create frameworks in which their different narratives can co-exist. That is also the problem that Old Towns pose. The question of how to represent plural and sometimes conflicting histories within them has a significance far beyond those highly charged symbolic spaces.

To explore it, we have to lift the cobbles and look at the layer of ash underneath. That stratum represents the devastation of cities by carpet bombing, urban battles and, in the case of Warsaw, systematic demolition by enemy troops. Cities in the core of Europe restarted their histories in 1945 upon three founding conditions: the destruction of urban fabric, the genocide of Jewish populations, and the replacement of pre-war inhabitants by people drawn or driven from other places. Although these conditions did not have a uniform impact throughout the region, they defined its post-war landscape. Journeys to the heart of Europe were journeys to the scenes of the most dreadful events in the continent's history, some of them still unfolding. Because it was the zone of greatest devastation, and because new ideological orders were being imposed upon it, this was the region where the most radical questions about reconstruction were posed. That is the decisive reason why this book explores places within the sweep of continental heartland east of the Rhine – Middle Europe can serve as a label for the region, so as to avoid the connotations of Mitteleuropa (Viennese-flavoured nostalgia, bygone German political ambitions) and historians' arguments about where Central Europe is – but not across the entire map of the continent.

The book spends much of its time in Polish cities, past and present. It was emotionally natural for me to use my personal heritage as a basis for examining a constellation of European heritage, and analytically logical. Middle Europe's eastern half offers many paths to understanding Europe as a whole, some of them clearer than the ones taken in regions to the west that are inclined to consider themselves more central and significant. In particular, the post-war role of nationalism can be followed more easily in the east than in Germany, where nationalist currents were stifled and confounded by the defeat of their Nazi variant. More fundamentally, awareness of the eastern half's history inculcates the awareness my first journey across Middle Europe helped to impress upon me, that peace cannot be taken for granted. The burned-out armour displayed against a backdrop of reconstructed Old Town houses in Warsaw serves as a dramatically apt symbol for that lesson. I did not know that an aggressor would start a war in Europe before I completed this book, but I wrote it because I was alarmed by the growth of the tensions and divisions that find their most extreme form in war. The centrality of the lands east of Germany has now become more widely apparent.

More of the book's time is spent in Warsaw's Old Town and its surrounding stories, of the people and the political forces that shaped its reconstruction, than in any of the other sites. The Old Town's wartime drama is uniquely compelling: a siege that became a crucial battle and ended in a tragic defeat, followed by massacres and the near-total destruction of the quarter. Its post-war story is also unique, for although it was not the only historic district in the region to be left almost completely in ruins, it was the only one to be entirely rebuilt in the image of its former self. The resurrection impressed foreign onlookers as a demonstration of national resolve, and presented a model for reconstruction that challenged internationally accepted views about the legitimacy of replicas. It became a landmark in post-war European debates about the preservation of heritage. France's minister of culture, the novelist André Malraux, invoked it when he spoke in support of a heritage law framed to protect districts as well as individual buildings. 'Let's not allow the old streets of Avignon to be destroyed at a time when Poland has rebuilt the oldest square in Warsaw stone by stone,' he urged. As a furiously modernising Europe remade itself in concrete, raising tower-blocks in place of houses and driving highways through city centres, Warsaw's Old Town offered the continent a lesson in values. Sometimes the past was so precious that it had to be recreated if it had ceased to exist.[8]

The story of the Old Town is the story of the people who tried to protect it in the war, and rebuilt it afterwards. Right from the start of the occupation, people trained in disciplines surrounding heritage risked, and sometimes lost, their lives trying to save it. Architects, conservators and art historians became soldiers of the underground state, with special responsibility for protecting the documentation that would be needed to repair the city's losses. They held soldiers' ranks, and some of them bore arms. After the war, they had to decide whether to work for the reconstruction under a regime that was locking up their former comrades and denouncing the state that they had served. They chose to rebuild, for the sake of the nation, directed by authorities that saw heritage such as the Old Town as a vital resource in the struggle for Polish hearts and minds.

Warsaw's Old Town is one of seven main sites in this book. They form a loose arc spanning Middle Europe, from Germany to Lithuania, and they offer answers to a complex of questions: how they fared before the war and what happened to them during it; how they were reconstructed afterwards and why; what they remembered and what they forgot; what stories they told, and what stories they could tell.

WARSAW

Chapter 1
Market to Monument

Warsaw's founding kernel has been old for a long time. The zone within the city's medieval walls first acquired the label in the fifteenth century, when a 'New Town' development began to arise next to it. At that stage, Warsaw was a provincial city of modest importance. Its status relative to that of Kraków, where the Polish kings had their seat, can be measured by the area of its central Market Square. At four hectares, Kraków's king-size Market Square is six times larger.[1]

The balance of power began to shift towards Warsaw in the sixteenth century. In 1569, the Kingdom of Poland and the Grand Duchy of Lithuania were joined together by the Union of Lublin, named after the southern city in which it was signed. The agreement created a dual state known as the Republic (or Commonwealth, as modern English-language texts conventionally have it) which in those days did not mean a state without kings. It was a vast, sprawling entity with two capitals, Kraków and Vilnius, far apart from each other. Warsaw lies roughly midway between them, so the Union of Lublin decreed that it should be the site for the dual state's parliament. In 1596, King Zygmunt III Waza decided to move his court there from Kraków. The castle that presided over the Old Town became the Royal Castle, and Warsaw became Poland's capital city.[2]

Within the walls, the Old Town began to acquire its definitive form, assisted by a fire that destroyed a large part of the quarter in 1607. Burned-out Gothic tenement houses were rebuilt in late Renaissance and early baroque styles; the neighbourhood became a showcase for mercantile prosperity. Its heyday lasted into the eighteenth century, but its prestige diminished as the nobility moved out to the suburbs where there was room for them to build palaces. Meanwhile the Polish-Lithuanian Republic grew increasingly weak and vulnerable to its neighbours, Russia, Prussia and Austria, which divided it up in a series of partitions. By the end of the century they had removed it from the map altogether, and Warsaw was no longer the capital of a sovereign nation. The Old Town lost its role as an annexe to the centre of political power, and went into decline. As the wealthy bourgeoisie moved out, the Market Square filled up with humble traders. The neighbourhood that had boasted Warsaw's wealthiest residents became home to many of the city's poorest inhabitants.[3]

At the beginning of the twentieth century, a plan to put a market hall on the Square was met with dismay in Warsaw's cultural circles. The Old Town was following a storyline similar to those that unfolded in historic quarters across Middle Europe, of deterioration in the nineteenth century and adoption by heritage protectors in the twentieth. Its principal advocate was a national organisation rather than a group of local enthusiasts. In 1911 the Society for the Care of Monuments of the Past established its headquarters on the Market Square, taking over a tenement house named after the building's seventeenth-century merchant owners, the Baryczka family.

The move reasserted the central place of the Old Town in Poland's symbolic landscape. It was followed in short order by the clearance of the market from the Market Square, which received a makeover that the heritage activists considered more appropriate to its status, giving it a more monumental character. The statue that served as its centrepiece and represented Warsaw's heraldic emblem, a mermaid brandishing a sword, was raised up and placed on a pedestal.

By turning the Baryczka house into a hub for gatherings and exhibitions, the Society furthered its aim of strengthening the cultural communities that were striving to protect the nation's heritage under foreign rule. Members of the Society supported the project with ventures into gentrification, buying Old Town tenement houses and doing them up. The new owners included several architects, a painter and a poet, known by the nom de plume Or-Ot, who wrote lyrical verse devoted to the Old Town. Visits to the Baryczka house and the surrounding quarter were not only fashionable but also, according to the Society's president, acts of opposition to the city's Russian over-lords. In 1916, the four rows of tenement houses framing the Market Square were named after eminent civic Varsovians who had been active in the years before Poland's independence was extinguished. It was a notable early step in the process of converting the Old Town into an exhibition space for the teaching of history and the promo-tion of national consciousness.[4]

At the end of the First World War, Poland returned to the map as an independent state, following the collapse of the three empires that had partitioned the Polish-Lithuanian Republic between them. The Second Republic resembled its predecessor in that it stretched a long way to the east and contained a variety of ethnic groups. Nearly four million Ukrainians found themselves within the borders of the new state, as did two million Jews, the second largest minority. In all, the minorities added up to more than 30 per cent of the population.[5]

Warsaw was thus the capital of a nation whose form was consistent with the vision of its dominant political figure, Józef Piłsudski, who became the head of the restored Poland. Piłsudski believed that the new republic needed territories beyond its heartland, so that it would be big enough to hold its own as a regional power, and he was confi-dent that it could incorporate ethnic minorities as citizens. He hankered after an even closer resemblance to the old 'Republic of Both Nations', but his proposals for a federation with Lithuania fell on stony ground. Instead he had to satisfy himself with holding

Vilnius, thereby creating a sacred cause for Lithuanian nationalists and setting the two countries at odds for the remainder of their spell of independence between the world wars.[6]

The dream of creating a new Polish-Lithuanian republic was not shared by Piłsudski's great rival, Roman Dmowski, the grand theorist of Polish ethnic nationalism and the leader of the National Democracy movement. Dmowski understood the nation as a single living organism with a unique spirit formed from culture, history, language, tradition and race. He maintained that minorities posed threats to the Polish nation simply by their presence, undermining Polish culture by exposing it to contact with their own. While he considered that Slavic minorities could be neutralised by assimilating them into the Polish majority, he denied that Jews could ever be Poles. In his view, Jewish culture was so strong and so alien that it posed a lethal threat to the Polish nation. Assimilation was even more threatening than the continued existence of separate Jewish communities, because it brought toxically incompatible Jewish elements into Polish Christian society. 'Mingling with the majority of them would lead to our destruction,' he warned.[7]

After the restoration of independence, Dmowski was faced not only with a country in which minorities comprised three-tenths of the population, but also a capital city in which a third of the population was Jewish. Warsaw was the scene of intense cultural mingling, in which Jewish Poles made some of the period's richest contributions to Polish literature and arts. It was a metropolis in the international style, boasting a city centre bright with neon lights and nightclubs – and that was an affront to nationalists who dreamed of a 'Great Poland' from which foreign influences would be purged. Piłsudski kept the National Democrats and their ilk in check, but they lost no time in stepping up their antisemitic agitation after his death in 1935. As well as organising boycotts of Jewish businesses, an increasingly radical nationalist front campaigned to exclude Jews from higher education and the professions. It scored a stunning success within Warsaw's architectural milieu, tearing a hole in the city's cultural fabric.[8]

For its part, the Old Town continued on the path of cultural gentrification set by the heritage society before the First World War. Tenement houses on the Market Square accommodated a publishing society, two writers' associations and the editorial offices of a historical journal. The priorities were those suggested by the pre-war redevelopment of the Square, which had entailed the eviction of the market stallholders. Concern for the status and appearance of the quarter was not matched by concern for the needs of its residents, many of whom lived in mouldering and overcrowded squalor. In 1928, the houses on the Market Square were painted with polychrome decorations to celebrate the Second Republic's tenth anniversary. The facelift was not a triumph. Commentators criticised both the quality of the painting and the decision to lavish money on facades, instead of repairing the decaying houses of the district and alleviating the living conditions of the people crammed into them. The parlous state of the quarter was highlighted by reports of the collapse of tenement houses, said to have been shaken apart by the increasing number of motor vehicles that rasped their way through the district.[9]

A number of buildings were demolished deliberately, to expose a surviving stretch of the medieval defensive walls that had defined the area of the Old Town. Directed by Jan Zachwatowicz, an architect and conservation expert, the project was intended to expand the quarter's function as a museum of itself, and to enhance it with a public amenity in the form of gardens between the double walls. Zachwatowicz also oversaw works for the conversion of the Baryczka house and two of its neighbours into a Museum of Old Warsaw, following the acquisition of the buildings by the city in the late 1930s. The Museum was planned to open in the autumn of 1939, but by that time the forces of the Third Reich had invaded Poland, the Second Republic had fallen, and Warsaw was under German occupation.[10]

Chapter 2
Soldier-Architects

When Maria Huber set out to meet her professors, she did not know whether her journey would end in a Warsaw apartment or a German labour camp. The train from Kraków left around midnight, but she had to get to the station several hours earlier, before the curfew, and then struggle to board amid the throng of people who pushed through the coach doors and clambered in through the windows. Many were traders, stuffing the carriages with huge bundles of goods, leaving little room even to breathe on the eight-hour overnight journey. All were vulnerable to roundups, in which passengers were ordered off the train and into trucks that took them away to forced labour in Nazi Germany. Maria made the trip to Warsaw about once a month, for a year and a half.[1]

Her luck almost ran out on one of those occasions, when her train was emptied for a roundup, but her acting skills saved her. She went up to the SS officer in charge of the operation and told him, in German, that she absolutely had to be in Warsaw the next day, in connection with matters very important to the Reich. The SS man let her get back on board, but nobody else. Maria continued her journey with just three other passengers for company, men who had managed to escape the sweep by hiding in the toilets.

There could hardly have been a more dramatic contrast with the beginning of her studies. Maria had spent the last part of her first year as an architecture student in the picturesque southern Polish highlands, surveying traditional wooden buildings. That was in the summer of 1939, though, and the exercise was terminated prematurely. When Poland mobilised its armed forces in the final days of August, the students were hurriedly cleared out of their summer lodgings. On 1 September, the Nazi regime launched its invasion; on 1 October, its forces took control of Warsaw. The country was overrun from both sides, Germany taking the west and the Soviet Union the east, and wiped off the map.

Maria had been enrolled in the country's leading architectural school, Warsaw Polytechnic's Faculty of Architecture. The German occupiers closed the Polytechnic, along with all the other higher education institutions in the territories under their control. Professor Oskar Sosnowski, the instigator of the students' fieldwork courses, was killed in the siege of the capital. He had moved himself and his family into the Faculty of Architecture building, in order to safeguard its collections; a few days before the city's surrender, he was fatally wounded by a bomb that hit the courtyard. Sosnowski was the founder of the Institute of Polish Architecture, a historically oriented body within the Faculty. The field surveys were a core element of the Institute's activities, and formed an important part of the archives that he had died trying to protect. They had a dual purpose, being intended not only to train students in core skills, but also to produce an inventory of Poland's built heritage. After the city sustained damage to its Royal Castle and trauma to its fabric from the German assault, Sosnowski's documents took on a profound new significance as records of lost or threatened national heritage, and blueprints for reconstruction.[2]

Sosnowski was succeeded by his colleague Jan Zachwatowicz, who risked his life to recover another archive of historic building documentation in the aftermath of Warsaw's fall. The records were stored in a basement of what had hitherto been the Ministry of Religious Affairs and Public Education, but was now the headquarters of the Nazi secret police, known as the Gestapo. An art historian who had been in charge of the state art collections heard that the occupiers were planning to throw the records out. Fortunately, the Gestapo had not yet dismissed all the building's Polish staff, one of whom opened a gate for Zachwatowicz, the art historian and several helpers from the Faculty of Architecture to drive through in a truck; even more fortunately, the Gestapo officers who saw them assumed that they were on authorised business. They made two trips, recovering 138 boxes of materials and transferring them to the Architecture Faculty building. The Gestapo subsequently used the basement to hold and interrogate prisoners; the architects used the documents to rebuild the capital.[3]

Warsaw's rebuilders also made use of fragments that Zachwatowicz had helped to recover from the damaged Royal Castle in the bitter winter after the conquest. Zachwatowicz had joined the army when the war broke out, and had been awarded the military Cross of Valour ten days before Poland capitulated. He was the model of the soldier-architect, a hybrid combatant variety on whom the nation's built heritage came to depend, both during the war and after it.[4]

Under the leadership of 'Professor Jan', Sosnowski's former colleagues and students continued the inventory work during the occupation, surveying buildings in Warsaw's Old Town and other districts of the city. It was a kind of unwritten testament, observed Maria Huber's fiancé, Kazimierz Maciej Piechotka, who had been a student and then a teacher in the Institute of Polish Architecture. He was also a soldier-architect, active in the 'Conspiracy', as the resistance against the occupiers was known.[5]

The lie that Huber told the SS officer contained a bold truth. By pursuing her studies, she was indeed engaged on a matter of great importance to the Reich. Nazi policy was resolved to destroy Poland's intellectual and cultural resources as well as the structures of its state.

The occupiers had made their intentions clear in the autumn of 1939, by arresting nearly 200 academics at the Jagiellonian University in Kraków and dispatching them to a concentration camp. Thousands of educated people perished in systematic campaigns of mass murder directed against the 'intelligentsia'. The aim was to deprive the nation of its elites, so that it would be incapable of reclaiming its place on the map.

In response, Poland built a state that conducted resistance through education as well as espionage and ambushes. The Polytechnic architects and their students set up a secret Faculty of Architecture, in which qualifications were awarded and plans for post-war reconstruction drawn up. Its dean, a civil engineer named Stefan Bryła, held classes and oversaw doctoral examinations in his apartment. Faculty members led a dual life, concealing their covert activities behind those that the occupiers still permitted, which included municipal work and interior design. They were able to return to their building in 1941, thanks to the German authorities' decision to install a technical school for construction skills in it. Although Nazi ideology held that Poles should be deprived of all but minimal education, the occupiers found that they needed local personnel with basic professional building qualifications in order to maintain the city they had battered and taken. With its railway links and munitions factories, Warsaw assumed major strategic importance after Germany attacked the Soviet Union.[6]

Many of the people involved with the wartime Faculty of Architecture served the military side of the secret state as well as the civil one. As the underground state was not in a position to pay its operatives proper salaries, they had to make ends meet as best they could. Kazimierz Piechotka had a job for a time as a salesman for a pharmacy glassware manufacturer, then meagre earnings from his work in the studio at the former Faculty of Architecture building, and occasional payments in kind, such as small quantities of flour or oil. He completed his studies during the occupation, rising early to make the most of the daylight for drawing. After working on his own projects, he went to the studio, where he spent the rest of the morning. His duties included the inventory of historic buildings, and he also worked as a draughtsman on the reconstruction plans.[7]

Then, around midday, he would 'go to the post office' – a rendezvous with a messenger who would pass on orders for the afternoon's secret work. The ability to execute plans and drawings was a skill that transferred readily to the forging of documents, a crucial requirement for the underground state's extensive network of intelligence operations, and architects formed a significant proportion of the forgery workshops' personnel. Agents always needed aliases, being vulnerable to checks and roundups at any moment. A courier travelling across Europe would need a sheaf of identity and travel documents, many of which were surreptitiously produced in the Faculty building. The industrious Polish forgers not only kept up with their own intelligence service's demands for 'legalisation', as the provision of fake credentials and passes was termed, but even supplied the French resistance with bogus papers too.

Piechotka was part of a three-person cell headed by Piotr Biegański, who completed his doctorate in architecture while working in the forgery studio, a room in the Institute of Polish Architecture's premises. The third member was Zofia Chojnacka, who had gone to study architecture in the secret Faculty after recovering from injuries she sustained while serving in the city's defence organisation during the siege. Her speciality was writing German texts; Piechotka's was forging signatures. As was standard practice in the resistance Conspiracy, they had noms de guerre. Piechotka was 'Jacek'; Chojnacka was 'Agata'; and Biegański was 'Paweł'. They struggled to decide what to call their cell, but ended up naming it after the local patisserie, 'Gajewski', in which they were sitting at the time.[8]

The forgery operation came under the control of the intelligence section of the Armia Krajowa, or Home Army, the main Polish resistance force. It was organised by another alumnus of the Faculty of Architecture, whose return to his alma mater was even more dramatic and hazardous than Maria Huber's journeys from Kraków. Stanisław Jankowski came all the way from England, reaching Polish airspace in a bomber and landing by parachute.

Jankowski had completed his studies and obtained a position as an assistant lecturer when the war broke out. Called up as a reservist, he was interned after his unit sought shelter in Lithuania, but he managed to escape and make his way to France. The Germans followed him there, and he became one of the thousands of exiled Polish servicemen who crossed the Channel when the country fell. On the day that he reached England, the SS and German police massacred 358 Poles in a forest near Warsaw. The action was part of the Nazi project to extirpate Poland's intelligentsia and its cultural life; the victims included politicians, lawyers, doctors, teachers, writers, artists and athletes. Among them were Jankowski's father and brother.[9]

The Polish forces regrouped in Britain and the government in exile also sponsored civil elements of resistance. It helped to establish a Polish School of Architecture at the University of Liverpool, where students learned the skills that would be needed for the reconstruction, and drew pictures of how it might look. Stanisław Jankowski was ideally qualified for the school, but he had already been selected to take the Polish armed forces' Military Administration Improvement Course in London. This came as an unexpected and unwelcome surprise to him, since he had not previously known of the course, displayed any aptitude for administration, or harboured any desire to serve his nation in an administrative capacity. The course's curriculum turned out to be more exciting than its title, though. It featured lectures on ciphers, Morse code, poisons, lock-picking and blowing up ships. Behind the cover name, it was the training programme for intelligence officers. They became known as the 'cichociemni', from cicho, silent, and ciemny, dark; their mission would be to return to their homeland and join the underground Armia Krajowa, or AK.[10]

They went by plane and landed by parachute – on the sixth attempt, in Jankowski's case. His first three missions were cancelled before take-off. The fourth succeeded in reaching Polish airspace, but was confounded by cloud that made accurate navigation impossible. They flew 3,000 kilometres and breathed Polish air, Jankowski observed, but the 300 metres of the parachute descent had proved beyond them. On the fifth flight, one of the Halifax bomber's four engines was knocked out by anti-aircraft fire near the Danish coast; the plane pressed on to the Baltic, but eventually had to turn back, weighed down by ice and buffeted by winds. The crew of the sixth flight evaded ground fire by crossing the sea at low level and Denmark at treetop height, then followed the pale snake of a frozen river to reach the drop zone north of Warsaw, where they unloaded Jankowski and five comrades. He jumped as a second lieutenant and landed a lieutenant: agents parachuting into action automatically went up a rank when they came down to earth. At seven in the morning on 4 March 1942, some thirteen hours after he boarded the Halifax, Jankowski got out of a train and read the station sign: Warschau Hauptbahnhof.[11]

Within a few weeks, he was assigned the task of organising the AK intelligence service's 'legalisation' department, code-named 'Agaton', and began to look for recruits among his colleagues at the Faculty of Architecture. By providing a room for the forgery studio and allowing three of his staff to run it, Professor Zachwatowicz made the building even more critically important to the national cause than it had been already. With its library, archives, classrooms and intelligence links, it was a bastion of integrated cultural and military resistance. Around three hundred students took part in the clandestine academy. Their professors legalised the degrees they awarded by backdating them to before the war.[12]

As well as providing materials for the intelligence network, the personnel of the Faculty themselves picked up information through their contacts with the German administrators. At the offices of the municipal board, Zachwatowicz saw a table-top model of a Nazi vision for the city, Die Neue Deutsche Stadt Warschau. The concept had been developed at the instigation of Oskar Dengel, whom the occupiers appointed mayor of Warsaw in November 1939. This was a vaulting promotion for an official whose most senior municipal positions to that point had been those of treasurer and deputy mayor of Würzburg, a provincial Bavarian city with a population of 107,000. Dengel engaged the head of Würzburg's planning department, Hubert Gross, who brought a twenty-strong team from the office with him. Gross had previously come up with a design for remodelling Würzburg, which he presented to Hitler in June 1939 at the Führer's Bavarian holiday residence near Berchtesgaden. Hitler took a close interest in the plans, and gave the project his approval. Now Gross and his colleagues came up with a plan that would cut Warsaw down to Würzburg's size.[13]

They lifted illustrations from a short book by Oskar Sosnowski on the history of Warsaw's street layout, published by the Institute of Polish Architecture in 1930, to show what they proposed to destroy. The plan envisaged the erasure of almost the whole main part of the city, the 'left bank' on the western side of the Vistula, apart from a few heritage showpieces. There would be ample room for the new population, which would be exclusively German, and much smaller than the pre-war one. By 1939 the capital had grown into a metropolis containing more than a million people on the western side of the river, and nearly a quarter of a million on the eastern or right bank: 1.3 million in all. Under the Würzburg team's plan, the New German City would accommodate less than a tenth of that number on the western bank, and a huddled mass of Poles would live in a township on the eastern side, crossing the river to provide labour for the Germans.[14]

The only district to be retained was the Old Town. In the Nazi view, its Gothic origins attested to German roots; it would accordingly serve as a seal of authenticity. A similar approach was conceived later by the architect in charge of planning the 'new German town' of

Auschwitz, Hans Stosberg. He proposed to keep the historic old town assemblage, defined by the market square, the town hall and the castle, as a symbol of the 'medieval German settler spirit' that had been reawakened by the Nazi drive to the East. The movement of settlers on which he based the idea had been instigated by the local Polish lords who lived in the castle. It had come to an end six hundred years previously, but it would serve as a foundation myth for the new town that was to be ordered around avenues, parade grounds and Party buildings, like the ones the planners modelled for Würzburg and Warsaw. The municipal authority's ambitions provoked boundary disputes with the SS, which was in charge of the adjacent concentration camp.[15]

In Warsaw there was no question of keeping the historic assemblage together, because the Royal Castle could not be presented as anything other than Polish. Even true völkisch believers would struggle to take in the notion that the Old Town was German in essence if the Royal Castle was still standing next to it. The medieval settlement had grown up in a symbiotic association with the castle, which occupied a position of supreme symbolic authority. The Royal Castle faced the city's founding quarter; it sat high on the scarp overlooking the river, and it formed the head of the Royal Route, a spinal column of prestige along which a succession of palaces was aligned as far as the monarchs' summer residence, thirteen kilometres to the south. But it did not appear on the plan for the New German City. Although the Nazis were inclined to keep the palaces, they were intent on demolishing the Royal Castle and thereby decapitating the historic complex. The act would assert that they had extirpated Polish nationhood.[16]

Oskar Dengel's tenure in the Warsaw post only lasted until March 1940, and the plan he sponsored was set aside after he was transferred to France. A relic of the project's supporting material survived in the form of a model of the Old Town, which was shown to the territorial governor, Hans Frank, and the Warsaw governor, Ludwig

Fischer, during the occupiers' 'Days of German Culture' festival in 1942. The model was not exhibited within the Old Town itself. By that stage, it was safer for Germans to contemplate the historical representation than to inspect the real thing. 'The Old Town had a life of its own,' recalled Stanisław Lorentz, the director of the National Museum. 'There weren't many Germans to be seen, and there were fewer and fewer of them as time went on, when they began to die in the Old Town alleys.'[17]

Lorentz had gone to live in a tenement used as an annexe to the Baryczka house, which together with its neighbours had been renamed the Museum Alt-Warschau, after the occupation authorities ejected his family from their apartment in the city centre. The museum's German overseer had planned to use it for an exhibition portraying German influences on Warsaw's architecture, but its Polish curator had other ideas. Before the First World War, the Baryczka house had been a hub for genteel cultural resistance to Russian rule. Now its ancillary buildings became a hub for conspiratorial armed resistance to the German occupiers, with a cache of weapons in a cellar. These remained undiscovered despite cavalier attitudes towards security that alarmed Lorentz. He reproved the curator for openly making offensive remarks about the Germans, but to little effect. That kind of behaviour was the Old Town's style at the time. Groups of musicians would often gather in tenement courtyards to play patriotic and anti-German songs. As the occupation went on, the inhabitants of the Old Town expressed their opposition increasingly openly. After a drinking session, two members of Lorentz's staff took their songs out of the annexe and onto the Market Square, shouting 'We've got something for the Germans!'[18]

It was not an empty threat. One of them took part in the attacks that reduced the number of occupiers at large in the district. He kept the guns he took from the Germans in his room, until a raid on an adjacent building sent him fleeing barefoot onto the rooftops. Lorentz ordered him to get rid of the weapons immediately, for fear that a raid would reveal the arms in the cellar. They were eventually handed over to the district's resistance command at the outset of the Warsaw Uprising, on 1 August 1944. The curator who had hidden them did not survive that long. He and a colleague were arrested for distributing underground newspapers. Both died in Auschwitz.[19]

The occupiers sustained their claims about Warsaw's Germanic character until they became seized with the urge to obliterate the city. At the beginning of 1944, Governor Fischer endorsed the message that Warsaw had 'a decidedly German past with great extant monuments of culture, which were created centuries ago by Germans and which speak to us today as stone witnesses of the erstwhile German rule on the Vistula river'. By the end of the year, the Nazi German rulers were in the last stages of a project to destroy as much of Warsaw as they could, silencing their supposed stone witnesses as they went.[20]

Afterwards, the Neue Deutsche Stadt plan formed a scandalous exhibit in Poland's indictment against Germany, serving to imply that the destruction had been planned from the outset. The charge has been sustained into the twenty-first century. A report published by the city council in 2004 described the plan as 'one of the most disgraceful documents in the history of European civilisation'. Prepared on the initiative of the then mayor of Warsaw, Lech Kaczyński, the report calculated the value of the city's material losses with a view to claiming reparations from the Federal Republic of Germany, and arrived at a total of what would have been US$45.3 billion in 2004. The claim that the destruction of Warsaw was a 'premeditated plan' was also incorporated into a campaign that the Polish government launched in 2022, demanding €1.3 trillion in reparations from Germany. The report containing the calculations for Poland's total wartime losses was presented at the Royal Castle on the anniversary of the Nazi invasion. Its cover image was a photo of the castle burning after a German air raid.[21]

After Dengel's exit, the Würzburg team's proposals became attached to the name of Friedrich Pabst, who became the construction superintendent for the city in 1942, along with other Nazi plans for the Germanisation of Warsaw. Pabst was particularly exercised by the fact that the Royal Castle was still standing. He repeatedly told a Polish official that it had to go. Grandiose plans appeared for an immense congress hall or Nazi party headquarters to occupy the site. A triangular edifice with a dome was proposed. Yet the German authorities allowed the castle to endure until almost the end of their rule, contenting themselves with wrecking the interiors and preventing repairs to the damaged structure, even though Hitler himself had approved its demolition shortly after the city's surrender in 1939. Its fate seemed imminent at the beginning of 1940, when engineers drilled rows of holes in the walls and packed them with explosives; the charges were wired up ready for detonation, but were removed a few weeks later. Something about the crowning symbol of Polish nationhood made the Nazis curiously indecisive.[22]

The first systematic area destruction perpetrated by the occupiers was the burning and subsequent razing of the Warsaw Ghetto in the spring of 1943. They had confined the Jewish population of Warsaw to a zone west of the city centre in 1940, and in 1942 they began to empty the ghetto they had created. By the beginning of 1943, more than a quarter of a million people had been removed, and it was clear that they had not been taken away to 'resettlement', as the SS had told them, but extermination. When the SS moved to complete the deportations, the remaining inhabitants launched a defiant uprising; the Nazi forces used flamethrowers to suppress it, house by house.

The destruction of the ghetto was therefore primarily an act of genocide, but also one of urbicide. In the dead zone, the razed terrain was used for mass executions. Later, a new SS commander took over and extended the killings to the streets where people still walked, the better to terrorise the populace. A catch-all charge of 'offences against German reconstruction work' was introduced, carrying the death penalty. People seized in raids or roundups were held as hostages and then shot in reprisal for AK attacks. Their names were published on notices describing them as convicted criminals. One of them was Stefan Bryła, the dean of the secret Faculty of Architecture. In November 1943 he was arrested, together with his family; on 3 December he was taken out into a street not far from the Polytechnic and shot, with a hundred others, in retaliation for an attack nearby that had killed six Germans the previous day.[23]

The secret state had its own courts, one of which pronounced a death sentence upon Emil Braun, the head of the occupation authorities' housing office. His crime was the mass eviction of Poles from their homes to make way for Germans, as the project for the replacement of the Polish capital by Die Neue Deutsche Stadt had envisaged. Like the occupiers' executions, the underground state's death sentence was to be carried out in a street – the one outside the municipal office building where Braun worked, as a warning to his colleagues in the higher ranks of the Nazi administration. This was a bold undertaking, since the offices were in the most dense and heavily guarded cluster of Nazi establishments in the city. As well as the men detailed to kill the target, 'Operation Braun' deployed a chain of observers, lookouts, armourers to deliver weapons and collect them after the attack, and shooters to provide covering fire.

They went into action on the morning of 13 December, after one of the observers, a 14-year-old girl, saw Braun drive away from the villa that he had taken for himself in an upmarket estate whose residents he had expelled. By the time his Adler Diplomat limousine pulled up to the municipal building, the operation's spearheads, 'Kastor' and 'Polluks', were in position. Braun got out, followed by another man and a woman. 'Polluks' and 'Kastor' shot all three of them down. With the guards in adjoining buildings kept back by automatic fire and grenades, the attack took less than a minute. The attackers escaped by car and melted away into the narrow streets of the Old Town. Afterwards they learned that the other man they had shot was Friedrich Pabst. They had unintentionally assassinated the official responsible for making the city German, on the doorstep of the offices in which the plans for Die Neue Deutsche Stadt had been kept.[24]

Towards the end of July 1944, Kazimierz Piechotka made the journey south to Kraków to meet Maria Huber, and then went east with her to the town where her parents lived. Piechotka had come to warn them that the Red Army was approaching fast, and who knew how things would be when the 'Bolsheviks' arrived? They would be safer in a big city. He urged Maria to go back with him to the biggest Polish city: they would be able to spend time together there, he told her, 'and you'll see you should be my wife'. While his argument that a large city would be safer than a small town was not unreasonable, his choice of destination was catastrophic. If they had just gone back to Kraków, they would have seen no bombardment or combat. In Warsaw, they were rapidly plunged into one of the war's most cruel and devastating urban battles west of Stalingrad.[25]

As passenger trains were reserved for Germans only, Piechotka bribed a railway policeman to let him and Maria climb aboard an open wagon on a freight train headed for Warsaw. When they arrived, on 26 July, Maria saw German troops pulling out of the city, taking their looted goods with them in their trucks. She also noticed large numbers of young people on the streets, carrying long packages wrapped in paper. Everybody was talking about an uprising, everybody in the Conspiracy was preparing for one, but through that last week of July, nobody knew if it would begin the next day or whether it would happen at all. Kazimierz Piechotka was waiting to find out if he was about to go into battle. While Piotr Biegański and Zofia Chojnacka were to continue the 'Gajewski' cell's forgery operation, Piechotka had been assigned to join an AK platoon commanded by Stanisław Jankowski, who had adopted the nom de guerre 'Agaton'; the unit would bear the same name. But after a few days, Piechotka brought his fiancée news that the rising had been called off.[26]

The uncertainty was not the product just of rumours, but of arguments and indecision at the highest levels of the secret state. Both in London and in Warsaw, the leaders were divided about the wisdom of a rising. Its purpose would be to assert Polish independence and agency as the Red Army drove the Nazis back towards German territory. Militarily, it would be directed against the Third Reich; politically, against the Soviet Union – and yet victory would depend on Soviet support, since little would be provided by the Western Allies. In Warsaw the AK could call on several tens of thousands of volunteers, but could only arm a fraction of them. Intelligence from outside the city was unreliable; communications within it were overstretched and haphazard. Messages could not be exchanged at night, because the messengers who carried them were unable to move around during the hours of curfew. According to the mobilisation plan, at least thirty-six hours would be needed to convey the orders, assemble the fighters and distribute the weapons.[27]

On 31 July, Jankowski was told that the rising would not begin the following day. Twenty-four hours later, he was informed that the AK would go into action in five hours' time. 'W' Hour was set for 17:00 ('W' stood for 'wybuch', meaning explosion in Polish). The decision failed to meet not only the requirement for thirty-six hours' notice, but also the need for surprise, flouting a directive that the insurrection should only be launched during the hours of darkness. 'Agaton' mustered his platoon, which comprised seventeen fighters and a nurse. Between them they had fifteen pistols, one rifle, a submachine gun bought from a German policeman, two bicycles and a car. With what would prove to be dreadful aptness, they were deployed to a cemetery.[28]

The insurgents quickly seized much of the city, including the central districts, but they failed to take some of their key objectives. What had been planned as a swift blaze of glory, lasting a few days or at most a week, turned into a desperate stand against a relentless counter-assault that the people of Warsaw had to endure for two

2. Lt Stanisław Jankowski, 'Agaton', leads a patrol in the early days of the Warsaw Uprising. The second of the men behind him is Kazimierz Piechotka.

months. Maria Huber narrowly escaped death on the third day, when Germans forced her and her companions out of the building in which she had found shelter. The Germans put them up against a wall, and it looked like they would meet the same fate as tens of thousands of other civilians whom the occupying forces massacred in the first two weeks of the Uprising. They survived because they were exchanged for a group of German hostages that Polish fighters had been holding nearby.[29]

Inevitably, the superior firepower of the occupying forces began to tell. As the pressure on the insurgents grew, the Old Town rediscovered its ancient role as a bastion. The narrow streets, barricaded with earth and rubble, kept enemy troops from entering the quarter. Instead, the attackers pounded the district from a distance with their most powerful weapons: rockets, siege mortars, shells from cannon mounted on an armoured train, bombs dropped by dive-bombers. They used remotely controlled vehicles, resembling miniature tanks and loaded with explosives, to blow up barricades. A larger bomb-vehicle, moved into position by a driver who then abandoned it, was taken over by a couple of insurgents who failed to realise what it was. They drove it triumphally through the Old Town, passing through the Market Square before the explosives detonated, killing more than 300 people.[30]

The district was packed with up to 100,000 civilians, for whom it proved to be more a trap than a shelter. Its fate was effectively sealed by the failure of an assault on a German firebase in the northern railway station. 'Agaton' and his men were sent to investigate the aftermath. They found massed corpses and 90 per cent casualties. A mad idea, Kazimierz Piechotka thought, sending young people armed with pistols to attack concrete bunkers defended with machine guns.[31]

Moving across the city at street level became all but impossible, so Jankowski's group had to descend beneath it. The sewers became the resistance's narrow arteries, vital to its survival, but exhausting and dangerous. Silence and darkness – the components of the collective nickname, cichociemni, that Jankowski and his fellow special operatives enjoyed – were essential to survival. Enemy soldiers listened and watched for lights at open manhole covers, through which they could shoot or drop grenades. Anybody who lost their footing in the dark risked drowning in sewage.[32]

The group's missions took them into the Old Town, where Jankowski met the Home Army commander General Tadeusz Bór-Komorowski, whose adjutant he later became. Towards the end of August, the general decided that the position in the district was hopeless, and evacuated with his staff via the subterranean route. The 'Agaton' group also left the quarter through the sewers, which they had to enter under artillery fire. They took four hours to reach the exit downtown, one and a half kilometres away. When Kazimierz Piechotka emerged, he saw smartly dressed people going to church, while the Old Town burned behind them. Those who remained there under the onslaught lacked water, food, medicine and hope. Among the civilians, the news that the military leadership had left them behind dealt a devastating blow to what was left of their morale. Several thousand people followed Piechotka and his comrades through the tunnels a few days later. Many of those left behind were slaughtered by the SS troops who then took possession of the area.[33]

Piechotka found Maria Huber, who had moved into Jan Zachwatowicz's office, along with two other women, both artists, and the daughter of one of them. Maria was sleeping under the professor's desk. Maciej, as she called him, looked more of a soldier than he had done when his platoon had first gone into action. He was wearing SS camouflage battledress, taken from a large stock that the insurgents had secured when they seized a German depot at the start of the fighting. A surviving photo shows him in his 'panterka' – from panter, meaning leopard. He has polonised his forage cap with an eagle badge, the Polish military insignia, and he has a smile on his face. Now's the time for us to get married, he told Maria, because I'm finally wearing trousers that are in one piece.[34]

The wedding took place in a half-ruined church, the floor strewn with broken glass. Maciej, or 'Jacek', was in his new fatigues; Maria, or 'Marianna', wore the same borrowed summer dress that she had worn throughout the Uprising. Both wore armbands in the national colours, red and white. Even the priest had a nom de guerre, 'Biblia': he was a senior AK military chaplain, holding the rank of colonel. The couple did not have wedding rings to exchange, nor did they ever, throughout the sixty-five years they were married until Maciej's death finally parted them in 2010. (He was ninety years old; Maria died ten years later, at the age of 100.)[35]

Maria worked for Zachwatowicz in the last weeks of the Uprising and the first days after the insurgents' surrender, helping him move the Faculty of Architecture's records to safety. He transferred the plans of the most important heritage, including the Old Town, to the basement of the Architecture Faculty building, against the objections of the medical staff who were running a field hospital in it and failed to see why patients should have to compete for space with documents. If the medics had prevailed, the plans would have been destroyed when fires burned out the floors above ground. Zachwatowicz doubted whether the post-war reconstruction of the Old Town would have been possible without them.[36]

One of the people who helped move the documents was Zygmunt Miechowski, an art historian. He had been arrested in 1939, along with Stanisław Lorentz and two other colleagues, while photographing German engineers drilling the holes for explosive charges in the Royal Castle's walls; Lorentz, released through some smart talking on his driver's part, managed to get Miechowski out of prison three weeks later. Miechowski lived in the same building as Lorentz behind the Old Town's Market Square, enabling them to work together after curfew, but he was arrested again in 1944 and sent to a concentration camp; once again, Lorentz interceded to secure his release. On the day before the Uprising began, he passed his examination for his master's degree in secret at the University of Warsaw. He was then assigned to look after the museum on the Market Square.[37]

In the Uprising he was a soldier-curator – he held the rank of second lieutenant in the AK, and 'Kustosz', 'Curator', was his nom de guerre. As the bombardments intensified, he organised the rescue of artworks and valuables from the churches and houses of the Old Town, bringing them to the museum buildings for safekeeping. He was assisted by Ewa Faryaszewska, an art student before the war and now a corporal in a resistance unit, together with Leszek Świderski, an artist, and his wife Kazimiera, both of whom were also enlisted in the insurgents' ranks. The team finished filling one of the cellars at the Baryczka house on 28 August. After Miechowski's helpers left the building, they were caught by a mortar shell explosion in the street. Faryaszewska and Świderski were fatally wounded. They were buried together at the foot of the city wall, the grave marked by a tall wooden cross. Kazimiera Świderska died subsequently in a makeshift hospital – not from the injuries she sustained that day, but in one of the massacres of patients and medical staff that German troops perpetrated when they finally took over the quarter. Miechowski himself escaped through the sewers in the evacuation of insurgent forces on 1 September, three days after his comrades fell. He was fatally injured three weeks later in the courtyard of the Faculty of Architecture, exactly four years after Oskar Sosnowski died from the wounds he received in the same spot.[38]

The Uprising formally came to an end on 3 October 1944, when General Bór-Komorowski signed the order for the soldiers under his command to capitulate. They were taken into captivity as prisoners of war. Having transferred along with Jankowski to Bór-Komorowski's personal guard, Kazimierz Piechotka ended up in hospital after falling ill with scarlet fever. Maria nursed him as best she could there, and then went with him to a prisoner-of-war hospital camp in eastern Germany. Stanisław Jankowski endured tougher regimes, including the one at Colditz Castle. Despite being moved from camp to camp, he managed to hold on to a typed document setting out guidelines for Warsaw's reconstruction, given to him by a fellow insurgent and Faculty of Architecture graduate during the Uprising.[39]

The non-combatants were taken out of the city as well, many of them to concentration camps or forced labour. Some managed to evade the transit camp though which hundreds of thousands of civilians were channelled, finding their way to refuges in towns and villages outside the former capital. The Third Reich was no longer in a position to entertain notions about building a new German city on the Vistula, but it still had the capacity to destroy the Polish one, as a punishment for its resistance, a blow to Polish nationhood, and an act of spite by a retreating power, trying to make sure that if it could not have Warsaw, nobody would.

Its forces might also have stood to gain some tactical advantage from the demolition, with the Red Army and a subordinate Polish force encamped on the eastern side of the river: buildings make stronger defensive bastions when they are reduced to rubble. When German troops made a stand in the Silesian city of Breslau, they destroyed tracts of its Old Town in order to create a line of defence against the Soviet attackers. But when the communist forces eventually entered the western side of Warsaw, the remaining German occupiers held out in the ruins for only a few hours.[40]

They began the demolition even before the Uprising ended, finally blowing up the Royal Castle after they took the Old Town. Then on 11 October, the governor of the Warsaw district reported that, after a meeting with the SS chief Heinrich Himmler, the commander of the forces that had defeated the Uprising 'has been given the new task of pacifying Warsaw – that is, of razing Warsaw to the ground'.[41]

This was not a brief outburst of apocalyptic fury by a fleeing horde, but a systematic programme of urbicide, conducted over a period of months. It proceeded by numbers, which were painted on buildings to ensure that the destruction squads performed their tasks methodically, house by house. As a Polish commentator later observed, Warsaw was not a village with thatched roofs that could be set ablaze by a single spark. Flamethrower teams worked through the streets, setting buildings ablaze; sappers beetled their way through the city, boring into walls and inserting explosive charges. The terms of the capitulation agreement provided for the removal of artworks and other cultural valuables, but the occupiers only permitted a small fraction of the material to be saved, and they intended the valuables to go to Germany. A covert operation was launched in parallel to the open one, spiriting objects and documents away to be concealed in safe hiding places on Polish soil.[42]

Jan Zachwatowicz had made his way to Podkowa Leśna, a garden-city settlement twenty-five kilometres from Warsaw colonised by displaced intellectuals, resistance leaders and black marketeers. The Faculty of Architecture reconvened there, forming a secret campus, and classes resumed in the villas discreetly screened by the trees. Zachwatowicz's most pressing task was to recover the collections that he had secreted away in the cellars of the Faculty building, a mission he organised with Stanisław Lorentz. A member of Poland's German minority, now known as 'Volksdeutsche', provided them with a ten-tonne truck, and helped them negotiate the passage back to the city by passing bribes to the German police who controlled the roads. Zachwatowicz had to carry a backpack stuffed with cash: each run cost half a million złoty, and there were six of them in all. It was worth it, though. The Architecture Faculty building had been burned out, and everything above ground level had been reduced to ashes, but the materials walled up in the cellar were preserved. Recruiting further assistance from firefighters, railwaymen and finally monks, Zachwatowicz ferried the collections out to a fire station near Podkowa Leśna, and then got them taken by goods train to a monastery further away, where they were hidden in the cloisters underground.[43]

When the German occupation was finally terminated, on 17 January 1945, the heart of the city was populated almost exclusively by the dead. A few hundred 'Robinsons' – so called after the solitary castaway Robinson Crusoe – had managed to survive hidden in the ruins. One man who ventured into the Old Town found a friend and her mother living in a wrecked shop on a street near the Market Square, cooking on a stove outside in the cruel January cold. The two women told him that they had survived the Uprising in the district by moving from cellar to cellar, and now had nowhere else to go.[44]

Post-war administrators estimated that there were also some 22,000 people living in a couple of southern districts, but the main part of the city west of the river was empty save for the Robinsons. The vast majority of survivors were tens or hundreds of kilometres further away. Many of them were determined to get back as quickly as they could, even though they knew they were returning to ruins. Within two months, more than 100,000 people were living in the devastated cityscape on the left bank of the river; by the end of the year, its population had grown by around 240,000, the vast majority of them former residents.[45]

Maria and Kazimierz Piechotka had to wait till May before they were free to find their way back. At the end of the war they found themselves by the river Elbe, at a border between the American and Soviet occupation zones picketed on both sides by drunken and loot-hungry soldiers. They slipped away the week after the German surrender, riding bicycles. Kazimierz armed himself with a rifle and Maria stuck a grenade in her belt, as protection against the liberators. They travelled part of the way with a larger group, which afforded them some protection against the additional threat of remnant German troops still at large in the countryside. When they reached the former Polish border, Soviet soldiers took the group's horses. On the advice of some Polish soldiers, members of the force set up and controlled by the Soviet Union, Maria and Kazimierz avoided main roads for the rest of their journey. When they got to Warsaw, they found a card from Jan Zachwatowicz and Piotr Biegański saying that there was work for them in the Bureau for the Reconstruction of the Capital.[46]

Chapter 3
Go to the Forests, or Get to Work

Zachwatowicz and Biegański had themselves been summoned to the task of reconstruction back in January, two days after the communist forces took control of the city west of the river. Some of their students had already gone there the day before, joining a continuous procession of people walking along the snow-covered railway line from Podkowa Leśna to Warsaw. There were no Germans left in the settlement, the small garrison having slipped away under cover of darkness, and not much food either. The professors ventured out into the fields with sledges, and came back around sunset with a haul of potatoes. They were dividing it up when they saw a lorry with Russian markings pull up outside the house. Three people got out, one of them a man in military uniform, and began to question passers-by. The ominous crunch of approaching boots was followed by a knock on the door, and the architects heard the officer ask for them by name – in Polish. They came forward and saw to their astonishment a former Warsaw Polytechnic architecture student, Józef Sigalin, who now stood before them as an army captain with a Polish eagle on his forage cap. The sight brought tears to their eyes.

Biegański was less than delighted to meet Sigalin's companion, though. He remembered him without affection from the school they had both attended, as a prefect who was always telling him off. But here he was, now a priest, hailing him as his dearest childhood friend. Like so many other people, the cleric was beginning the new era by rewriting his history.

The visitors brought news about another of Biegański's former fellow students, one of his contemporaries at the Faculty of Architecture. Marian Spychalski, who joined the communist party the year that he graduated, had now returned to Warsaw as the city's mayor. Would the architects come back as well, to help rebuild the capital? They would! Within a couple of hours, Zachwatowicz and Biegański were on their way, aboard the Soviet truck. Sigalin said little during the journey – characteristically, for he was to become the éminence grise of the reconstruction – but told them that the work had to start right away. It was clear both to him and to them, Biegański later recalled, that the real Warsaw had to be rebuilt – especially the Old Town.[1]

At nine o'clock the next morning, they presented themselves at the mayor's temporary headquarters on the eastern side of the river, where Colonel Spychalski invited them to create a Bureau for the Organisation of the Reconstruction of Warsaw. He had assigned them a truck and a driver; they were to go and set the bureau up forthwith. Zachwatowicz would be in charge of the Organisation until the government made permanent arrangements.

Accompanied by Sigalin, they crossed the river to look at a building in a district on the western side that was less damaged than most, because the Germans had taken it for their own use. The modernist interwar townhouse had since caught the eye of the Soviets, who planned to use it as accommodation for officers of the NKVD – the Soviet system's principal organ of enforcement and repression – but Spychalski secured it for the municipality. Reassured by seeing the words for 'no mines' at the entrance, the architects placed a notice on it announcing that it had been requisitioned. This modus operandi was subsequently scaled up to encompass the entire city. Later in the year, the government requisitioned the whole of

Warsaw on behalf of the reconstruction project, taking all the land within the city limits into municipal ownership.[2]

They spent the rest of the day touring the city in the jeep Spychalski had provided, finding themselves halted in places by banks of snow-covered rubble that stood two storeys high. The worst devastation they encountered was in the historic district. Sigalin had ventured there already, with a party of architects who had come from Lublin with him. In a memoir he recalled how, entering the Castle Square, he had seen a form in the piled snow. 'Watch out!' he shouted to his driver, 'A corpse in the road!' He got out and began to brush the snow away. It was the prone statue of King Zygmunt III Waza, which had overlooked the square for 300 years until the Germans felled the column on which it stood. 'He was lying on his back, with his eyes to the sky. I wept.'[3]

Already he had to chase away looters. Hyenas, he called them. They had begun to pour into the ruins almost as soon as the sound of the last shots died away, columns of horse-drawn carts rolling in from the surrounding villages. Former residents had good reason to get back to whatever was left of their homes as fast as they could, despite the dangers of mines, unexploded munitions and continuing Luftwaffe air raids; but however much haste they made, many of them found that looters had got there first. If the buildings in which they had lived were still standing, their apartments might have been taken by squatters, who often secured official permission to remain in them. A new word entered the popular vocabulary during the war, and took command of it in the aftermath: 'szaber', 'loot'. It came from criminal slang and spread through a population that had become increasingly detached from legality. Some of the looters were 'hyenas', but in truth everybody took things that did not belong to them, for better reasons and worse. One day Zachwatowicz and Biegański foraged in frozen fields for potatoes because they had nothing to eat; the next day they helped themselves to a building so that they could begin to reconstruct Warsaw.[4]

Within a month, the government imposed a definitive form upon the Bureau that Zachwatowicz had set up. He moved down and sideways, taking charge of the Department of Heritage Architecture. Sigalin took a seat at the top, becoming a deputy director of what was now the Bureau for the Reconstruction of the Capital, known by its initials as BOS (standing for Biuro Odbudowa Stolicy). The change of name represented a victory for Marian Spychalski. Daunted by the scale of the destruction in Warsaw, the new authorities had considered designating a new capital for the new Poland; perhaps Łódź, an industrial city that was both proletarian and relatively intact, or Kraków, which had once been the capital and had emerged from the war unscathed. Spychalski had argued for Warsaw – and found support from the most powerful of all possible backers. A week after Spychalski summoned the architects to Warsaw and told them that the city must be rebuilt without delay, Stalin summoned Bolesław Bierut, whose position in the emerging state approximated to that of president, and told him exactly the same thing. Bierut returned from Moscow in no doubt that as far as Marshal Stalin was concerned, the capital of the new Polish Republic should be Warsaw.[5]

Stalin's view strengthened Spychalski's position, which was reflected in his appointment as a junior defence minister and a rapid succession of military promotions that took him to the rank of major-general, giving him two stars to wear on his cap when he showed General Eisenhower around the ruins of the Old Town. The future Soviet leader Nikita Khrushchev, sent to Warsaw by Stalin to help restore electricity and water supplies, was struck by Spychalski's taste for conducting his civil duties in army uniform. Sigalin likewise insisted on wearing uniform to the office, and likewise enjoyed a promotion, from captain to major.[6]

Both men were, of course, power-dressing. But it was an assertion of power within a complex of insecurity. They were soldier-architects whose status was ambivalent, in an environment that was neither stable nor at peace. In addition to the uncertainties that surrounded

Sigalin's place in the new order, his status was undermined by the fact that he had not actually qualified as an architect, the war having broken out just as he was about to start the final year of his course at Warsaw Polytechnic. His military rank also bolstered his sense of personal security, because it enabled him to go armed as he went around the bandits' paradise that the ruined city had become. The dangers were close and always present. A BOS driver was found dead the day after he took an official car for his journey home, having obtained special permission to do so precisely because he feared attack by bandits. It is easy to see why Sigalin carried two guns: a small pistol in his trouser pocket, and a larger one in his coat. He applied for permission to hang on to them when he was demobilised at the end of the year, but was only allowed to keep one.[7]

The challenge that faced the two men, and the order they represented, was ultimately one of authenticity. They claimed to be Polish; they believed themselves to be Polish; and in their way they were – but they looked like Soviet puppets in Polish costumes. They claimed legitimacy, but they knew that while being visibly in charge was sufficient for them to be acknowledged by foreign powers, they would need to be more than that in order to achieve legitimacy in the eyes of the people. The strategy that they developed had the Old Town as its keystone. Perhaps the germ of it was in Sigalin's mind as he brought Zachwatowicz and Biegański back to Warsaw the day after what was officially termed its 'liberation'. He and Biegański might well have agreed on the importance of rebuilding the Old Town, as the latter recalled, but for different reasons. Sigalin had not hitherto shown any particular interest in built heritage, but his experience as a pre-war communist agitator and a wartime political commissar had taught him about the propaganda value of symbolism. With a whole metropolis to rebuild, the first door he knocked on was not that of an urban planner, but of the city's leading architectural conservator.

Securing the city for the reconstruction project entailed dealing with nearly 100,000 mines and unexploded munitions, a task undertaken in the first few months after the new authorities took control. As the sappers went about their hazardous work, the nascent regime stepped up its efforts to secure the political terrain, vilifying and demonising rival claimants to patriotic authenticity. Remnants of the AK who refused to lay down their arms, having survived mass arrests by the NKVD, were 'fascist criminals'. In narratives of the struggle against the Hitlerite occupiers, the AK's combatants were replaced as heroes by the much smaller communist underground groups, the People's Guard (whose intelligence section Marian Spychalski had headed) and its successor, the People's Army. Instead of insurgents stained with sewer filth, wearing their mortal enemy's uniforms, the new power offered the vision that greeted Biegański and Zachwatowicz on the doorstep that January afternoon: a Polish officer, properly dressed and equipped, wearing the eagle that confirmed him as a rightful heir to Poland's revered military traditions. There was one vital difference between the eagle on his cap and the one Kazimierz Piechotka had pinned to his German one during the Uprising, though. The eagle of the Polish People's Army had lost its crown.[8]

By wearing their uniforms, Józef Sigalin and Marian Spychalski automatically triggered feelings of respect, admiration and love for country that cast a favourable light upon them. The reason that the sight of Sigalin brought tears to the architects' eyes, Biegański wrote in a reminiscence published in 1984, was that the captain was the first 'real Polish soldier' they had seen for five years.[9]

That was the way he had become used to telling the story, judging by a similar version from around the same time, in which he said that Sigalin was 'the first Polish officer' he had seen since 1939. What about his comrade in the forgery cell, Kazimierz Piechotka, who left the workshop to go and fight in the Uprising? What about their AK intelligence supervisor, Lieutenant Stanisław Jankowski, who led Piechotka's platoon? What about all the soldiers of the AK who emerged from the Conspiracy to fight the occupiers in the streets? Nearly forty years had passed since the Home Army officially disbanded. Its place in Polish history remained a highly sensitive topic, but its name was not taboo. Although the run-down city museum on the Old Town's Market Square still pretended that the resistance had been a communist movement, Biegański could have acknowledged the AK without repercussions. But he had spent half his life negotiating between what could be said in public, at any particular stage in the progress of 'People's Poland', and what everybody privately knew to be true. Piotr Biegański had not forgotten his comrades, or ceased to honour them. He had just ceased, perhaps, to notice that he was gaslighting himself.[10]

Józef Sigalin's experiences as an architecture student at Warsaw Polytechnic in the 1930s were not the sort that leave fond memories of college days. He began his course just when radical nationalists launched a campaign to exclude Jews from the country's universities and schools of higher education, part of the broader wave of antisemitic agitation launched by nationalists following the death of Józef Piłsudski, the country's dominant political figure. Their first demand was that lecture theatres should be segregated, with Jewish students sitting apart from the others on 'ghetto benches'. Being Jewish by descent but not by self-identification, Sigalin protested angrily when a crowd of nationalist students tried to enforce segregation at a lecture on, aptly enough, the Middle Ages. 'I feel myself to be Polish,' he shouted, 'so it is insulting that I cannot sit where I want.'[11]

Across the country, nationalist students added injury to insult as they escalated their campaign. Riots closed all Warsaw's higher education institutions during Sigalin's first term, in November 1935. The radical-rightists made their 'autumn manoeuvres' an annual event to mark the start of the academic year. In March 1937, the governing body of the Polish Architects' Association addressed an open letter to the Warsaw Polytechnic authorities, declaring that an 'atmosphere of ethical and moral depravity' had enveloped the Faculty of Architecture, enforced by 'the law of iron bars and knuckledusters'.

The institution's response to the violence was to inscribe ghetto benches into its own laws.[12]

Flushed with their success, the militants of the National-Radical tendency dealt with the resistance they had met from the leaders of the Architects' Association. Young Faculty of Architecture graduates formed a rightist cadre that seized control of the organisation and inscribed a so-called 'Aryan paragraph' into its statutes that barred Jews from membership. To be precise, persons of 'Jewish nationality' were denied membership; persons of Jewish descent would have to be approved by a committee, which would reject new applications from individuals whose parents were born into the Jewish faith, or ones from existing members who could not produce a certificate of baptism dating from before the restoration of Poland's independence.[13]

The ultranationalists continued to recruit fresh supporters at the Faculty of Architecture, making the most of their presence within the architecture students' association. 'Young Polish Architecture is National-Radical', their newspaper gloated. The report suggested the acquiescence of the Faculty authorities, describing a speech made at a meeting of the students' association in the presence of the dean, Stefan Bryła. It included a warning about the 'three-million-strong Jewish menace'.[14]

Those words indicated the extent of the National-Radicals' antisemitic ambition, which they shared with the nationalist movement as a whole. The nationalists dreamed of a Poland entirely without Jews. Their motivating axiom was that a Jewish presence of any kind posed an existential threat to the Polish nation. The more influential they perceived a sector of society to be, the more urgently they strove to curtail Jewish involvement in it. In the 1930s the nationalists concentrated their assaults on two main fronts, both of which offered ethnic Poles the prospect of reduced competition for employment and business in the punishing economic conditions of the time. One was the commercial sphere, in which they promoted boycotts of Jewish-owned shops and firms. The other was that of higher education and the professions to which it led, where the National-Radicals used a highly effective combination of violence followed by the capture of institutions whose doors often seemed to be left open to them. Their campaign through the Faculty of Architecture and the Architects' Association was a textbook operation. It was a step towards their ultimate goal, a 'Great Poland' constituted as a species of fascism.[15]

By then Sigalin had accumulated years of experience as a radical agitator himself. Born in 1909, he grew up in Warsaw, made friends with young leftists as a teenager, and joined a communist youth organisation the year he graduated from high school. After he was called up for military service in 1930, he joined one of the Communist Party's army cells. These clandestine rings had two missions: agitation and intelligence-gathering. Hoisting banners outside barracks probably caused the authorities little more than annoyance, but intelligence was another matter. The cells were tasked with providing information about soldiers' units, equipment, morale and combat-readiness, which the Party then passed on to Soviet military intelligence. They were spying for a foreign power, though as believers in an international workers' movement, they did not see it that way.

Neither, as time went on, did the foreign power itself. The Soviets became increasingly suspicious that their Polish comrades were actually spying on them. Eventually they decided that the Polish communist leadership had been infiltrated by 'fascists' to such an extent that they dissolved the organisation altogether. The liquidation of the Party was accompanied by the liquidation of many of its members.

For those who escaped execution, loyalty to the communist movement created inner conflicts that could not be resolved, but had to be withstood. Józef Sigalin and others like him had felt themselves to be part of Polish society, but many members of that society refused to accept that Jewish identification with Poland might be deep and genuine. The internationalist ideology of communism had offered Polish Jews a way to resolve the tensions created by exclusive conceptions of national identity. Instead it compounded the contradictions, and introduced terrible new ones of its own devising. Józef Sigalin's biographer Andrzej Skalimowski persuasively suggests that such contradictions were what made the agitator, architect and éminence grise the man he was. Sigalin's ability to turn those fractures into strengths was the secret of his success.[16]

The system that commanded his loyalty put his older brothers to death. Both Grzegorz and Roman Sigalin were architects: Józef followed them into the profession, gaining work experience in Roman's Warsaw studio. Seeing employment opportunities in Moscow's great construction projects, Grzegorz went there in 1935. Two years later he tried to escape Stalin's 'Great Terror' by returning to his homeland, but was arrested and shot as a spy – a fate shared by more than 100,000 ethnic Poles and others accused of spying for Poland during the bloodbaths of 1937 and 1938. The NKVD shot Roman two years later. He was one of the victims of the Katyn massacres, in which more than 20,000 Polish officers and civilians were murdered because they were deemed to be enemies of the Soviet Union. Many of them, like Roman Sigalin, were reservists called up from civilian professions. The effect of their loss on Polish society was similar to that of the parallel massacres perpetrated by the Germans on the country's intelligentsia – though its nationalists did not consider Jewish Poles like Roman Sigalin to be part of the Polish nation.[17]

Józef Sigalin had followed in his brother's footsteps upon completing his military service, becoming a second lieutenant in the army reserve, but he took a different path when the war broke out. He headed east to relatives in Vilnius, spent the next few years in the Soviet Union, and in 1943 joined a new Polish infantry division set up to help achieve Stalin's objectives in the lands west of the USSR. After a brief spell as a political commissar, Sigalin became adjutant to the division commander, General Berling, and then a staff officer. He saw action, too. The two pistols that he was so concerned to keep after leaving the army were trophies from the battle of Lenino, a baptism of fire that became a glorious feat of Polish arms in propaganda myth, but took a devastating toll on the unready and inadequately supported troops. His mementoes of it included a medal for valour as well as the guns.

When the communist forces advanced into Poland and set up a provisional authority in Lublin, he took his place in it. By then he had accumulated a portfolio of acquaintances that included many of the most influential figures in the post-war regime. His acquaintance with Marian Spychalski, who initiated the reconstruction of Warsaw as the city's mayor in the bitter January of 1945, dated back to the pre-war coup by radical right-wingers in the Architects' Association; he was one of a group of leftist architecture students whom Spychalski gathered at his apartment to plan a response. The two men encountered each other again as soldiers in May 1944, at a military parade; Spychalski had just come from an audience with Stalin.

None of Sigalin's connections helped him in the matter that was most personally important to him, though. Trying every possible channel to find out what had happened to his elder brothers, he even prevailed upon the Polish communist leader Bolesław Bierut to ask Stalin personally. Józef entertained some hope that Grzegorz might still be alive, even though seven years had passed since his disappearance. He had not known that when he and his comrades in the Polish division raised a cross over the site of a mass grave in the Katyn forest, the victims they were commemorating included his brother Roman. Though he believed the Soviet lie that the massacres had been committed by the Germans, he must have had little doubt that the Soviet regime was responsible for Grzegorz's fate. Yet he did not waver in his dedication to the communist movement and his readiness to meet whatever demands the Party made on his loyalty. The Marxist historian Eric Hobsbawm noted how some comrades embraced the most unbearable demands as the proof of their commitment: 'Test me some more: as a bolshevik I have no breaking-point.' Sigalin may not have craved the tests that his life as a communist imposed on him, but he met them without breaking.[18]

His painfully accumulated experience in defying contradictions was a powerful asset in his role as a leader of Warsaw's reconstruction programme. Despite the impressive range of his communist contacts and old comradeships, they were not sufficient for the project. He needed to recruit people who had the necessary skills, but many of them viewed the emerging political order with suspicion or hostility. That meant being ready to work not just with old comrades, but also former members of the nationalist camp they had opposed before the war. One of the Faculty alumni he recruited, Piotr Biegański, had been on the other side when the nationalists took over the Polish Architects' Association. Biegański was a delegate from Warsaw at the organisation's general assembly in 1938, at which the 'Aryan paragraph' excluding Jews was added to its statutes. Only one delegate, representing a provincial branch, voted against the proposal. The Warsaw branch was the first to be purged when the rule came into force: fifty-six Jewish members were expelled.[19]

When Sigalin knocked on the door of the house in Podkowa Leśna and invited Jan Zachwatowicz to join the reconstruction, Zachwatowicz agreed on the spot. Two weeks later, he signed an appeal calling on all Polish architects to do likewise. It told his colleagues that the whole country was looking at them, and counting on them to take up the great cause immediately. 'The Polish architect must fulfil his duty, must prove himself worthy of the Polish soldier. That soldier has already rebuilt the foundations of the Republic – Now rebuild its capital!' The appeal put national history first, calling for King Zygmunt's column, the Royal Castle, the Old Town and the highlights of the Royal Route to be raised from the ruins, before going on to declare that the new estates to be built for the capital's heroic inhabitants must be healthy, sunny and green. Zachwatowicz's signature represented heritage; Marian Spychalski's stood for the new political authority: together with that of the president of the Architects' Association of the Republic of Poland, they signified a grand project of national unity.[20]

A number of Polish architects, including Maria Piechotka and her husband Kazimierz, were unable to respond to the call immediately because they were in German prison camps. By the time they were freed, the prospects for AK veterans and anybody connected with the London-based government were looking increasingly ominous. In March 1945, the NKVD arrested political representatives of the secret state that had been established under the German occupation, together with a former AK commander, and took them to Moscow for a show trial. The remnants of the underground state attempted to sustain their networks without confronting the communists openly, but had little control over partisan groups across the country that waged guerrilla campaigns against the new government and those they regarded as its collaborators. The struggle went on for years, taking perhaps as many as 50,000 lives, and the government conducted its side ruthlessly. Among the casualties of the conflict was a Faculty of Architecture student who had served in the wartime resistance. Arrested on Christmas Eve in 1948, he was officially reported to have jumped to his death from a window in the Ministry of Public Security headquarters, along the street from the Architecture Faculty.[21]

Against the background of political tension and what amounted to a low-level civil war, the prevalence of architects formerly involved with the underground state in the staff of the Bureau for the Reconstruction of the Capital is striking. Jan Zachwatowicz had been the London-based government's delegate responsible for heritage; he now held the equivalent position under the government that had taken power, as well as heading BOS's heritage section. Piotr Biegański had forged documents for the AK's 'legalisation' department, working with Kazimierz Piechotka, who then fought in the Uprising alongside Stanisław Jankowski. Zofia Chojnacka, the third member of the forgery cell, was reunited with her former comrades when she became a colleague of theirs in BOS. Józef Sigalin estimated that 80 to 90 per cent of his colleagues and friends in the Bureau were AK veterans. They not only got their jobs despite their resumés, but kept them despite the intensification of the state's efforts to suppress all opposition to it. Zofia Chojnacka was arrested and held for three months, having also reconnected with former comrades from Jankowski's unit who revived the underground forgery operation under the name 'Agaton II', yet even she was able to return to her work at BOS after her release.[22]

Stanisław Jankowski was called in for questioning by the secret police a number of times after he returned to Poland in 1946, having earned a diploma in Civic Design from the Polish School of Architecture in Liverpool. They knew he had been the AK commander's adjutant, and they wanted to know where he had buried the general's documents. He said he didn't know: it had been dark; shells were exploding and buildings burning around him. After a while they left him alone, having found out by other means. Although they must have investigated him thoroughly, they revealed no deeper interest in him. That was remarkable, given his military record. Not only had he been aide-de-camp to the commander of the Uprising, but he was also a trained intelligence operative who had spent extended periods of time in Britain both during and after the war. His potential value as a reconstruction professional evidently outweighed any perceived risk that he might start practicing his intelligence tradecraft again.[23]

In at least one instance, when Jankowski was picked up while photographing a church unfortunately located near a building used by the secret police, he obtained a swift release through Sigalin's personal intervention. Jankowski recounted the incident – without mentioning the telegram that his wife Hanna sent to Sigalin, asking for help – in a chapter of his memoirs entitled 'Why did I not go to prison?' He did not provide an answer to the question. But the main reason, for him and his colleagues alike, was that the appeal to Polish architects had been successful. They had consented to take part in a project controlled by the new authorities because they believed it was their duty to the nation. Jan Zachwatowicz's argument was as powerful as it was simple. He told Maria and Kazimierz Piechotka that they had two choices. They could go to the forests – in other words, they could go off and join the partisans – or they could stay and get to work. 'Professor Zachwatowicz convinced us that whoever was in power, this was still Poland, this was our country, and it was our duty to rebuild it,' Maria recalled.[24]

Jankowski and Sigalin, contemporaries at the Faculty of Architecture before the war, had hitherto been on opposite sides. In 1939, Jankowski was among the contributors to a collection of articles about 'national' architecture in a right-wing cultural magazine. They included a piece by Jan Poliński, a Faculty of Architecture graduate and National-Radical activist, in which he excoriated 'Jewish' building design and contended that even the ban on Jewish membership of the Architects' Association was insufficient to protect Polish architecture from foreign influences. By contrast, Jankowski's essay was relaxed in tone, portraying foreign influences as fads rather than as malign alien threats. But in an earlier article for the Association's bulletin, he took a clearly nationalist ideological line, calling for nationally conscious architects and allied trades to help build a 'Great Poland'. Such a country could not exist without adequate homes for working Poles, he declared, but private capital, which was 'largely Jewish, and therefore asocial', would not deliver the necessary housing. 'The fact that a whole range of sectors of the construction industry is now in the hands of Jews should be considered abnormal and highly harmful,' Jankowski claimed.[25]

When the war broke out, five months later, Jankowski and Sigalin both went to Lithuania. Jankowski then headed west, to France; Sigalin moved into the Soviet Union. Each served as adjutant to a Polish commander, one loyal to the exiled government in London, and the other loyal to Moscow. Each was awarded a decoration for bravery, one by the Home Army and the other by the Red Army. With so many opposites in common, it is perhaps no wonder that when they began to work on rebuilding Warsaw together they became friends, and remained so for nearly forty years. Their friendship outlasted Sigalin's faith in the Party, as he acknowledged to Jankowski when the latter visited him in hospital a few days before his death.

Chapter 4
A Brigade of Goldsmiths

The architects could not begin to rebuild until they had updated their records. Before the war they had made inventories of historic buildings; now they had to make inventories of ruins. They started to survey the Old Town in March 1945, most of them travelling into the city each day on goods trains or bicycles along the railway line that passed through Podkowa Leśna, then making the rest of the journey on foot, first to the building that Zachwatowicz and his colleagues had claimed for a base, and finally through the ruins of the city centre to the Old Town; about twenty kilometres a day, there and back.[1]

As they worked, they set up the first heritage plaques of the new era, red tablets bearing a Polish eagle emblem. 'Historic Building Standing as a Document of National Culture', these declared: 'Violating the Condition of the Building Is Strictly Forbidden'. This seemed strange to a teenager called Bogdan Wyporek, who would grow up to be an architect and urban planner, because many of the plaques stood in front of completely demolished buildings. What, he wondered, was the point of protecting rubble?[2]

Part of the point was to conserve architectural fragments that might lie buried beneath. Anna Czapska and a friend walked down the railway line from Podkowa Leśna to join BOS in early February, having received one of Piotr Biegański's invitation cards. The two young women, alumni of the secret campus where Biegański had lectured until the end of the German occupation, were among BOS's early recruits. Their first assignment took them through the Old Town to save fragments from the rubble of a church. If walls had to be built anew, then at least they could serve as a matrix for whatever shreds of the original buildings remained. Although they would not themselves be authentic, authenticity would be embedded in them. BOS's Architectural Heritage section was already preparing for reconstruction on a scale and of a kind unprecedented anywhere in the world. And that was the deeper reason to protect rubble. The BOS tablets asserted that a historic building still existed if its substance remained, even though its form did not. They laid a claim to the space and volume that it had occupied, creating a moral hologram of the structure that awaited the restoration of its material form.[3]

Those claims had an especially profound significance in Warsaw's Year Zero, where the principle of ownership had ceased to apply. Instead, everything from a spoon to a townhouse was szaber, actual or potential. The word expanded beyond its concise expression, 'loot', to signify all appropriation of objects, portable or immobile, that for whatever reason were not in their owners' possession. Since people had almost nothing left of their own, szaber became the source of almost everything. Its ubiquity was nicely captured by a satirical verse in which the narrator meets the man who first introduced the word 'szaber' to the marketplace. The narrator asks him where he got that 'beautiful expression' from. 'I szabered it,' the man replies.[4]

According to BOS lore, the state of employees' shoes determined whether they were sent out to survey the ruins or stayed in the office. The ones with intact footwear went out wearing backpacks in which to carry food, and bring back szaber. Like everybody else, they contrib-uted to the feral circulation of objects in a city where the fabric of ownership had been disrupted as massively as the power cables, phone lines and water pipes. All the structures that gave the city coherence – physical, social, legal and moral – had been shattered. Varsovians saw a new political order being imposed, but could not be sure how far it planned to go. Nor could they be sure how their city would be rebuilt, or what form it would take, or whether they would be able to recognise it when it was done. By placing its tablets at the sites of historic buildings, BOS offered reassurance that Varsovians would still be able to see a constellation of heritage in their 'new' city. In marking out the sites as fixed points of departure for the reconstruction, it asserted that Warsaw's past would be the basis of its future.[5]

BOS sent three architects into the Old Town to establish a base there. It had already been prepared for them before the war, unintentionally, by Jan Zachwatowicz. When the city bought the three houses on the Market Square to house the Museum of Old Warsaw, the conversion works carried out under Zachwatowicz's direction included the installation of reinforced concrete slabs to strengthen ceilings. A few years later the slabs provided significant protection against the fires and blasts that devastated the other sides of the square, preserving not only walls but also several decorated wooden ceilings. One of the houses was even marked on the hand-drawn BOS survey map as 'undamaged', though photographs show that to be an overstatement. The architects also found a couple of undamaged rooms on the ground floor of one of its neighbours, the Baryczka house. They put up a BOS plaque outside, and made themselves some desks from planks and boxes.[6]

At that stage, they had the place almost exclusively to themselves. Few living human beings were to be found in the quarter, which had now become a charnel house. The authorities estimated that across the city, some 200,000 corpses had been left behind when the Germans drove the surviving residents out. Their remains lay in ruined buildings, in the sewers, buried under rubble, out in the open, and in makeshift graves. Some of those hastily buried in the tract between the medieval walls, a space originally intended to accumulate the bodies of attackers rather than defenders, were becoming visible as the rains washed away their scant covering of earth. There was no rubble to conceal them because the walls themselves, carefully exposed by Zachwatowicz before the war, had survived strangely unscathed. Several corpses lay in the museum houses, and remained there throughout the winter. It became impossible to ignore them in the spring, as temperatures rose and decomposition resumed. In April, Zachwatowicz asked the municipal authority to take the remains away.[7]

Survivors began to reappear. Anna Czapska saw them increasingly frequently by the end of February. A family moved in next door to the Baryczka house, putting a stove in a ground floor room and arranging shards of broken glass in a plywood frame to make a window. Stovepipes projecting from doorways or poking up from cellars revealed the presence of recolonising occupants. In June, a newspaper report estimated that 3,000 people were living in the area. The reporters described a family 'vegetating' in a tenement house on a street leading to the Market Square: a builder, his wife and four children, with a goat tied up in the courtyard. They found eight families living in the square itself. All were born in the district, 'and do not want to die anywhere else . . . Because that's how it is: whoever inhabits the Old Town remains under its spell.' There was another builder, and a shoemaker, and a shopkeeper who had just reopened his shop, the second to resume trading in the district. While playing in the rubble by the Baryczka house the previous day, the builder's son had noticed a shoe sticking out from under a slab. It revealed the remains of a man, a woman and a child. The 'last of the Mohicans of the Old Town Square' pressed the reporters to let the authorities know, so that these and other corpses could be removed as quickly as possible.[8]

The figure of 3,000 living inhabitants may refer to the Old Town police district, which covered an area much larger than the ten hectares within the line of the medieval walls. Official statistics for the year recorded 7,318 inhabitants and 1,412 occupied premises in the district. The total population of the city was heading for 400,000 – but the capital still had far more war dead than living inhabitants. As many as 800,000 people were estimated to have died, a number approaching two-thirds of Warsaw's pre-war population.[9]

As for the fabric of the city, it was calculated that around 84 per cent of Warsaw had been destroyed. This figure continues to be widely repeated, without elaboration on what it actually means. It does not mean that 84 per cent of the city was razed to the ground. The skeletons of buildings still lined the streets in nearly every area, the most conspicuous exception being the zone the Nazis had turned into a ghetto and then reduced to rubble. While parts of the 'Small Ghetto' nearer the city centre survived, the occupiers succeeded in levelling large tracts of the 'Large Ghetto' before they called a halt to the operation, a year after they finally suppressed the Ghetto Uprising. Its fate has in effect been appropriated as that of the city as a whole, intertwined with the claim, memorable but of uncertain provenance, that the infamous order to raze Warsaw to the ground was given by Hitler himself. (The city governor, Ludwig Fischer, ascribed it to the Führer, but when questioned on the point at the Nuremberg trials after the war, the SS commander said he was unable to confirm whether it had in fact come directly from Hitler.)[10]

The headline figure does not mean that 84 per cent of the city was left in ruins, either. BOS surveyors recorded that 75.2 per cent of the buildings on the western side of the river had been destroyed: 57.8 per cent were completely lost; 17.4 per cent could be rebuilt. On the eastern side, the figures were 16.2 and 10.7 per cent. Across the entire city, 80 per cent of the buildings had suffered more than 10 per cent damage – but the total proportion of buildings classed as destroyed, adding together those considered rebuildable and those deemed beyond repair, was just under 60 per cent. It appears that the figure of 84 per cent for the extent of the destruction was arrived at by averaging the percentages for the various categories of building: residential, 72.1 per cent; heritage, 90; cultural, 95; educational, 70; industrial,

90; health services, 90; a mean of 84.52 per cent. The statistic conveyed a message of near-total destruction to the wider world. It was dramatically illuminated by images from the two most devastated areas, the wasteland of the former ghetto and the ruined Old Town.[11]

Already the Starówka (its colloquial name, from 'Stare', 'Old') was becoming idealised. According to a newspaper article from June 1945, the intact quarter had been a place out of time, in which nobody would have been surprised to see one of the Baryczka family emerge from a townhouse in the garb of a rich Warsaw merchant, his robe sweeping the pavement. By reporting that a builder, a shoemaker and a shopkeeper had returned to the Market Square, the article presented Varsovian readers with an image of the Old Town's pre-war population that was both sanitised and politically resonant. A local shoemaker had led a militia in the Warsaw Uprising of 1794 against the imperial Russian forces occupying the city. The communists seized upon him gratefully as a revolutionary ancestor, though his trade suited their narrative better than the fact that he prospered from it sufficiently to buy a house in the Old Town. Although the shopkeeper was not strictly proletarian either, he was plebeian, and for good measure was said to have been a member of the communist People's Army resistance group. That was entirely possible, since the People's Army did take part in the defence of the Old Town district (and its command staff was based there, until they were all but wiped out by a bomb that struck the house in which they were gathered). But it was a relatively small fraction of the insurgent forces, and the emerging regime needed to magnify it retrospectively. The authorities appropriated dead combatants, recording their remains as those of fallen People's Army fighters.[12]

It was not a worker or a soldier who came to personify the spirit of the ruined Old Town, however, but a retired bank clerk. Before the war, Kazimiera Majchrzak used to feed the Old Town's pigeons, on a considerable scale: it was said that she bought more than five kilograms of grain for them a day. She had carried on through the

3. Kazimiera Majchrzak in the street where she lived and looked after the pigeons of Warsaw's Old Town, 1945.

occupation, and had returned to look after them again, even though her meagre pension was insufficient to keep her out of abject poverty. Her life echoed the examples of the saints, bearing privation in a kind of desert while devoting herself to the care of other living creatures. It was an image that came to symbolise Varsovian endurance. Another elderly woman lived in a neighbouring ruin, keeping rabbits in a corner of her room for company. 'It's a little nicer with living things around,' she told a reporter from *Życie Warszawy* (*Warsaw Life*).[13]

Majchrzak criticised the restoration of the houses for the museum in the Market Square. 'It would be better to restore them for people,' she told a writer who described an encounter with her in *Robotnik* (*The Worker*), the Socialist Party newspaper. She herself was rehoused elsewhere, leaving the pigeons to serve the press as symbolic doves of peace that 'accompanied the builders of the East–West Route' – a throughway that ran past the edge of the Old Town – 'in their efforts to lay the first foundations of socialist, peace-loving Warsaw'. When the ruined house she had lived in was rebuilt, it featured a sculpture of a group of pigeons above the door, as though they had lighted upon the arch.[14]

Shortly before the two women spoke to the press, their street was cleared up by a brigade of goldsmiths. This was part of a major operation in which 3,000 craftsmen and tradesmen tackled the wreckage of the Old Town, dismantling barricades left over from the Uprising. They deployed in their guilds: as well as the goldsmiths, there were barbers, shoemakers, grocers, woodworkers, tailors, grocers, butchers and allied trades. Exercises of this kind would become a familiar feature of the reconstruction as the regime bedded in and sought to mobilise the people. 'We formed a chain and passed the bricks from the demolished houses from hand to hand,' recalled one of the participants, a student at the time. 'Nobody had gloves, and we scraped the skin off our hands, but we didn't complain. There was huge enthusiasm for the work.' People would surely have volunteered even if they had not been volunteered by the authorities.[15]

Some of them, however, were driven by the need to survive in the present, rather than to rebuild for the future. 'We had nothing,' remembered a woman who had still been in her teens when she returned to Warsaw from forced labour and a series of concentration camps in Germany. 'What we brought from Germany we sold, so as to have something to eat. We would go to the Old Town and clean up bricks. Nobody paid money for that, just a piece of sausage and a roll or a slice of bread. We had to go early in the morning to get into those teams.' Many people did get paid for clearing rubble – but only for a few months, until the city decided it could no longer afford their wages. By one estimate, about a third of Warsaw's inhabitants may have depended on the brigade workers' earnings during the summer of 1945.[16]

The brigades' efforts were mirrored in Berlin, which now resembled Warsaw in its devastation, and where the authorities also directed people to shift the city's remains by hand. As in Warsaw, many of the labourers were female. The 'rubble-women', Trümmerfrauen, came to symbolise the new start that the German people had to make after the end of the Reich. In East Germany, they were remembered as pioneers for the building of socialism, a role in which their Polish counterparts had also been cast.[17]

In those first post-war years, Polish socialism had yet to assume its fully stereotyped Stalinist form. A short film made in 1947 opens with scenes of Warsaw coming back to metropolitan life, with shops and businesses reviving the private enterprise that had surrounded Varsovians before the war. These images serve to establish a dramatic contrast with the subject of the film, a 'quiet and lonely' backstreet of the Old Town. It hardly seems to be part of the same city, or any living city at all. Every wall is scarred and mutilated. One of them bears a BOS plaque declaring what is left of the building to be historic. The line of the street has disappeared under weeds, with a path winding through it as if through a forest.

At first sight it appears abandoned, but it is populated by 'Robinsons', mostly in the cellars that afford shelter from winter cold and summer heat. They are making the best of the ruins in which they have nested. This is a story of individual self-help, not of brigades directed by the state. The Old Town is honoured as 'the most heroic neighbourhood of Warsaw', but the scenes in the street are homely. Flowerpots line windowsills; a girl mops the tiled floor of what was once a shop; children play hopscotch on battered flagstones. A boy in a cellar builds a wooden glider (and from the ceiling hangs a model of a bomber with Royal Air Force markings, which would have been hastily removed if the filmmakers had visited a year or two later). He looks up through the window: there are children outside, gazing at builders who are putting the roof on the first house in the street to have been rebuilt. 'Before long all the inhabitants of cellars and ruins will move into sunny houses,' promises the narrator.[18]

Nevertheless, the Old Town continued to be a backwater of the reconstruction for some time, and the street remained a backwater within it, with walls still left unsecured a decade later. By then the children in the film would have grown up, probably on housing estates elsewhere in the city. In People's Poland, the Robinsons themselves were reconstructed.[19]

On the first day of September 1947, the start of what the government had declared a Month of Rebuilding the Capital, crowds of workers tackled the rubble of the Old Town with spades and pickaxes, helped by public employees diverted from their regular duties in state and municipal offices. They were joined by government ministers and the President of the Republic, Bolesław Bierut, who wielded a spade for the newsreel camera. 'Let's get to work,' he urged, 'and build a new Warsaw, the splendid future capital city of Poland!'[20]

His appearance in the Old Town Market Square signalled his commitment to the reconstruction of the quarter, and his words placed the historic kernel of Warsaw at the heart of the national reconstruction project. It was a powerful expression of the government's national vision, and suggests Józef Sigalin was right to claim that Bierut took a close personal interest in the reconstruction of the Old Town. But, like the President's efforts with the spade, it made little impact on the rubble. Nor did the brigades of students and office workers, although they did provide rousing newsreel footage. That was unsurprising, since there was nearly half a million cubic metres of debris to shift. The brigades lacked machinery, the city lacked funds, and the state had yet to adopt a clear concept that would drive the reconstruction forward.[21]

The new power had to consolidate itself and establish a permanent form before it could decide upon the form it should impose upon its capital. It was midway through the process when Bierut bestowed his blessing on the Old Town with his spade. In June 1945 it had constituted itself as the Provisional Government of National Unity, which was dominated by the communists but included representatives of other parties. While stepping up its repressive efforts against its opponents, armed and otherwise, who remained loyal to the wartime underground state, it undertook a series of measures that gave the communist party an institutional monopoly of political power. In 1946, it falsified the results of a referendum in order to weaken the communists' most significant rivals, the Polish Peasants' Party, and it then falsified the results of the elections the following January, giving the communist-dominated Democratic Bloc 394 parliamentary seats against the 28 taken by the Peasants' Party. Bierut became President of the Republic, and most of the remaining partisans accepted an amnesty. At the end of 1948, the communist Polish Workers' Party absorbed its main partner in the Democratic Bloc, the Polish Socialist Party, and renamed itself the Polish United Workers' Party. Although the Peasants' Party and a centrist party were allowed to persist as shadows of their former selves, so that the regime could still claim to be pluralistic, the transition to a one-party state on the Soviet model was complete.

Stalinist Poland duly resounded to stentorian clichés about 'building socialism' and 'Polish–Soviet friendship'. But its new ideology was not simply a transcription of Soviet communist precepts. It was an unholy alliance between communism and a mutant version of Roman Dmowski's National Democracy, opportunistically founded on Poland's re-emergence after the war within altered borders and without most of its pre-war ethnic minorities. The new Soviet satellite state exploited this convulsive transformation to claim a patriotic authenticity based on an ethnically exclusive vision of nationhood. It also took brutal measures to reduce its ethnic minority population still further. This project was the background to the reconstruction of the Old Town and architectural heritage elsewhere in the country, which was shaped to tell the stories about Polish history that those in power needed the people to hear.

Poland was shifted to the west by the Potsdam Conference, in 1945, when the leaders of the Soviet Union, the United States and the United Kingdom agreed that its western border should run along the line of the Oder and Neisse rivers. On the eastern side, the Soviet

Union claimed the territories it had seized in 1939. By an uncanny historical coincidence, Poland now occupied almost exactly the same territory that the first Polish state had claimed a thousand years before, under a family of rulers known as the Piasts. The new state's propagandists hailed it as a country that had recovered its original and true form. Its leaders presented themselves as the modern heirs to 'Piast Poland', a concept that had emerged between the wars to distinguish the National Democrats' ideal of an ethnically homogeneous state from Piłsudski's more expansive vision of the republic. Now it served as a useful basis for the communists' historical narrative – especially since according to legend, the eponymous founder of the dynasty was a working man, a wheelwright by trade. At the same time, the Piast idea connected the new state with the 'Baptism of Poland' in 966, when the Piast ruler Mieszko I embraced Christianity. By claiming Piast lineage, the officially atheist People's Poland gave itself Christian roots.[22]

The communists claimed the credit for bringing Piast Poland back into existence, hailing the territory gained from Germany as the 'Recovered Lands' that had rightfully been Polish since the previous millennium. 'You have returned to your own country – as the rightful owners of these territories,' the communist party leader Władysław Gomułka told the settlers in 1946. To develop this idea, the authorities supported the establishment of bodies devoted to providing historical arguments for Polish territorial claims to lands bounded by the Oder river and the Baltic Sea. This intellectual movement, known as Western Thought, dated back to the nineteenth century and was associated with National Democracy. It now suited the communists to nurture the nationalists, using them to provide scholarly support for the new regime's claims to legitimacy, and to counter an obvious source of political opposition by giving it an incentive to collaborate instead. Whereas the authorities had chosen to overlook architects' previous political associations when the Bureau for the Reconstruction of the Capital was set up, they encouraged the exponents of Western Thought precisely because those thinkers were nationalistic in outlook.[23]

Poland's dramatic crabwalk across the map was accompanied by mass transfers of millions of people across the region, turning the redrawn state into a cauldron of expulsions and coerced migrations. The government's General Plenipotentiary for Repatriation declared that Poland would no longer have ethnic minorities: it had moved to a conception of itself as an ethnically exclusive nation state, because minorities would inevitably become fifth columns. He was a member of the Polish Workers' Party, but his words would have been cheered to the echo if he had uttered them at a gathering of National Democrats before the war.[24]

The main thrust of the government's efforts was directed against those Germans in the western territories who had not already fled the advance of the Red Army. Their removal was part of the largest forced exodus in history, which relocated some twelve million Germans westwards from Soviet-dominated regions to the other side of the new German border – a mass ethnic cleansing that was sponsored not only by the Soviet Union but also by the Western Allies, who broadly shared the Polish view of minorities as potential sources of trouble. More than three million Germans were expelled from the 'Recovered Lands' between 1945 and 1947. Nearly a million Poles were sent to those lands from what was now Soviet territory in the east.[25]

On the other side of the country, nearly half a million Ukrainians and Lemkos, a group classed by the government as Ukrainian, were transferred to the Soviet Union in 1946. After the Soviet authorities refused to take any more, Polish forces drove a further 140,000 from their homes the following year, in what they called 'Operation Vistula'. This was partly a counter-insurgency measure against Ukrainian nationalist partisans, who had themselves conducted a bloody ethnic cleansing campaign against Poles several years previously. Emptying the villages would drain the sea in which the guerrillas swam, and also eradicate the habitats in which minority ethnic consciousness could be sustained. Their inhabitants were dispersed throughout the Recovered Lands, to be assimilated in the way Dmowski had envisaged at the beginning of the century.[26]

The largest minority had been largely annihilated. Only about 10 per cent of Poland's pre-war Jewish population survived the Holocaust, the majority of them in the Soviet Union. Most of them returned; most of them left again. Many found that their homes had been destroyed, or occupied by others. By the beginning of July 1946, 244,000 people were registered with the Central Committee of Jews in Poland. That month, more than forty Jews were murdered in a pogrom in the town of Kielce, and another thirty in the surrounding area. The attack precipitated a wave of emigration. By September, 100,000 Jews had left the country; thousands more followed them over the course of the next few years.[27]

Across the country as a whole, many individuals with minority backgrounds, especially Jewish ones, probably felt it best to conceal their heritage and identify themselves as part of the majority. To all visible intents and purposes, Poland had become an ethnically homogeneous state. For the new regime, that counted as an achievement. The country was felt to have attained an ideal ethnic condition, and its rulers promised that it was on its way to an ideal social order.[28]

Chapter 5
The Whole Nation Is Building
Its Capital City

Amid the seismic shocks that reverberated through Polish institutions as the regime consolidated its power, the Bureau for the
Reconstruction of the Capital remained a pluralistic body in which
non-communists like Jan Zachwatowicz retained both presence and
influence. Although he had not been put in charge of the Bureau,
despite having led the preparatory organisation, his position as
director of its Architectural Heritage department was a powerful
one. His authority was further enhanced by his appointment as the
nation's Conservator-General, responsible for heritage across the
entire country.

It would in any case have seemed somewhat out of balance to put
a conservator rather than an urban planner in charge of rebuilding
the capital as a whole. The man chosen to head the Bureau known as
BOS was both professionally and politically suitable for the position.
Roman Piotrowski represented Warsaw's architectural left, which
was oriented towards urban planning in general and housing in
particular. Between the wars he had been part of Praesens, a Polish
manifestation of the international modernist movement in architecture. During the war, the Praesens architects regrouped in the
Architectural and Urban Planning Studio, based in an apartment in

a northern suburb; it formed an alternative centre of urbanist thought to the Faculty of Architecture in the Polytechnic building on the other side of the city. Many of the people associated with the Studio were members of the Polish Socialist Party, or joined the Polish Workers' Party when it was established in 1942. The Studio architects had little interest in heritage and an iconoclastic attitude towards tradition.[1]

When BOS was established, with one of their number in charge of it, they reassembled in its planning department. Another former associate of the Studio, Marian Spychalski, had become first the mayor of Warsaw and then a government minister. The political environment suited them, and the need for what they hoped to build – modern, healthy mass housing for working-class people – had never been greater. But in some respects, the regime treated the conservators' dreams more indulgently than it did theirs. Palaces and Old Town merchant houses were rebuilt as idealised versions of their former selves, at least on the outside. Housing estates and administrative buildings were obliged to conform to the tenets of socialist realism, a doctrine that strengthened the regime's control over culture and displayed its totalitarian ambitions. Introduced to Poland by the architect Edmund Goldzamt, 'socrealizm' rejected functional modernist forms in favour of ornament intended to tell glorious, inspiring stories of progress towards socialism. Architects could usually satisfy its requirements with the use of classical columns and friezes depicting workers in heroic profile.[2]

Its promulgation in 1949 was a strategic political adjustment intended to resolve the tensions between the regime's nationalism and its communism. Rattled by Yugoslavia's split from the Soviet camp, Moscow was especially alert to 'nationalist deviation'. To achieve what it regarded as the proper ideological balance, it handed down the maxim 'national in form, socialist in content'. In doing so, it directed Poland's leftist architects to turn away from international currents, thereby removing themselves from Western influences.

They were now to look for examples in the country's own heritage, and to apply them in a Soviet-designed framework. This resulted in stylistic farragoes such as a steelworks building topped with a crenellation of the kind known as 'Polish parapets', or 'attics', modelled on the one that adorns the sixteenth-century Cloth Hall in the vast main square of nearby Kraków. The 1950s steel-town development of Nowa Huta was built as a modern socialist showpiece to outshine the ancient royal city, yet its creators felt the need to adorn an administrative building at an industrial facility with pseudo-Renaissance trappings. Polish attics were placed atop reconstructed buildings in the Recovered Lands, even in places where no such decorations had previously existed, to help the new settlers feel that they really were in Poland.[3]

Crenellations also featured prominently in the Six-Year Plan for the Reconstruction of the Capital that Bolesław Bierut publicly previewed in July 1949, hard on the heels of the proclamation of socialist realism. By putting his name to the Plan, and himself forward as the patron of reconstruction of the capital, he underlined its central place in the national project. He was also in the process of strengthening his own place at the centre of political power. This was a pivotal development in the struggle within the Party over the balance between its function as an element of the Soviet order and its nationalist tendencies, personified in the rivalry between Bierut and Władysław Gomułka. The latter was accused of 'right-wing nationalist deviation' and lost his position as First Secretary of the Party to Bierut in 1948. A week after Bierut's speech, the Soviet ambassador sent a letter to his minister claiming that the pre-war Polish regime's military intelligence service was still active in the country, and that Gomułka's close ally Marian Spychalski was one of its agents. According to the ambassador, the deputy defence minister had engineered the removal of Soviet personnel from the Polish army, and brought in officers returning from ideologically suspect exile in London. Spychalski was purged, jailed, tortured, and forced to testify at a show trial that sent Gomułka to prison in 1951. It was thus Bierut who presided over the early years of Warsaw's reconstruction, one of the highlights of which was the resurrection of the Old Town's Market Square.[4]

In his Six-Year Plan speech, Bierut denounced the chaotically 'cosmopolitan' development of the city centre between the wars, and decried the 'heritage of bourgeois cosmopolitanism' that produced 'colourless, box-like houses'. Cosmopolitanism covered a multitude of sins, from capitalist building development driven by 'greed and speculation', to the 'formalism' embraced by architects with communist sympathies. It did not carry the same force as a codeword for Jewishness in Poland as it did in the Soviet Union, where an anti-semitic purge against 'rootless cosmopolitans' was under way, but the undertones were present. There are unmistakeable resonances between the President's rhetoric in 1949 and the diatribe that the architect Jan Poliński published in 1939, attacking tenements built by 'Jewish capitalists', and 'box-like' 'Jewish' designs.[5]

Poliński himself took to the post-war Polish environment like a duck to water, despite having spent much of the war in England, where he helped to set up the Polish School of Architecture at the University of Liverpool – and also took part, as a representative of the National-Radical 'Falanga' party, in a semi-clandestine nationalist alliance opposed to the Polish government in exile. After returning to Poland in 1947, he enjoyed a successful career designing interiors, for everything from cafés to government buildings. He was not required to publicly recant his pre-war views, unlike Helena Syrkus, one of whose works he had singled out as an example of 'Jewish boxiness'. She had been a leading light of the avant-garde Praesens group, but at a meeting of the communist party's architect members held the month before Bierut's speech, she condemned modernist currents of thought – 'abstractionism, constructivism, formalism' – as manifestations of the 'destructive cosmopolitanism' from which card-carrying Party architects had to cut themselves off.

Being Jewish, Syrkus was particularly vulnerable to accusations of cosmopolitanism.[6]

Bierut made it clear that architects should henceforth draw more extensively upon the nation's 'sound traditions'. Against this background, the political incentives to reconstruct the Old Town became sharper. After all, it was the point of origin for the capital's traditions, and it could serve a valuable didactic purpose by highlighting the ones that were held to be sound. Unlike other new building projects, it came ready with its own answers to the question of how to make it national in form. And the government had grasped the perfect way to give it socialist content. The Old Town was to be part of an archipelago of model housing estates in the centre of the city, reconfiguring the area as a zone for the benefit of workers instead of capital. On the outside, the historic facades would be recreated; on the inside, working people would live in well-designed modern apartments. With its clarity, simplicity and compelling symbolism, the concept was politically irresistible.

Jan Zachwatowicz elaborated the idea in an article published a couple of months after Bierut's speech. He seemed very comfortable hailing the successes of People's Poland and sketching the future place of the Old Town in its capital. That was not altogether surprising, since what he was describing was a development of what he had already begun to do before the war. He saw the district as a site that offered 'not just the charm of old streets and squares, but also the key to understanding the character of the city'. The Old Town could illuminate how the city had developed, and how it might develop in the future. It also had to be a living quarter, not a museum that was deserted after closing time. Zachwatowicz had envisaged that the rebuilt Old Town would resume the direction in which he had helped take it before the war, functioning principally as a centre for cultural organisations and museums. He argued that events held by those bodies would keep the quarter alive in the evenings, but he was willing to accept that the Old Town should have people actually living in it too. Happily, the two functions would complement each other, and would require the same architectural measures. Making it more historically legible would also make it a more pleasant place in which to live.[7]

The vision of a quarter fit for workers promised a radical change of strategy from the gentrification espoused by admirers of the Old Town in the early part of the century. They were supported by the Old Town property owners' association, according to which the wretched conditions in the quarter's tenement houses were the fault of the occupants, whom it described as 'not only poor, but morally depraved'. In later years Zachwatowicz took a more jocular tone, recalling his discomfiture when he wanted to show somebody the medieval walls on which he was working, 'and the local prostitutes bowed to me'. He gave the impression that he got on well with the locals. That is easy to imagine, since his wartime heritage-rescuing activities evidenced his ability to strike up cooperative relationships with people from diverse walks of life. But his project was a step towards a different kind of community for the Old Town, modifying its appearance and displacing some of its inhabitants.[8]

Aesthetic and social critiques of the Old Town converged on the idea that its original forms had been degraded by subsequent modifications. Houses built for prosperous merchants had been divided up into batteries for impoverished tenant families, with deplorable consequences both for the well-being of the occupants and for the fabric of the buildings. 'Dampness, leaks, cracked walls, rotting beams, door and window frames, sagging floors and ceilings, unceasing general decay' were typical pathologies. Courtyards were blocked up with outbuildings and annexes, increasing the number of occupants while diminishing the outside space available to them. Those additions were excrescences that had to be removed, for the sake of the past and the present alike.[9]

In 1938 Zachwatowicz made a start between the inner and outer medieval walls, which had long been hidden by houses that had been set up against them. He revealed the walls by demolishing the infill, and repaired their 'missing teeth' with reconstructed sections. In retrospect, the project looks like a kind of pilot for the much larger one he undertook ten years later, demonstrating principles and arguments that would be applied to the ruins of the quarter as a whole. Its basic aim was to reverse the balance of history, asserting the priority of the Old Town's oldest structures. In the reconfiguration of the quarter to tell a suitable historical story, the Middle Ages had to come first. Structures that stood in their way would have to be demolished even if they were themselves old – the strip between the walls had begun to fill up when the fortifications became militarily redundant in the seventeenth century. The stories they could tell would spoil the line of the grand narrative.[10]

Here Zachwatowicz was following an internationally controversial precedent. When the French architect Eugène Viollet-le-Duc and his successor Paul Boeswillwald rebuilt the medieval citadel of Carcassonne in the nineteenth century, they knocked down more than a hundred textile workers' houses and other buildings between the inner and outer walls, enhancing the spectacle by erasing part of the site's history. Viollet-le-Duc sought not to return a monument to its original condition, or to any particular stage of its development, but to give it an ideal form. Parts of it could be removed, restored, or reconstructed as he believed they should have been, rather than as they had been. That view guided him when he designed a replacement for the original spire of Notre-Dame Cathedral in Paris, which had been taken down in the previous century.[11]

His spire (which collapsed into the nave when fire swept through the cathedral in 2019) was roughly contemporaneous with the English art critic John Ruskin's treatise *The Seven Lamps of Architecture*, and anathema to the principles Ruskin advanced in it. The Englishman denounced the very idea of reconstruction as 'a Lie from beginning to end'. Restoration, he insisted, was 'the most total destruction which a building can suffer', because the act would turn it into a new building. 'You may make a model of a building as you may of a corpse, and your model may have the shell of the old walls within it as your cast might have the skeleton, with what advantage I neither see nor care: but the old building is destroyed . . .' The 'greatest glory' of a building lay not in its form or its substance but its age, the fact of its having passed through time. Ruskin thought that 'a building cannot be considered as in its prime until four or five centuries have passed over it', a condition that the Old Town of Warsaw had met by the point at which it was destroyed.[12]

Questions of preservation became ever more highly charged as modernising cities and nations struggled to decide what their past meant to them. Ruskin's diatribe was echoed in the 1900s by Georg Dehio, a German art historian, who formulated the dictum 'Conserve, do not restore'. Alois Riegl, Austria's Conservator-General, also affirmed oldness as a value in itself. He distinguished between intentional monuments, constructed as commemorative objects, and unintentional ones, which become monuments because they come to stand for the history through which they have passed. In the old quarter of Warsaw, the intentional kind was exemplified by King Zygmunt's column, overlooking the square outside the Royal Castle, and the unintentional variety was represented by the merchants' townhouses on the Market Square, which grew into monuments as they acquired the patina of the centuries.[13]

Opponents of restoration had to accept that objects could not be preserved forever, and so would eventually be lost, but they were not contemplating the possibility of cataclysms such as the one that would bring down the column and the townhouses alike. If Alois Riegl had lived to witness the reconstruction of Warsaw's Old Town, he might have regarded the rebuilt townhouses as intentional monuments, commemorating the fate of the buildings in whose place they stood. UNESCO did more or less that in 1980 when it inscribed the quarter on its World Heritage List. After wrestling with the question of the Old Town's authenticity for two years, it eventually adopted the site as 'an exceptional example of the comprehensive reconstruction of a city that had been deliberately and totally destroyed', founded upon 'the inner strength and determination of the nation'. The argument may have been contrived, but the conclusion was sound. Heroically intentional, the Starówka is an authentic national monument.[14]

The authenticity debates of the century's early decades gave rise to the Athens Charter for the Restoration of Historic Monuments, adopted at an international congress of architects and conservationists in 1931. One of its precepts was that new materials used in the reconstruction of ruins should be recognisable as such, so people could tell what was new and what was original. After the war, Zachwatowicz honoured that particular principle in the breach rather than the observance, presenting the rebuilt quarter as a seamless unity. Before the war, however, he dutifully marked each reconstructed portion of wall off with a black line. Where only fragments of walls and arrow-slits remained, the newer surfaces in which they were embedded were plastered, so that the medieval bricks stood out red against a white background.[15]

The final element of the colour scheme was green, added by sowing grass and planting shrubs in the cleared tract. This, Zachwatowicz claimed, was hugely important for the overcrowded quarter, providing it with public gardens. He did not mention what happened to the occupants of the houses that he had 'cleaned' away.

A year after the war ended, Zachwatowicz outlined a 'programme and rules for the conservation of historic buildings'. It was also a declaration of principles and a manifesto: 'Being unable to accept the tearing of our cultural monuments away from us, we will reconstruct them from the foundations, to pass on to future generations, if not the authentic monuments, then at least their exact forms, alive in our memory ...' The axiom underlying the programme was that 'the nation and the monuments of its culture are one'. Rebuilding the nation therefore entailed the rebuilding of its heritage.[16]

As the Conservator-General acknowledged, the conclusions that followed from the axiom were 'not always in agreement with scholarly views'. Faced with such cataclysmic losses, architects and conservators would have to embark on a reconstruction project of an unprecedented character. They would have to go much further than simply replacing 'missing teeth'. In effect, Zachwatowicz was proposing a derogation from the Athens Charter for the Restoration of Historic Monuments, on the grounds that Poland's national interests had to take precedence over 'the principles proclaimed at conservation congresses'. National interests had prevailed over the purist doctrine of non-intervention after the First World War, and not just in Poland. He noted that the cathedral of Reims had been reconstructed after the damage it sustained in the earlier conflict. If a historic building was important to a nation – and historic buildings were especially important to nations that were just regaining their independence – it would not be left in ruins. Now that nearly every historic building in the capital had been destroyed, responsibility to future generations demanded 'full reconstruction, conscious of the tragedy of the conservation falsehood being perpetrated'. Among all the falsehoods and breaches of principle that were being perpetrated in Poland at that time, this was probably the one that least deserved to be described as a tragedy. But Zachwatowicz evidently felt he needed to show that he had wrestled with his professional conscience, and felt John Ruskin's pain.

Although he did not mention it, the principle of authenticity had been overridden by Polish national considerations even before the recovery of independence. In the early years of the century, which turned out to be the next-to-last years of the Habsburg Empire, the imperial authorities in Vienna handed over Kraków's historic Wawel Castle to the local Polish administration. It had been indifferently rebuilt after it burned down in the eighteenth century, and had latterly been used as a barracks. As it had been the seat of Polish monarchs until 1596 when King Zygmunt III Waza decided to move the court to Warsaw, Wawel demanded the restoration of something approaching its former glory. That required the reconstruction of the roof and other parts of the structure. The Austrian Conservator-General objected to the plans, regarding them as a proposal to violate the authenticity of the monument, but he was eventually overruled. After the First World War, the castle's interiors were restored by Adolf Szyszko-Bohusz, an architect who argued that the object of conservation was not the substance of the monument but its 'spirit'. He subsequently brought his historically creative approach to the restoration of the interiors of the Royal Castle in Warsaw.[17]

Observing that historic buildings were not just for the cognoscenti, Zachwatowicz argued that they performed didactic and emotional services for the masses. The more complete they were, the greater the emotional response they evoked in people, and the more they taught them about the history of the nation. Completeness mattered more than authenticity: 'The significance of an architectural form is independent of when it was made.' And unlike a bare relic, a complete building was capable of playing its part in the life of its neighbourhood. 'Whether it becomes a busy office building or a peaceful museum ... a historic building must become active and perform a social role, making its full impact as a vital element of the district.' Each historic building, he declared, 'must find the most appropriate living content for itself'. In the Old Town, it subsequently transpired, the most appropriate living content for the rebuilt tenement houses would be workers and their families.

Zachwatowicz returned to the theme of opening up the space between the Old Town's medieval walls in 1949, linking it with the clearance of the additions that had overburdened and disfigured the quarter's houses. His first steps in that direction had provided residents with open space, light and access to fresh air, he wrote, echoing the Six-Year Plan's mantra of space, light and greenery. Now he promised that the residents would benefit from interiors equipped with all modern conveniences as well. He anticipated that the tenement houses would become homes for workers, craftsmen and public service employees. They would also provide studio spaces beneath their skylights for artists. The implication, which proved to be correct, was that the people who worked with their hands to reconstruct the Old Town would be rewarded by being allowed to live in it.[18]

None of this required him to alter his views to conform to the new ideology. Architects and urbanists before the war had not needed to be on the left to agree that Warsaw's housing was deplorably over-crowded and its inhabitants deserved healthier homes. That was hardly disputable in a city where only a third of the dwellings had toilets, and the average single-room flat was shared by four people. Zachwatowicz's approach to uncovering the walls showed that he was ready to recognise historic districts as community neighbour-hoods, and to incorporate features into his heritage work that bene-fited the residents. It also demonstrated that he took a pragmatic view of authenticity, and was prepared to replace lost features with reconstructions. His arguments about how to bring the district back to life as a heritage quarter that was home to a flourishing commu-nity would have been as appealing to nationalists or democrats as it was to the communists. If it had been the Western Allies that liber-ated Warsaw, and had either established a democratic system or allowed the authoritarian right to take back the power it lost in 1939, his proposals for the Old Town might have been much the same as the ones that met with Bierut's approval.[19]

According to legend, however, Bierut initially objected to the restoration of the defensive walls, because he feared that there might at some point be an uprising against the regime. He imagined insur-gents seizing the Old Town, turning it into a stronghold and using the walls as battlements from which to fire on government forces. Zachwatowicz is said to have countered the President's anxieties by drawing a sketch of what the view of the Old Town would look like without the walls in front of it. 'What do you see?' he asked. 'Nothing but churches!'[20]

This was one of several anecdotes that depicted him and his colleagues thwarting unwelcome ideas from the upper levels of the Party by mischievously playing on communist sentiments. In another version of the story, which Zachwatowicz himself was said to have told, a senior party figure declared that the area beyond the walls should be turned into lawns. 'Why yes, that's a splendid idea!' the Conservator-General exclaimed. 'I've seen that somewhere before,' he added, as if musing aloud: 'Ah yes – that's just what Mussolini did in Rome!'[21]

Did he really praise a senior communist's idea and in the next breath associate it with the inventor of fascism? The tale implies a striking degree of confidence on his part that he could make such remarks without them coming back to haunt him. It also prompts a question about what he actually did think of Mussolini's Italy, which had considerable appeal in eastern Europe between the wars as a model for building strong new states. In 1937, as the editor of an architectural journal, he had published an article by Piotr Biegański which highlighted the central role of architecture in the new Fascist order. Biegański found much to praise about Italian architecture under Mussolini, from its design aesthetics to its social provisions.[22]

If the architects had ever fallen foul of the authorities, the article might have featured in the case against them. But they never did. The only prominent architect to be jailed by the regime was the communist Marian Spychalski, but that happened because he was also a politician, and found himself on the losing side of a power struggle within the Party. By recruiting architects to the reconstruction project, regardless of their pre-war political leanings or wartime loyalties, BOS harnessed their sense of patriotic duty. It gave architects who had served in the AK a way to finish the struggle against the Nazi occupiers without embarking on a struggle against the new power. Warsaw had to be rebuilt precisely because it had been deliberately destroyed by the Nazis, who tore out 'whole pages of our history, written in the stone letters of architecture', as Zachwatowicz put it.[23]

The reconstruction of the capital, with the Old Town in its historical form at the heart of it, was the final act of the resistance. BOS's recruits had promised it publicly on May Day in 1945, when they marched to the ruins behind a banner vowing 'We Will Rebuild the Old Town'. Their leaders committed themselves to it in the spring of 1946, when Zachwatowicz and Biegański led them 'to work', as Sigalin put it, in the Market Square. They gathered outside the precarious shell of a house on the corner of the museum row, where bricks and a trowel awaited them on scaffolding rigged up from planks. Roman Piotrowski clambered up and laid a few of the bricks, followed by Zachwatowicz, Biegański and some of the others. Among them was Józef Vogtman, an architect and former AK combatant who had served in the Old Town during the Uprising. 'It wasn't just about saving one more historic building, of course,' he recalled. 'We all felt that it was a very important moment for our city. It was a symbolic act, a decision to rebuild the Starówka.'[24]

The first public step in the reconstruction was another symbolic gesture: the raising of King Zygmunt's column in the Castle Square. It was combined with the opening of the capital's first major new infrastructure project, the East–West Route. This was a dramatic engineering coup, driving a highway nearly seven kilometres long through the northern half of Warsaw. From the eastern bank of the river, it ran along the base of the scarp where the Royal Castle had stood, and through a tunnel below the approach to the square. This would be the first bold stroke in the reconstruction of the capital as a modern metropolis, around a lattice of carriageways designed to speed the passage and circulation of motor vehicles.

As such, it represented everything that the heritage conservationists feared. Tensions between the aims of preservationists and modernising urban planners had intensified in cities across Europe as the century gathered pace and motor traffic grew. Now the balance between the camps had shifted decisively. For a preservationist, the shattering of a historic building could only be a loss, but for a moderniser, it could be a valuable opportunity. Each ruin diminished the preservationists' moral capital, by reducing the stock of material to be preserved, and increased that of the modernisers, who could claim emptied urban spaces as resources for building a better future. In many cities, the planners' claims were irresistible. The future took precedence over the past, and effaced it. But in Warsaw, the first highway into the future was presented as a means to protect the past. The new regime needed history as well as infrastructure, and the East–West Route would show how a harmonising balance could be struck between the two. Modern engineering would come to the relief of the Old Town.

A page in the magazine *Stolica* (*Capital City*) set out the scheme's benefits under two headings, given equal weight. On the left of the page, its advantages for 'historic Warsaw' were listed, with an accompanying text by Jan Zachwatowicz. It would divert traffic from the Castle Square, the centrepiece of the 'Acropolis of Warsaw'; it would relieve the narrow streets of 'Old Warsaw'; and it would improve views of the scarp, surmounted by the Castle. On the right-hand side, the scheme's role in national defence was outlined. The new throughway would speed military transport to battlefronts, and the tunnel could be used as an air raid shelter for 10,000 people.[25]

There was scepticism about whether that military traffic would really be for national defence. Maria Dąbrowska, a major figure in twentieth-century Polish literature, figured that the crosstown route was intended as a strategic artery for Soviet army offensives. To her mind, it was Russia's way of exploiting the aftermath of the Uprising, turning the immolation of the Old Town to Moscow's benefit. Having sarcastically remarked that the road should be opened by Konstantin Rokossovsky, a Red Army commander of Polish descent who was both a Marshal of the Soviet Union and Poland's Minister of Defence, she was staggered to read subsequently that Rokossovsky did indeed conduct the ceremony, together with President Bierut. It took place on 22 July 1949, the fifth anniversary of the 'July Manifesto' that had proclaimed the embryonic communist-controlled government to be the country's sole legitimate authority, dismissing the exile government as an illegal body based on a 'fascist' pre-war constitution. That date loomed large on the calendar in Stalinist Poland as the default deadline for showpiece reconstruction projects.[26]

The architectural studio responsible for the Route was led by Józef Sigalin; Stanisław Jankowski was a member of the core design team. Rumour had it that Edmund Goldzamt, the herald of socialist realism, suspected Jankowski to be a British intelligence asset whose initial designs for the tunnel had deliberately made it too low for the passage of Soviet tanks. Goldzamt's suspicions would doubtless have been heightened by Jankowski's proposal that the Route be named after the 'Heroes of the Starówka' – a group in which the former lieutenant known as 'Agaton' could have claimed membership himself. The SS officer in command of the Reich forces during the Uprising had stated that the stronghold completely blocked the passage of the German army from east to west; so, Jankowski declared, 'let the route be named after the Starówka that once defended it'. His personification of the Old Town, merging the district with the insurgents who had fought in it, showed how the Uprising had transformed its value and meaning. Before the war, its reputation had been compromised by its degraded condition. Now, in blood-steeped ruins, it had won honour. It was a concentration of national heroism, sacrifice and loss.[27]

By this time Sigalin was properly qualified for the job. Although it was hardly his fault that he had been unable to complete his studies in 1939, his lack of a diploma prompted unsympathetic comment in architectural circles. The Council of the Faculty of Architecture made an official protest about his use of the title 'Engineer'. After the matter came to the attention of the Ministry of Reconstruction and the Architects' Association, Sigalin went back to the Faculty and completed his course. As one of his professors, Jan Zachwatowicz found himself in the curious position of being simultaneously his academic superior and, at BOS, his professional subordinate. For his diploma project, Sigalin designed a modernist concrete structure to house the Gajewski café, after which Piotr Biegański's wartime forgery cell had been named. It offered a hint of the kind of architecture he would have promoted if the Party had not imposed socialist realism.

Sigalin was not a hack who dutifully followed where the Party line took him. His success as a rebuilder of the capital arose in large measure from his political nous and his readiness to take initiatives. Not being wedded to modernism or conservation or any other architectural school, he approached planning questions pragmatically, weighing up what was politically desirable and what was possible. When it came to heritage, he neither wanted to sweep it away, as a true-believing moderniser might, nor to preserve it unaltered, as a faithful conservationist would. He understood its value, but he did not regard it as sacred. That made him a powerful but ambivalent ally for Zachwatowicz and the BOS 'monumentists', who had been at odds with the 'urbanists' in the planning department since the first few weeks of the Bureau's existence. Much of the time he positioned himself as the conservationists' adversary, in order to curb what he regarded as their excessive influence. At one meeting, he declared that there would be no 'heritage ghetto' in Warsaw. His stance gained him a reputation for hostility to conservationism that was misleading, although not unfounded. It may have helped him reduce his level of political risk, in a period when questions might be asked if people appeared to care more about national forms than socialist content.[28]

The East–West Route was exemplary in the balance of its approach, scrupulously offering features to please modernisers on the one hand and conservationists on the other. As it approached the tunnel from the river, a new showpiece housing estate arose on its left, replacing tenement houses that were levelled whether or not they could have been rebuilt. Conservationists and modernising planners were united in their detestation of the city's nineteenth-century tenements, which were considered to have blighted the lives of the people who had been forced to crowd into them as Warsaw mushroomed into a metropolis, as well as spoiling the views of the historic buildings that defined the silhouette of the city. Now a palace was visible, on the scarp at the edge of the Castle site, that before the war had been hidden by a viaduct. The palace signified that the new Poland would take care of its history; the estate asserted that the new capital city would be built for the well-being of the working class, not for capitalist profit. And the bridge that carried the road across the Vistula, named after the regions of the country where the funds to pay for it had been raised, was a satisfyingly prominent affirmation of the endlessly repeated slogan, 'The Whole Nation Is Building Its Capital City'.

Although the project threatened historic buildings that lay directly in its path, it served the conservationists' broader cause by drawing attention to the Old Town and the Castle site below which the route ran. Sigalin pointed out the potential for synergy between the historical and the modernising elements of the capital's reconstruction. As he told Roman Piotrowski, 'The moral and political significance of completing the East–West Route would be greatly increased by simultaneously unveiling the reconstructed King Zygmunt's column, and by the fact that the rebuilding of the Royal Castle had begun.' They could make the most of the equipment assembled for the throughway works by using it to erect a fragment of the Castle overlooking the road.[29]

It was not just Piotrowski that he needed to convince, though. The reconstruction of the supreme symbol of Polish statehood would require Soviet backing. Sigalin needed an excuse to pitch the idea to the senior leadership of Soviet architecture – and Moscow provided him with it in the form of a pair of large escalators, promised as the Soviet Union's contribution to the East–West Route. Carrying pedestrians between the tunnel and the Castle Square, they would be the first moving stairs that Warsaw had seen. Even today, they leap out from the plans as exactly the kind of novel, technically demanding feature that torments construction managers facing deadlines not to be missed on any account. The escalators had still not arrived by the end of 1948, so Sigalin went to Moscow in pursuit of them. While he was there, he made an excursion to meet with a group of senior Soviet architects at their country retreat outside the city. They spent seven hours discussing the Royal Castle, and decided that it should be rebuilt in its historic form, housing a museum of Polish culture.

Sigalin and his colleagues made the case for this 'treasury of the Polish Nation' in a brochure they prepared for the Party leadership in Warsaw. One of the main tasks of socialist education was the cultivation of 'patriotism in a spirit of international brotherhood', they declared. Patriotism was based on love of one's country, and that love was based on the thousand years of the nation's history. Sigalin's communism and the nationalism with which Jankowski had aligned himself before the war were cementing their alliance, under Russian auspices.[30]

In directing its satellites to build socialism upon national foundations, the Soviet Union was actually telling them to follow the model that it had adopted for itself, having fought what it called the 'Great Patriotic War'. But Sigalin's example illustrates that Polish communists were not simply following a line that meant nothing to them beyond the disciplined implementation of Party strategy. They could and did harbour authentically patriotic sentiments, which provided a basis of shared values for rebuilding the nation in collaboration with non-communists. Back in September 1939, when Sigalin heard that Soviet forces had crossed the eastern frontier, his reaction was reflexively Polish. He immediately saw it as the fourth partition of Poland, after the three that had wiped the country off the map towards the end of the eighteenth century. Sigalin felt himself to be Polish, and he responded as a Pole, construing the Soviet action as a new chapter in the Polish narrative of national independence. That shared and felt understanding of history helped Polish communists to sustain nationalism as the one great ideological continuity in Poland's history since the nation's return to the map in 1918, keeping it going until their own time was over and it was free to flourish again without restraint.

The Polish parliament subsequently approved the reconstruction of the Castle after the prime minister urged it 'as a testament to the inexhaustible strength of the nation and the majesty of People's Poland', in a speech that Sigalin wrote for him. By then, however, the opening of the East–West Route was only three weeks away, so the raising of King Zygmunt's column was the sole historical focus of the ceremonies on 22 July. The manoeuvre raised a large cross, taller than the figure of the monarch holding it, high above the Castle Square. Once the statue had been carefully winched into position, atop a new column made from granite mined in the Recovered Lands, a worker placed a traditional wreath upon the symbol of Christianity.[31]

Jan Zachwatowicz was furious about Sigalin's proposal to link the start of the reconstruction with the completion of the East–West Route. 'The plan has been produced by incompetent people who have consciously isolated themselves from conservation specialists all along,' he told a meeting in the mayor's office. While the conservationists had gained views of the old city skyline as the road came in from the river – and that skyline had always been important to Zachwatowicz – they had sustained losses once it reached the tunnel. The ruins of several eighteenth-century townhouses and a palace were demolished instead of being rebuilt; historic cellars were sacrificed to make way for the escalators from Moscow. Tensions between the monumentists and La Scala were inevitable.[32]

Zachwatowicz and a team of his fellow conservators were brought into the East–West Route studio, and new plans for the Castle were discussed. It was now to be the seat of supreme political authority, as well as the site of the museum of Polish culture that the top brass of Soviet architecture had recommended. Acquiring those responsibilities seemed to weigh it down instead of lifting it up, though. The focus of activity shifted to the other side of the Castle Square, to the streets of the Old Town. It might well have been physically easier to rebuild the Castle, which the Nazis had left a brownfield site. The heavy machinery was on hand, and there were no narrow streets in its way. But the project never got going after the false start caused by Sigalin's political misstep in securing the approval of the higher Soviet authority while omitting to win that of his subordinates.

That loss of impetus, at a time when funds were stretched and there was only room for one showpiece reconstruction project at a time, may have been fatal to the initiative in the early 1950s. The resulting hiatus continued until the 1970s. There were doubtless many reasons for that, but one that stands out was the unshakeable hostility of Władysław Gomułka, the senior communist who had been ousted in Bolesław Bierut's favour and subsequently jailed. Released from prison in 1954, he became the most powerful figure in the land two years later. In March 1956, Bierut died; in June, a sudden wave of strikes in the city of Poznań became an uprising in which dozens of workers were killed; in October, riding a wave of demands for reform, Gomułka became First Secretary of the Party. He remained in power until the end of 1970, when the newsreel of his career seemed to go into reverse. Sudden price rises provoked another outburst of protests; state forces shot workers down again; and the Party decided it had to make a fresh start with a new First Secretary.

Gomułka's successor, Edward Gierek, was quick to announce that the Royal Castle would at last be rebuilt. It was a highly effective move, showing that the new leader understood the power of national sentiment, and recognised that the people wanted more from their rulers than just affordable food. Unsurprisingly, Gomułka was bitter about it. 'I was never, and never will be, a supporter of rebuilding the castle, or to be more precise, building a new castle, since there is nothing left of the old one,' he declared. As far as he was concerned, it represented 'anarchy'. It was the place where the parliaments of the nobility assembled and were rendered futile by the right of any single nobleman to veto their decisions, undermining the viability of the state. It was the home of Poland's 'venal and despicable' kings; it was the place where the partitions of Poland were made law. The Castle, he concluded, was not a symbol of Polish statehood, but of the destruction of Polish states. Even allowing for the anger provoked by his downfall, his scorn conveys a compelling sense of why the reconstruction plans were left in a drawer for the fourteen years he was in power.[33]

The Castle was eventually completed in 1984.

Chapter 6
The Stones Speak Polish

When the government said that the whole nation was rebuilding its capital city, it meant first and foremost that the whole nation was paying for it through a tax on earnings of 0.5 per cent, channelled to the Social Fund for the Reconstruction of the Capital. Additional revenues were raised from cash collections, and a tax on vodka. The nation abroad contributed as well. A group of 46 Poles in Istanbul committed themselves to fund the reconstruction of a house in the Old Town's Market Square, raising 20,000 Turkish lira towards it. The building had been allocated to the city's historical museum, which was now to occupy not just three houses but the whole of the terrace on one side of the square. A few doors away, the costs of reconstructing the Baryczka house were met by a department store. Neither sponsorship worked out as the donors had hoped. The Turkish lira were appropriated for other projects; the department store was expropriated in 1950 by the state, which then presented it with a tax bill beyond its means and declared it bankrupt.[1]

The state also drew heavily upon its new western possessions, especially the city of Wrocław, treating the Recovered Lands with a highly charged combination of piety and rapaciousness. Their 'return' to Poland was exalted as a restoration that enabled the nation to assume its original and truest form, but the honour paid to them in rhetoric contrasted with the ruthless way that their assets were stripped and conveyed to the capital. Wrocław's material resources were rendered to Warsaw like tribute from a vassal city to the imperial centre. In the early 1950s, the tribute was paid mainly in bricks salvaged from rubble, sent in their hundreds of millions to rebuild the capital 300 kilometres away. A railway track was laid through Wrocław's Old Town to help move them out of the city. Buildings that could have been repaired were demolished to supply the capital's apparently insatiable demand for bricks, and some that had already been reconstructed were knocked down again. Although the authorities now maintained that Wrocław had always been Polish, they treated it as though it was still German.[2]

It must have been hard for them to do otherwise, since the city had only ceased to be German very suddenly and recently, right at the end of the war in Europe. To see its Polishness, they had to stare through the six centuries of history it had spent under Bohemian, Hungarian, Prussian and German rulers since the Middle Ages. It had owed its allegiance to the Piast dynasty nearly a thousand years before, after its conquest in 990 by the first Christian Piast duke, but had spent much of its subsequent development becoming steadily more German. By the beginning of the twentieth century, only a few hundredths of its population were Polish, and nearly all of them left when Poland regained its independence. Then, in 1945, it underwent a cataclysm that rendered it unrecognisable. The city formerly known as Breslau was swiftly declared to be Polish, but looking at the rubble and the scattered belongings, the columns of people leaving and people arriving, all as disoriented as each other, nobody could really tell what it now was, or what it would become.

Hitler had set the train of events in motion by ordering that Breslau was to be a 'fortress', which would not surrender to the enemy even if the territory surrounding it was overrun. It held out for eighty days, from January 1945 until May, when the Nazi regime finally capitulated. During those months the Red Army and the German defenders fought over it house by house, turning it into what the historian Gregor Thum called 'the Stalingrad on the Oder'. Civilians who had been left behind when the city was evacuated were forced to join the captive labourers working on the defences, the centrepiece of which was the levelling of a tract more than a kilometre long through the university district to create an airstrip. Thousands died on it, children as well as adults, under strafing fire from Soviet planes. Only one German aircraft ever used the strip, to fly the SS commander out just before the surrender.[3]

The expulsion of the remaining Germans and their replacement by Poles began a few days later. Breslau had ended the 1930s with a population of 600,000 Germans; Wrocław ended the 1940s with a population of 250,000 Poles. Most of the so-called 'pioneers' came from central Poland; some came from the eastern lands annexed by the Soviet Union. Among the latter group were former residents of the city now known as Lviv, who seeded a lasting myth that Wrocław was a western re-creation of the city they called Lwów. Their distinctive accent may have helped the idea take hold, along with their salience in particular occupations, notably tram driving and university teaching. The majority of the settlers were new to city life altogether: 40 per cent had lived in villages, and another 40 per cent in small or medium-sized towns. It took time for them to find what they had in common, as they concentrated on finding themselves a place in the remains of the former 'Fortress Breslau'.[4]

The first step for many of them was to find a habitable dwelling, take possession of it, and hang a Polish flag from the window to advertise that they should not be targeted for eviction. Furniture, furnishings and housewares were there for the taking, as were a host of other items that had once made dwellings into homes. Soviet soldiers had a particular craving for pianos, which they rounded up and sent east. As a city full of things left behind by inhabitants who would not be coming back, Wrocław became the capital of the szaber economy. The szabrowniks, traders who made a living out of abandoned goods, rode the 'szabrobus' into town from the railway station, and converged on what was dubbed 'Szaber Square'. Hugo Steinhaus, who had been a professor of mathematics in Lviv before the war, described the scene in his memoirs: 'On the one side, thousands of vagrants in top boots, with knapsacks on their backs, swindlers, szabrowniks, wandering soldiers, Soviets, Jews – jacks of all trades, modestly speculating matrons and ordinary thieves; on the other, German men with white armbands, German women wearing trousers, dragging trolleys, belongings, bundles.' The women were selling possessions that they knew they would not be able to take with them when they were expelled.[5]

The szabrowniks' industry was driven in part by the sense that their window of opportunity might be limited. An air of doubt hung over the city. People found it difficult to believe that the western lands would remain under Polish control, so suddenly and unexpectedly gained. The very idea of taking over Breslau was novel, having been entertained by only the most ardent of Polish revanchists before the war.[6]

Now that the city found itself on Polish territory, its authorities had to rebuild it in such a way as to instil a belief in its Polishness into its new population. 'The Polish Wrocław will become the antithesis of the German Wrocław,' promised the architect Emil Kaliski. In his view, its oldest historic buildings were of especial significance because they were 'the Polish birth certificate of this city'. They were required for the new narrative that used the Piast era to identify Wrocław's foundations with Poland's. That meant according supreme historical value to relics of the period, and also to later Gothic buildings, which were treated as honorary Piast relics. A map produced for an exhibition about the Recovered Lands, held in 1948, highlights the Piast survivals – a dozen or so, thinly scattered across an area that by the nineteenth century had accumulated a rich concentration of Renaissance and baroque buildings.[7]

The Piast relics were mostly Catholic churches, but the diocese lacked the money to rebuild them. Having decided that the 'Polish birth certificate' needed to be prominent and entire, the authorities had to pay for its restoration, thus subsidising the one major ideological adversary the regime was unable to neutralise. The investment was worth it, though, for the Catholic Church embraced the Piast cult fervently. In 1965, as the millennium of the 'Baptism of Poland' approached, the Primate of the Church gave an address 'standing on Wrocław cobblestones, by this venerable cathedral which is also celebrating its millennium'. He spoke of holy Polish sites 'in which we read stone relics, we see signs from the past which say: We were here! Yes, we were here! And we are here again! We have returned to our native home; we have recognised the signs that have survived; we understand them. We understand this speech! It is our speech! The stones call out to us from the walls!' Cardinal Wyszyński's charismatic certainties doubtless helped to secure a belief in the Polishness of the city among its inhabitants, and his arresting metaphor may have helped to popularise the saying that 'in Wrocław, the stones speak Polish'.[8]

Some of its masonry was sent off to go and speak Polish in Warsaw. Wrocław's Old Town was a different proposition to that of the capital city. It was larger, more diffuse, and had acquired a flotilla of new buildings around the turn of the twentieth century. Although it was heavily damaged during the siege – not least by the defenders' actions, demolishing streets to create defence lines and stationing artillery in it that drew retaliatory shellfire down on the quarter – more than half of it was still standing when the German garrison capitulated.

The biggest difference, however, lay in the ideological value bestowed on buildings of similar age in the two historic districts. In Warsaw, the buildings of the second half of the eighteenth century represented an Enlightenment flowering whose further growth was terminated by the partitions that brought the era of the Polish–Lithuanian Republic to an end. In Wrocław, buildings of the same period represented the early stages of Prussian rule, which turned into German rule after the unification of Germany in 1871. In Warsaw the eighteenth century was Polish and good; in Wrocław it was German and bad.

German associations could be fatal even to older structures in Wrocław. If the Rubble Clearance Department wanted permission to demolish ruins, whatever their age, it would claim that they were of a German building. Its deputy director dismissed the surviving portion of a Renaissance house as 'a worthless foreign souvenir'. With such a precarious status, Wrocław's heritage was vulnerable to szaber. Stone portals, window frames, facade ornaments and even Gothic bricks were transported from the Old Town of Wrocław to be used in the reconstruction of its unequivocally Polish counterpart in the capital.[9]

Similar architectural szaber was sent from the old centre of Nysa, a town south of Wrocław that had been celebrated as the 'Silesian Rome', to adorn rebuilt houses in the historic environs of Warsaw's Old Town. The plundering of Nysa was denounced in a conservationist report that described how the town's old buildings, fire-damaged but still standing, were sabotaged by the demolition of internal walls, so that the consequent collapse of the facades could then be blamed on 'the wind'. Between 1945 and 1955, 103 historic townhouses were destroyed in the drive to meet the local authorities' grandiose targets for brick acquisition. In 1952, conservation bodies managed to cut the planned haul from 15 million to 6 million, but the demands rose again, and were only curbed when the city architect was sacked for fraud. Brick trafficking afforded lucrative opportunities for private profit in socialist Poland, as a similar scandal in Wrocław illustrated.[10]

The contradictions in the Poles' treatment of Wrocław were unsustainable, and had to be resolved. A dozen old churches might be enough for a 'Polish birth certificate', but they were insufficient to claim the whole of the city's rich heritage. Wrocław's Renaissance and baroque history had to be appropriated. Marian Morelowski, an art historian, supplied the necessary ideological rhetoric in an article published at Christmas in 1950. He denounced the 'bourgeois-speculative disfigurement' of the city's historic centre, and urged rebuilding as 'a correction to the grave sins of a spiritless bygone epoch'. A lifelong cultural nationalist, Morelowski was one of the Polish intellectuals obliged to leave Vilnius after the war. He was noted for his irascible temperament and his belief that slights to his honour demanded satisfaction through ritual combat. On one occasion he fought a double duel with two brothers, members of the Vilnius literary intelligentsia, whom he believed had disrespected him in a roman à clef: he exchanged pistol shots with one, harmlessly, and then engaged in a sabre bout with the second, sustaining a slight wound that terminated the encounter in accordance with the rules of the duelling code. Transplanted to recently German lands, his passionate resentment of Germany seemed to give him a ready fluency in communist idiom.[11]

His declaration heralded a reconstruction project based – perforce, for want of alternative documentation – on the pre-war work of a German conservationist, Rudolf Stein, who cherished the Market Square as the heart of a city built by the 'German tribe of the Silesians', and wished that it could be restored to its appearance before the turn of the nineteenth century. Some 340 townhouses were eventually rebuilt. They were supplemented by a number of twentieth-century buildings whose steel frames had defied the bombardments, and were now clad with imitation Renaissance or baroque facades. One of them was the House of the Golden Crown, built upon the skeleton of the Golden Crown department store, which had replaced a sixteenth-century townhouse and taken its name. It was several metres taller than its Renaissance namesake and had a portal taken from another building, but it harmonised with the Gothic town hall across the Market Square.[12]

Chapter 7
We Will Come to Believe in It Ourselves

There were pictures that told the story. Twenty-odd Canaletto paintings, displayed in the Royal Castle until 1939, formed an album of Warsaw at the summit of its sophistication and elegance as the capital of the Polish-Lithuanian Republic. After the war, the architects of the new historical narrative took them up as models for the reconstruction of buildings along the Royal Route leading south from the Castle Square. The high street of Warsaw's history was made to look like the paintings.

That inevitably entailed deviating from historical accuracy, since Canaletto was an artist, not an architectural draughtsman. Like any other painter, he adjusted scenes to enhance their composition. He took a similar approach with his own personal branding. Bernardo Bellotto was actually the nephew of the celebrated Venetian painter known as Canaletto; he helped himself to the name after falling out with his uncle, and also with his father, who denounced his 'bestial brain' to the prime minister of Poland. Despite that testimonial, Bellotto enjoyed twelve years of royal favour as painter to the court of Stanisław August Poniatowski, the last king of Poland, until his death in 1780. Among his subjects was the reconstruction of the Royal Castle, following a fire that destroyed one of its wings. After the Second World War, Bellotto's paintings provided the architects with idealised models that were all the more attractive because they gave off their own historical glow.[1]

As with all unintentional monuments, which acquire layers and alterations in the course of becoming historic, the reconstruction of the adjacent Old Town posed the question of what particular historical form or forms it should take. The heritage architects had become archaeologists as they investigated and documented what had survived in the ruins. They took some comfort from the unexpected number of medieval remains that turned out to have been concealed within the townhouses and the defensive walls. These fragments lent support to the planners' proposals for disposing of the quarter's nineteenth-century alterations, according to Piotr Biegański, who became Warsaw's chief conservator in 1947. Unfortunately, he acknowledged, there were not enough of them to rebuild the Old Town in its Gothic form. On the other hand, that left the reconstruction free to depict a proud historical sequence from the Middle Ages to the last flowering of Polish baroque. And that enabled the new regime to present the rebuilding as a restoration of the Old Town to 'its original condition, so shamefully destroyed during the capitalist period and the period of the Hitlerite occupation'.[2]

The heritage architects' ambitions extended far beyond restoring what the Hitlerites had destroyed. Jan Zachwatowicz succeeded in reconstructing the medieval Barbican, which had been demolished in 1794 – a massive addition to the outer face of the Old Town, rising up 15 metres in height and projecting thirty metres forward. The Party's Central Committee ruled out the reconstruction of the defensive walls along their entire original course around the perimeter of the settlement, however, and Zachwatowicz had to persuade it not to demolish stretches that already existed.[3]

The authorities also rejected the conservationists' proposal to rebuild the town hall that had stood in the Market Square until 1817. Whereas the Barbican was reconstructed around the surviving rump of its original bulk, the town hall would have been an entirely new build from the ground up. As a component of an ideal Old Town, it was essential: the two most important buildings in an old northern European city were the cathedral and the town hall, complementing each other with their respective commands of the spiritual and temporal domains. It might have served a contemporary purpose too, such as providing a home for the museum – which would have freed eleven of the quarter's 181 tenement houses to provide much-needed homes for workers. But it was said to have been rejected because of the communist passion for mass gatherings and open public spaces in which to hold them.[4]

That seems somewhat unlikely, since the nearby Castle Square is larger, more accessible, and ideally situated to welcome parades processing along the Royal Route. As a central symbolic space that can readily be occupied, it remains the capital's prime site for rallies and demonstrations. The claim does, however, serve as a coda to the best of the tales that entered the lore of the Old Town's reconstruction. Leaving the square empty was said to have been a compromise agreed after the heritage architects cunningly foiled a grandiose communist plan. Little was left of the buildings along the eastern terrace of the Market Square, known as the Barssa side. Józef Sigalin conceived the idea of creating a spectacular three-dimensional assembly space over-looking the Vistula, by levelling the Barssa ruins and building an amphitheatre on the scarp below. According to the story, an anony-mous phone caller tipped Piotr Biegański off that the Party leadership would shortly conduct an inspection to decide whether the Barssa side would be rebuilt. Biegański hastily arranged for a brigade of building workers to erect a single-storey frontage along the length of the terrace. A few days later, Sigalin showed President Bierut round the square and outlined his idea. 'Well, yes,' Bierut replied, 'but we won't knock down what the working class has already put up.'[5]

Although Sigalin and Zachwatowicz would have tackled the reconstruction of the Old Town very differently if it had been up to either one of them alone, they were both frustrated by the slow pace at which it proceeded. A few houses had taken shape, and a railway track had been laid as far as the Market Square so that steam locomotives could haul the rubble away, but the works lacked a unifying focus. After discussing the problem with Zachwatowicz late in December 1951, Sigalin came up with the concept that finally galvanised the process: the Old Warsaw Route. This heritage trail would run through the streets from the Castle Square through the Old Town, forming a kind of branch line off the Royal Route. Sigalin proposed that the first stage should be opened in 1953, as the centrepiece of the government's anniversary celebrations on 22 July. It would reach the Market Square from the Castle Square via Piwna Street, where the pigeons had flocked to be fed.[6]

The idea had the necessary political clout behind it. Sigalin had outgrown BOS, which had been wound up in September 1951, and was now the Chief Architect of Warsaw. At the beginning of 1953, the scheme was given priority over other major building projects. The director of the city museum recalled that in June, with the opening date just a few weeks away, Sigalin set up a cabin in the middle of the Market Square to serve as a command post, emerging from time to time to urge the workers on through a megaphone. According to the project manager, the structure resembled a lighthouse and was fitted with a battery of communications devices: three telephones, a radio link and a public address system which the manager used to remind the workers of the impending deadlines.[7]

They were not helped by the sightseers who gathered to watch them and got in their way, but they finished the job in time for the 22 July celebrations. Bierut made his appearance on a balcony, to take the principal credit on behalf of himself and the Party. A plaque on a corner of the Market Square declared the place to be a 'monument of national culture and the revolutionary struggle of the people of Warsaw, reduced to rubble by the fascist occupiers in 1944. The Polish People's Government raised it from the ruins and returned it to the nation in 1951–1953.' By using a phrase that made the recon-struction sound like the raising of a sunken ship from the seabed, the statement contrived to suggest that the destroyed Market Square and its replacement were a single enduring monument.[8]

The government also succeeded in conveying its implicit message about the nation, as a fraternal socialist visitor from East Germany demonstrated the following year. Marvelling at the Square's 'inde-scribable beauty', the mayor of Leipzig testified that 'here I recognise the creative power of this constantly oppressed people, which seeks forms to give shape to its national folk art'. His excitement was romantic with a small 'r' – 'I feel like I've been taken centuries back in time,' he exclaimed, like countless thousands of Old Town tourists in Middle Europe before and since – and his reading was Romantic with a capital 'R'. In speaking of the Volk, the mayor implied that the ensemble was an expression of the Polish people's essential character. The regime would probably have been quite happy for outsiders to see it that way.[9]

By approaching the Market Square along Piwna Street, the first phase of the Old Warsaw Route avoided passing the problem of the ruined cathedral. Jan Zachwatowicz took charge of it, recruiting Maria and Kazimierz Piechotka to help him. His main design chal-lenge was to create a new frontage for the building, which had been rebuilt in an English neo-Gothic style around 1840. Although he had promised to reconstruct the 'exact forms' of monuments when he outlined his programme in 1946, he found the proportions of the nineteenth-century one unsatisfactory. He thought about giving the cathedral a modern face, but could not shake off the feeling that it would be out of place in a quarter full of recreated historic forms. Finally, he decided that the new facade should be Gothic, but of a 'more local' character.

The style he chose is sometimes known as Vistula Gothic, though he described it as Mazovian, referring to the region in which Warsaw is situated. It enabled him to give one of the quarter's most important buildings a medieval appearance, upholding the priority he sought to give the Middle Ages, while replacing a foreign influence with an indigenous one. And it gave him considerable freedom as a designer, since there had been no Professor Sosnowski to organise architectural surveys in the fourteenth century. A couple of seventeenth-century images indicate the general form of the building, with its steep pitched roof, but the rest was up to Zachwatowicz and his colleagues. They produced a striking facade in which the rise of the gable was measured out by columns made from recovered medieval bricks and specially made copies.[10]

The contrast between what he called his 'contemporary interpretation' and the stiff, pompous design it replaced was telling. Its simplicity was a riposte from the architects of the middle decades of the twentieth century to their nineteenth-century predecessors, who helped to define them by representing everything they were against. Elsewhere in the city, their campaign against the generations before them led to the loss of buildings that could and should have been reconstructed. 'Maybe future generations will bear a grudge against us for not keeping art nouveau buildings,' Zachwatowicz mused in 1946, 'and who knows whether it might not be a good idea to keep one such house?'[11]

While the authorities accepted the restoration of the Old Town's churches, they relieved some of their anti-clerical feelings by replacing a few of the religious figures that had featured as ornaments on other buildings in the district. An obelisk was substituted for a figure of Christ; the Lamb of God was replaced by a boar, the Virgin Mary by the goddess Diana. The pettiness of these jibes suggests just how powerless the communists felt in the face of the Catholic Church – not least because as well as being national in form, it was nationalist in content. By spiritualising patriotism, it dissolved the distinction between the spiritual and temporal domains that the cathedrals and town halls of medieval cities had symbolised. While the Party was systemically vulnerable to the tensions between the nationalism it needed and the socialism to which it was committed, the Church seemed to incorporate nationalism without the slightest hint that there might be a fundamental contradiction between it and Catholic universalism.[12]

A host of other figures also appeared in the square, as artists covered the frontages of the houses with polychrome decorations. These were not recreations of historic features, nor of the polychromes that had received mixed reviews in 1928. National themes ran through them, but the degree of licence enjoyed by the artists resulted in an effusion of whimsy and fantasy. Satyrs, squirrels, dancers and kite-flying children suggested a desire for fairy-tale escapism rather than socialist realism.[13]

One of the motifs was the legend of the Old Town basilisk, a frightful creature that now perches, in the form of an exuberant metalwork figure, above a restaurant bearing its name. The story was a local tale, dated to 1587, in which two children ventured into the cellar of a ruined house and were struck dead by the lethal gaze of a basilisk that had made its home down there. A man clad in a suit of protective mirrors went down and extracted the creature from its lair.[14]

Even the milder versions of the story had a chilling resonance in a place where so many people had perished in the cellars of ruined houses less than ten years before. Indeed, workers clearing the rubble of what became the Basilisk restaurant building found the desiccated remains of a local shopkeeper sitting on a chair in the corner of an underground chamber. Monika Żeromska, a writer who had served as a nurse in one of the Old Town's improvised hospitals during the Uprising, recalled that in a townhouse across the Market Square, 'water from a burst pipe inundated a crowd of people packed so tightly that they were drowned standing up. All the cellars were tombs, as far as the eye could see.' Perhaps the images of the basilisk represent the desire to sublimate traumatic visions into the realm of fantasy. Or perhaps time had passed more quickly in people's minds than anybody might have expected. But whatever the reasons, the visitors who made their way in growing numbers to the Old Town were evidently ready to be enchanted.[15]

The decorations were not universally appreciated, though. In the week that the magazine *Stolica* hailed the achievements of the workers who had finished the 'cradle of the city' in time for 'Rebirth Day' ('They were proud that thanks to their efforts, the Old Town could host the leadership of our Government and Party on this day of general joy') it also ran a letter from a reader complaining that the fixtures and fittings of the flats inside the tenements were inadequate. Echoing the criticism of the decorative works in the 1920s, the writer accused the architects of concentrating on the facades and forgetting the people who were to live behind them.[16]

Those who had recently lived behind the original facades were certainly forgotten. In recreating the Old Town as an ensemble monument to the grand sweep of Polish history, the reconstruction effaced the memory of the common people who had given the district its human character before the war. Some of the flats in the new socialist residential quarter were occupied by workers who had helped build it, but as Stanisław Lorentz noted, its population mostly comprised 'intellectuals, scientists and artists'. Their plebeian predecessors were not considered worthy of commemoration, because they were associated with a neighbourhood regarded by both pre-war and post-war elites as disreputable.[17]

Jewish memory was excluded from the Old Town in the process. The district was not identified with Warsaw's Jewish population, but many Jews lived and worked there. According to the city's *Warsaw in Numbers* report for 1939, a document at pains to highlight the proportions of Jews in its various population statistics, 38 per cent of the Old Town administrative district's residents were Jewish. A different account of the Old Town's history might have given Warsaw's exterminated Jewish population a place in the city's symbolic centre of memory, but it was kept separate, in the former ghetto area. Warsaw was not unusual in this regard, for the margin-alisation of former Jewish presence is a phenomenon found in Old Towns across Middle Europe.[18]

No other Old Town could compare with that of Warsaw in its ambition, though, and outside observers were awed by its execution. The quality of the work carried out in the reconstruction's first phase came to be rated highly by the people who maintained the buildings in subsequent decades, despite the pace at which the buildings had been completed. Standards were not maintained as the rest of the Old Town was rebuilt, however. On Brzozowa, the street that had featured in the 1947 film about Robinsons living in the ruins, cracked walls testified to the deficiencies of later reconstruction works. Not only were the new walls inadequate; Gothic ones had been demol-ished to make way for them.[19]

The slippage in standards might to some extent have been a side-effect of the end of Stalinism. After the change of leadership in 1956, the regime ventured to win public support by relaxing its grip on culture slightly, and exhorting the people a little less stridently. It had lost its old enthusiasm for construction projects as heroic theatre, so the first phase of the Old Town's reconstruction belonged to a phase of national history that was now over.

Józef Sigalin and Jan Zachwatowicz never did see eye to eye over the Old Town walls. Sigalin had a lasting aversion to them, for reasons that are hard to grasp. Perhaps it was precisely because Zachwatowicz was so keen on them. Possibly Sigalin disliked the idea of a clearly bounded Old Town because of his opposition to 'heritage ghettos'. He certainly preferred opening it up to enclosing it. That was apparent not only in his notion to turn the Market Square into the upper deck of an amphitheatre overlooking the Vistula, but also from what he valued most in the reconstruction as a whole. When he showed foreign visitors around it, he would take them on a three-hour tour of the courtyards that afforded post-war residents the space denied to their predecessors by infilling. Creating space was his generation's 'true, progressive contribution to the reconstruction of Warsaw's Starówka'. And on this, he and Zachwatowicz were at one. Sigalin went out of his way to give credit for the gift of space to Oskar Sosnowski's students and former colleagues, gathered together in BOS's Architectural Heritage department under Zachwatowicz's leadership.[20]

Before the war, Zachwatowicz had been careful to respect the international conservationists' charter by ensuring that visitors could see which parts of the medieval walls were original and which were modern reconstructions. By the 1950s, he was committed to creating a simulacrum. The idea now was to make the new and the old indistinguishable from each other. At the site where the rebuilding of the Barbican was under way, he showed Sigalin a method of treating new bricks so that they acquired a patina quickly. Presenting a pair of bricks for comparison, he asked whether Sigalin could tell which one was new and which was a medieval original. The Chief Architect shook his head. 'But that one is new as well,' the foreman interjected. Evidently Zachwatowicz couldn't tell new bricks and medieval ones apart either.

Next to them, a tour guide was telling a party of tourists that 'these walls remember the Swedish invasions' of the seventeenth century. The rapt visitors touched the walls 'as though they were relics,' Sigalin recalled. 'That almost all of this is new, inauthentic? My god, in a couple of years' time nobody will remember it, except the historians, who will be duty bound to record this truth somewhere,' he reflected. 'Hundreds of thousands of people will pass by here each year. Their feelings and dreams will lend these walls the patina of history. We will come to believe in it ourselves.'[21]

WÜRZBURG

Chapter 8
Christmas Trees in Lent

By the middle of March 1945, most of Würzburg's hundred thousand inhabitants had an idea of what might be coming. People packed belongings into boxes and suitcases which they entrusted to friends, so that they might still be able to reclaim a few possessions if their homes were destroyed by an attack from the air. Half a dozen raids had struck the city in a month, and its residents had no reason to think that the Allied air forces had finished with them yet.[1]

Until then, they had not expected to suffer the devastation visited on cities throughout Germany by the Royal Air Force and America's strategic bomber fleets. They told each other Würzburg would be safe because it contained a large number of hospitals, which it did, or because Churchill had studied at its venerable university, which he had not. Similar mythical stories about the protective effects of links with Britain's prime minister circulated in a number of German cities. The first to have been falsified by the Royal Air Force, three years previously, was the claim that the port city of Lübeck was safe because Churchill's grandmother lived there. Half way through the war, German civilians were apparently confident that Churchill would not kill his own grandmother. By the end of it, they might not have been so sure.[2]

Würzburg had been given a preview of its fate in July 1944, when a flight of American aircraft appeared over it at noon one day and dropped twenty tons of bombs that landed among houses, killing forty-two people. When US bombers returned seven months later, they destroyed the railway station which sits on the perimeter of the Old Town, or Altstadt, the city's central district. More than 170 people died in the raid, which was the deadliest of the six attacks that took place in February and early March. The other attacks were more ominous, though. In the first, a pair of Royal Air Force Mosquitoes turned up and dropped two bombs, hitting a bridge and taking about twenty lives. The aircraft did not simply strike and fly off, but spent seventeen minutes over the city. That worried Hermann Knell, a young man who was still there because he had been exempted from military service on medical grounds, and his father, a Würzburg business owner. They knew from friends and relatives in other cities that operations of this kind were often the harbingers of massive raids, their purpose being to gather preparatory intelligence. The Mosquitoes, fast light bombers suited to conducting reconnaissance, had indeed been on what was classified as an 'experimental' mission, sizing up the target.

Four more Mosquitoes visited Würzburg the next day. Another quartet came a few days later, and then a flight of six, which left 112 people dead behind them. After that, they came in force: thirty-one planes that dropped forty-seven tons of bombs, killing eighty-six people. Hermann Knell and his father had taken to spending their nights in a shack on a garden plot they owned a few kilometres outside the city. When they returned the next day, checking the buildings where they had cached supplies and valuables, they found that a bomb had wrecked one of the family businesses, a printshop. They had to dismount from their bicycles because the streets were strewn with debris and broken glass. The American bombers had targeted the ganglia on the railway lines that ran through the city; the RAF had attacked the city at large. That reflected the differences in doctrine between the two allies' air forces. American bombing strategy was based on the identification of target classes within urban areas, such as factories and transport infrastructure. For the RAF, the cities themselves were the strategic targets. The term used officially was 'area bombing'; informally, it was 'carpet bombing'.

When the Mosquitoes next came back, on the night of 16 March, they were leading a fleet of more than 200 Lancaster heavy bombers. Two Lancasters preceded them to drop the first markers, guiding them in so that they could pick out the Old Town with coloured flares, known to those on the ground as 'Christmas trees'. The main force followed the illuminations and unloaded their bombs upon the Altstadt, raising a firestorm that subjected the people of Würzburg to horrors of conflagration like those that had been visited upon Hamburg, two years before, and Dresden, a month previously. Several thousand of them were killed that night.[3]

More air raids followed, and also an artillery bombardment in support of the American assault that captured what was left of the Old Town, wresting it from the German troops who were ordered to hold a line in the rubble; a thousand of them died, and so did three hundred American soldiers. At the end of it all, 89 per cent of the Altstadt was destroyed, according to the RAF's assessment. That put it on a level with Warsaw's Starówka, and made Würzburg one of the most heavily destroyed cities in Germany.[4]

Hermann Knell, eighteen years old at the time of the raid, was left bitter and angry in the city's ashes. He had felt the wind of the fire-storm and witnessed its consequences; he had sheltered from the high-flying bombers and taken cover when fighters came in at low level to strafe the ruins with bullets. His family's apartment and busi-ness properties were gone, leaving just the shack at the garden plot for shelter. Whatever was left of people's property was at risk. Just like their counterparts from the villages around Warsaw, local farmers rode their wagons into the city and loaded up with loot, including 'beams, girders, cables, pipes, fittings and bathtubs', according to a

4. Old Town streetscape in Würzburg, 1945.

former district mayor. Food and fuel remained in short supply long after the fighting was over. On New Year's Eve in 1946, as a bitterly cold 'hunger winter' began to tighten its grip on the country, Cardinal Josef Frings of Cologne preached a sermon in which he declared that people could take the necessities of life if they had no other way of obtaining them. The people gratefully took his name and turned it into a verb, fringsen, to describe what they did when they helped themselves to coal from trains.[5]

Knell conceived the idea of writing a victim's history of the air attacks, in which he would denounce the men responsible for raining destruction upon his home town. He eventually completed his book in 2002, having acquired an engineering qualification fifty years previously and used it to roam across the globe, as so many engineers do. By then, time and travel had altered his perspective. He lost the urge to condemn, and set himself instead to address the question of what led to the city's destruction. His researches took him to archives in England, Germany, Canada and the United States, but left him without an answer. 'And today,' he wrote, 'after years of reading and studies, I still do not understand why Würzburg was destroyed.'

That is a remarkable statement, for he provides his readers with more than enough background and detail to leave them feeling that they understand all too well what led to the cataclysm of 16 March 1945. His account of the history of strategic air warfare is wide-ranging and detailed, enabling the reader to grasp how military doctrines, commanders' personalities and the self-propelling momentum of campaign operations sealed Würzburg's fate. He knows what happened, and he accounts for it, so why does he say that he does not understand it? He is not uttering a plaint – 'why, oh why?' – about human folly or cruelty: he accepts that such things are in the nature of war. Although he regrets that the archives failed to yield explicit detail about the purpose of the mission, it did not need to be spelt out; the attack was entirely typical of RAF strategic raids in its targeting and the manner of its execution. What he means is not obvious, but it is significant, and it has a bearing on the question of why the reconstruction of German historic quarters is still a work in progress.

Knell's failure to attain understanding seems to result from the obstacles he faced, as a German, in engaging with the moral dimensions of the history he documented. Similar obstacles stood in the way of reconstructing German cities' built heritage, and still do. Their stories were complicated for the same reasons that Warsaw's was simple. In Poland, the story was the rising of the national phoenix from the ashes; the care and reconstruction of historic buildings were understood as part of that narrative, in which there was no question about Poland's victimhood or its right to national pride. Its history had not been compromised by its recent actions. German cities had no such consolation or support – least of all from national pride, for that was what had led to their destruction.

In many places it seemed simplest to raze the site completely and start afresh. The expression 'Stunde Null' had originally meant what its English equivalent, 'zero hour', continues to mean: the moment at which a military attack is launched. It came to denote the moment at which the Nazi regime surrendered; the point at which Germany was reduced to zero, and at which its historical clock was reset. The idea of Stunde Null implied that there was more hope in the future than there was comfort in the past.

One of those comforts had been the image of the tranquil but busy German town, home to a harmonious community, at ease with itself and its hinterland. Hermann Knell cast Würzburg as a model of the type, 'a city that lived the life of an unobtrusive, self-supporting central European community, a pleasant and peaceful place'. History had largely passed it by, except to leave it with an accumulation of baroque and rococo splendour. 'There had been no great political, social, racial, or religious problems,' Knell averred. It is true that Würzburg had avoided the conflicts ignited by the Protestant Reformation through remaining steadfastly Catholic; and that during the time of the Weimar Republic, Würzburgers' loyalty to the Centre Party, the political wing of German Catholicism, made the Bavarian city relatively unrewarding territory for the Nazis. But Würzburg had not always been as innocent as Knell implied. He did not mention the anti-Jewish riots that erupted there in 1819 and spread throughout Germany, nor the deportation of 2,000 Jews from the city during the war. Indeed, he did not mention Würzburg's Jews at all.

By contrast, he took pains to survey the townscape and note everything that could have been considered a legitimate target for Allied bombers. As well as the railway lines and marshalling yards, Würzburg's transport infrastructure included a harbour for the barges that carried freight along the river Main, on the banks of which the city had grown up. There were a couple of manufacturing plants, and army barracks. Although the industrial facilities were not large, they did contribute to the production of items that were central to the German war effort. One plant repaired machine tools damaged in raids on the ball-bearing factories at Schweinfurt, forty kilometres away, and one of the smaller Schweinfurt factories was relocated to

Würzburg. Another of the city's manufacturers made hull sections for U-boats, sending the completed units off up the river for assembly in shipyards elsewhere.[6]

The RAF was apparently unaware of all this, though. Würzburg was among the 518 towns and cities covered by the 1944 edition of *The Bomber's Baedeker*, a survey of potential targets compiled by Britain's Ministry of Economic Warfare. The report took its name from the celebrated Baedeker range of guidebooks to Europe, making a pointed allusion to the 'Baedeker raids' that the Luftwaffe conducted against heritage-bearing cities such as Canterbury, Bath and York. It rated Würzburg's factories as being of relatively small importance to Germany's war effort, and made no mention of the submarine hull construction or the ball-bearing works. 'What goes on in Würzburg?' asked an RAF squadron commander, Peter Johnson, when he learned on the morning of 16 March 1945 that it was to be his target that night. 'Nothing very much, according to the book,' the unit's intelligence officer told him. 'No big factories. Bit of a railway junction.' The Baedeker entry was padded out with items it acknowledged to be militarily unimportant, such as a workshop which Knell described as 'five ladies . . . knitting sweaters'. It looked to him as though it had been compiled using a telephone directory and a bit of guesswork.[7]

On the evening of 16 March, the bombers did not attempt to pick out individual objects anyway. Würzburg had been classified as an 'industrial area target' – but the bombers did not aim at its industrial areas either. Their bullseye was the Altstadt that formed the centre of the city. The target zone was extended slightly on its northern edge, covering the railway station and the plant that built the U-boat sections, but the barracks and the main industrial zones were several kilometres away.[8]

This was how the RAF's Bomber Command conducted its war against Germany. Its planes marked out the old hearts of cities and set them ablaze. A city's Altstadt was likely to suffer more destruction than the districts around it, and would be targeted precisely because it was the easiest quarter to immolate. According to the historian Richard Overy, the RAF's campaign against cities was 'predicated from the start on causing as much general damage and loss of life as possible by means of large-scale fires'. The bombers used the Old Towns as the kindling.[9]

Area bombing was the product of both doctrine and exigency. The idea that wars could be won by attacking enemy nations from the air, rather than by doing battle with their armed forces on land and sea, held an obvious and powerful appeal for RAF commanders between the world wars. It helped them assert that Britain's new air arm could equal or even supersede the army and navy in importance. After the British land forces retreated from the Continent in 1940, aerial bombing was left as the only means by which Britain could take the war to Germany. Targeting urban areas made the task less difficult for the bomber crews, who embarked on the offensive with little in the way of electronic aids for locating German cities, let alone particular industries or installations within them. Carpet-bombing cities at night had a powerful cost–benefit logic as a way to maximise damage to the enemy while minimising losses to the attacking force.

It was also an end in itself. The aim was expressed most clearly and uncompromisingly by Arthur Harris, who became commander-in-chief of the RAF's bomber forces in February 1942. 'Bomber' Harris believed that the way to defeat Germany was to destroy its cities, one after another. He directed a campaign against the industrial region of the Ruhr, but he regarded the destruction of factories themselves as a 'bonus'. In his unwavering view, the way to degrade Germany's ability to wage war was to disrupt the infrastructure of its cities and to bomb its people's homes.[10]

From the start of the campaign, Peter Johnson had accepted that it was his duty to implement the Harris doctrine without questioning his superiors' judgement, although he found himself troubled at a deep level about waging war upon the populations of cities. On one occasion, while showing the Chancellor of the Exchequer around the base, he was shocked by stereoscopic reconnaissance images of Düsseldorf taken by aircraft to review the effects of a raid. There were 'just rows and rows of apparently empty boxes which had been houses. They had no roofs or content.'[11]

After visiting the Operations Room on the morning of 16 March and inquiring about the nature of the target, then taking his Lancaster bomber up for a test flight, he returned to his quarters, where he spent half an hour of haunted reflection. In his memoirs he describes looking at a book of drawings from the London Blitz, and thinking about a letter examining the doubts it had provoked in him that he had written to a lover, who had died on air raid rescue duty before she could read it. He says that he contemplated refusing to fly that night, but reasoned that it would only result in another crew being assigned to face the hazards of the mission, and that he would in any case have remained 'an essential cog in the machinery which was to carry out the destruction of Würzburg', as he had been in organising the destruction of Dresden the month before.[12]

When they gathered for the final mission briefing that afternoon, the crews were informed that there would be a fairly strong wind blowing across Würzburg at ground level. Johnson knew that it would fan the flames that their bombardment would light. 'I remember thinking that seldom had destruction been so carefully prepared,' he recalled. 'It seemed impossible that any house would be spared or any individual escape.'[13]

Feeling he had to say something, he elliptically remarked that his intelligence officer had given him little information about Würzburg other than that it was a residential town with some light industry, and inquired whether there was there any special reason for the attack. The Air Officer Commanding told him that the city contained 'thousands of undamaged houses, sheltering tens of thousands of Germans'. Ending that state of affairs would be 'another nail in the enemy's coffin'. It resulted in the burial of the remains of three thousand of those Germans without coffins, in a mass grave. The RAF was reluctant to acknowledge that its campaign killed civilians, preferring to speak of 'de-housing' them in order to weaken their 'morale'. Nazi media called the raids 'terror-attacks', and they were echoed by many of those people against whom the bombs were directed.[14]

Peter Johnson did his duty that night. He was first to the target, flying one of the two Lancasters that guided the rest of the fleet to the Altstadt. As well as releasing marker flares, his plane dropped six thousand-pound bombs on the town.[15]

Those were not the most destructive munitions in the RAF's arsenal. Nor were its massive blockbusters, containing thousands of pounds of explosive. As Johnson knew, Bomber Command's most devastating weapons were its four-pound incendiaries. It learned that lesson from studying the effects of the Luftwaffe's Blitz on British cities in 1940 and 1941: the figures indicated that a ton of incendiaries had five times the destructive potential of a ton of high-explosive munitions. Blasts could smash buildings one by one; fires could burn out entire quarters. High-explosive bombs had a key role in fire-raising too. They broke open the shells of buildings, allowing the incendiaries to use the wooden floors, rafters and furniture inside as fuel. Explosives also played an important part in sustaining fires, by fracturing pipes and thereby depriving firefighters of water. The principal fire-sustaining weapons, however, were the delayed-action bombs that were dropped to deter firefighters and rescuers from approaching the scene of an attack, or to neutralise them if they did.[16]

The maximisation of destruction was the subject of intense research, covering questions such as the ratio of high-explosive bombs to incendiaries, the intensity of the bombardment – the RAF bombers dropped 300,000 incendiaries in the seventeen minutes they spent over Würzburg's Altstadt on 16 March – and, most basically, the flammability of German houses. Information about the construction of staircases was obtained from a German book called *Residences and Houses of the Middle Class*; exiled German architects (among them Walter Gropius, the modernist founder of the Bauhaus design school) were consulted about the thickness of roof beams. Model roofs were experimentally burned at the Road Research Laboratory on the outskirts of London.

German city districts were assessed and mapped into zones; it was obvious that the most easily immolated quarters would be the oldest ones. The buildings were densely packed along narrow, often winding streets that impeded firefighters but not flames; they tended to contain a lot of wood, in their structures as well as their fittings, while lacking parapet firewalls. As a report by the Bombing Directorate put it, the 'terraces of box-like buildings dating from the Middle Ages' should 'yield good dividend'. Würzburg was registered as a potential target even before the fire-raising campaigns began, appearing on a list compiled in 1941 that identified seventeen cities as being suitably combustible for incendiary attack.[17]

After the surveys and the laboratory studies came the fieldwork. Arthur Harris had a specific research objective for the attack he ordered on the Baltic port city of Lübeck in March 1942. The main purpose of the raid, he explained in his memoirs, was to find out how effectively a wave of bombers could guide a second wave to the target by setting it alight: 'I ordered a half-hour interval between the two waves to allow the fires to get a good hold before the second wave arrived.' Harris described Lübeck as 'an industrial town of moderate importance', but that was not why he chose it as the site for his experiment. He selected it because it was identifiable, less heavily defended than the great industrial cities of the Ruhr, and flammable. 'It was built,' he observed, 'more like a fire-lighter than a human habitation.'[18]

The Old Town of Lübeck occupies an island, the Altstadtinsel, nested within a loop between two rivers that were joined by a channel in 1900. In an aerial plan view, it looks somewhat like a diagram of a plant cell in a biology textbook, a dense internal microstructure contained within the waterways that form the wall. With an angled perspective, its secular buildings appear as ranks of sawtooth roof lines; its seven slender church spires are spikes in the graph, pointing heavenwards. Lübeck's Altstadt is the heritage of its glory days, which lasted from the thirteenth to the sixteenth century, as the 'Queen City' of the mercantile Hanseatic League. Although Harris considered the city to be only moderately important as an industrial centre, the section of it that he sent 234 planes to burn was generally acknowledged to be of immense cultural importance. Decades later, UNESCO classified the parts of the Old Town that the bombers failed to destroy as a World Heritage Site of 'outstanding universal value'.[19]

UNESCO's appraisal notes that the Old Town's 'uniquely uniform silhouette' is visible from afar. That was helpful for the bomber crews, who also had the benefit of a coastline by which to orient themselves, a clear night, and an almost-full moon whose light reflected off the water that surrounded the Altstadtinsel. Planes came in over the great twin pepper-pots of the Holstentor, the western gate, and dropped their payloads immediately beyond it. Much of the area they struck was destroyed, including the Gründungsviertel, or Founding Quarter, one of the oldest parts of the Altstadt. The town hall was damaged, two Gothic churches were burned out, and the twin spires of the cathedral collapsed. A survey conducted for the German authorities reported that the zone of complete destruction covered twenty hectares, a sixth of the Altstadt's total area, and almost the entire Old Town suffered damage to varying degrees. More than 300 people were killed.[20]

Hitler chose to respond to the bombing as an attack on German culture and heritage, ordering the reprisals against historic provincial cities in England that his foreign ministry's press office dubbed the 'Baedeker raids'. The RAF followed it up a month later with four nights of raids on Rostock, a port city further east along the Baltic coast. Rostock was built with a layout like that of Lübeck, one of a chain of Baltic cities modelled on their Hansa 'Queen' that stretched as far as Tallinn. Harris reported with satisfaction that the attacks on it 'fully confirmed the lesson of Lübeck', which was that 'a fairly important, but not vital, German town could be at least half destroyed by a relatively small force dropping a high proportion of incendiaries'.[21]

Lübeck itself was spared much further punishment, despite having considerable military industry in its environs. It is said to have been saved thanks to the efforts of Eric Warburg, a scion of a Hamburg banking family, who quit Germany in 1938 and served in the American military during the war as an intelligence officer. Though he had been forced to get out of the Reich because he was Jewish, he continued to feel himself to be German. According to one account, he heard in June 1943 that a second major attack on Lübeck was imminent. Appalled that the city's cultural patrimony faced further devastation, he got in touch with the President of the International Red Cross in Geneva and persuaded him to route the Red Cross's packages for British prisoners of war via the city, thus sparing it further attention from the RAF. Despite its happy ending, the story has an unsettling undertone, since in depicting a Jewish banker pulling strings behind the international scenes, it employs tropes that have spawned a host of antisemitic conspiracy fantasies. But Eric Warburg came to be regarded as a saviour in Lübeck, which named a river bridge on the Altstadt bypass route after him in 2008.[22]

After the attacks on the Hansa ports, the next question for Harris was whether the method could be scaled up to saturate the defences of major industrial areas. He deemed that question to have been answered by the 'Thousand Bomber Raid' he staged against Cologne on 30 May 1942. Hamburg, rated 'outstanding' as a potential target for fire-raising attack, had been the first choice, but it was spared by unfavourable weather. Its turn came the following year, in the last week of July. 'Operation Gomorrah' took around 37,000 lives in a series of raids, the most apocalyptic of which killed 18,500 people in a firestorm that rose over two miles into the sky and burned out twelve square miles of the city. The storm was raised by dropping 1,200 tons of incendiaries upon two square miles of densely packed workers' housing. Hamburg did not have an Altstadt that could be

used as kindling, as much of it had already burned down in a catastrophic fire a hundred and one years previously, or been demolished
in sanitary clearances after a cholera epidemic fifty-one years before.
Elsewhere, attacks on timber-framed town centres amply confirmed
the Bombing Directorate's anticipations of 'good dividend'. In
Hannover, just 32 of the city's 1,600 half-timbered buildings survived
the war.[23]

Harris believed that the bombing campaign against German
cities, together with the Soviet struggle against Hitler's forces in the
east, would bring the war to an end in 1944, sparing the Western
Allies from having to mount an invasion. The Ministry of Economic
Warfare provided him with a table of a hundred German towns,
compiled from *Bomber's Baedeker* data, rating them according to their
economic importance. He crossed them out one by one as his planes
worked through the list. Although the campaigns did not have the
effect that he had predicted, they continued after the D-Day invasion in June 1944, and were sustained almost up to the moment at
which Germany finally surrendered.[24]

During those last terrible months before the clock stopped at
Stunde Null, Allied bombers made sure that they had left few
German cities unvisited. The major targets had all been struck over
and over again; minor potential targets now attracted increasing
attention from the mission planners. With hindsight, speculative
remarks in the *Bomber's Baedeker* entry for Pforzheim read like a
death sentence upon the Black Forest town and its inhabitants, who
specialised in making jewellery and watches. 'These industries were
formerly carried out largely in the homes of the individual workers,'
the report observed, 'and it may be said that almost every house in
this city is a small workshop ... As was the case in the 1914–1918
war, most of the factories and workshops of Pforzheim will have now
been turned over to the manufacture of precision parts for instruments, small-arms components, fuzes, clockwork movements and
similar products ...'[25]

In his post-war report on Bomber Command's operations, Harris rewrote the *Baedeker's* presumption into a statement of fact. As if the RAF's reconnaissance aircraft could see through roofs and ceilings, the chief of Bomber Command asserted that 'almost every house was a small workshop engaged in the production of instruments, small arms and fuzes'. Every house was therefore confirmed as a legitimate target, and so was everybody in it. The RAF bombed the town towards the end of February 1945, raising a firestorm. 'Hardly a building remained intact,' Harris claimed: the accepted figure for the extent of the destruction is 83 per cent. He noted that Pforzheim had a population of 80,000, but not that the raid killed 17,600 of those inhabitants. It was the third highest toll from an Allied raid in Europe, after the firestorms that left 18,500 dead in Hamburg and 25,000 in Dresden. The scale of the whole campaign is indicated by the estimate of 350,000 for the total death toll.[26]

In hindsight, looking back along a timeline in which the war against the Third Reich ended in May, the attacks carried out against modest German towns in February and March seem to defy any strategic justification. Pforzheim and Würzburg were the most horrific instances of bombing that was, in Richard Overy's measured judgement, 'evidently punitive in nature and excessive in scale'. At the time it may have looked different to many on the Allied side, after the Western Allies' slow progress towards German territory and the Reich's deployment of new weapons, including the V-2 ballistic missiles that represented a new technology for bombing cities. The first American troops did not manage to get across the Rhine until early March, little more than a week before the climax of the British raids on Würzburg. In January, Britain's Bombing Directorate had advocated inducing 'a state of terror by air attack'. Hitherto, the RAF had euphemistically talked of attacking 'morale'. Now the word 'terror' was slipping into the Allies' usage, as they cast about for ways to win the war.[27]

Even with hindsight, and even with decades in which to reflect upon how to locate right and wrong in the history of the air war against Germany, the campaign poses questions that are intractable even when they are answered. The period of reflection seemed to last until almost the end of the century, and then the books began to appear. Peter Johnson wrote his memoirs, subtitled *Reflections and Doubts of a Bomber*, which were published in 1995. The writer W.G. Sebald produced a series of essays that came out in 1999 under the title *Luftkrieg und Literatur* (*Air War and Literature*). Lighting his argument with firestorm scenes, he criticised his fellow German authors for having failed to write about the bombing war in a satisfactory fashion, or at all. Then, in 2002, came Jörg Friedrich's *Der Brand* (*The Fire*), the best-seller that thrust the Bombenkrieg, and German suffering, to the forefront of national public debate about the Second World War. Written by a freelance scholar-journalist, *Der Brand* was not an argument about morality or a detached academic summation of events in their broader context. It was a literary enactment of agony, its testimony unbearably eloquent, and a lament for loss. To describe it as repetitious is not to deprecate its narrative structure, but to recognise the depiction of similar horrors in city after city as an assertive act of remembrance. Professional historians criticised its standards of scholarship, while acknowledging its literary power. Pushing its readers onward through inferno after inferno, *Der Brand* insisted that their gaze should be fixed upon the lives consumed in the fires, and the agonies in which those lives ended.[28]

It also dwelt upon the places that were lost, prefacing episodes of destruction with nostalgic local histories and myths. The historian Jörg Arnold observed that the book empathises with urban land-scapes as well as the people in them, treating towns as 'living organisms with distinct identities whose loss is irreplaceable'. Friedrich finds no comfort in reconstruction, at least not in the ways that were done in the years after the war. His accounts of those curtailed histories seemed to resonate with his readers, and perhaps strengthened a collective sense that the reconstructions needed to be revisited. 'The new town is receding,' he observed in an interview, 'the old one coming closer and closer to the memory of people.'[29]

That imagined municipality came bathed in a nostalgic glow, lyrically evoked in Friedrich's elegies, and reproduced in the autumnal tones of old postcards. The appetite for it shows no signs of diminishing. Roland Flade, a former editor of Würzburg's local paper, finds that posts featuring photos from before the war are always the most popular ones on the Facebook page about the city's history that he runs. 'People in Würzburg cannot believe how beautiful Würzburg once was,' he says. 'It was one of the most beautiful towns of Germany, and maybe of Europe. People said it was Florence put into the north of Europe. There's a certain fascination with how beautiful Würzburg was.'[30]

Jörg Friedrich's depiction of Würzburg resembles Hermann Knell's in the sense it conveys of a well-mannered town, long nestled peaceably in the heart of Europe, that had its history terminated in the space of seventeen merciless minutes. (Knell completed his book in the year that Friedrich's was published, evidently without reading the latter, so their accounts are independent.) Unlike Knell's narrative, with its scrupulous cataloguing of anything that could be construed as a military or industrial target, Friedrich omits all of the city's contents other than its cultural wealth. 'There were no warmongering industries here, just spinets and altars,' he imagines the residents thinking, as they denied the risk of attack – though they would not have felt the same once the locally built U-boat sections began to pass the edge of the Altstadt on their way to the river, and even the city's printing press manufacturers were reassigned to carry out essential repairs on military-industrial machinery.[31]

Friedrich heightens the implication of violated innocence with his claim that the city 'had previously been left virtually untouched by the bombing war', and that its people were doomed by their unfamiliarity with air raid conduct. But they had already been subjected to seven raids, including one the previous summer, which had killed several hundred of them. Knell's account makes plain that they knew what to expect and how to respond, as best they could. A fire-raising attack on the heart of the city by more than 200 bombers was simply too much for them.[32]

Behind the narrative details, the fundamental difference between Friedrich's narrative and Knell's is one of certainty. Friedrich's radiates conviction – not the kind that emerges from rigorous analytical scrutiny, but the kind that emanates from the righteousness of testimony and eulogy. Knell's inability to attain certainty after a lifetime's reflection and inquiry makes a poignant contrast.

Some of the difference can be attributed to their capacities as writers: Hermann Knell was a retired engineer trying to make sense of a formative encounter with history; Jörg Friedrich was already a published historical author before he wrote his bestseller. But the key difference between them is that of where they appeared on the timeline. Friedrich was born in the summer of 1944, by which point Knell was on the verge of adulthood. For Friedrich, there was no question of complicity in the National Socialist project, or indeed of responsibility for the manner of the reconstruction after it. He had the additional biographical asset of involvement in the radical left-wing student movement that almost became a revolution in 1968 and was, in Germany, a conspicuous rejection of what the students' parents did or might have done in the war.

Knell's more ambiguous position created complications for him that he was unable to resolve. He was an engineer who could not construct an entirely stable structure for himself, because he could never be confident about where he stood. There was no framework without fracture-lines available to him, even by the end of the century; nor had there been one for Germans in mid-century, working out how to move forward along the timeline that had been reset at Stunde Null. It was not so much an engineering problem as a psychological complex.

Across the eastern border, by contrast, Germany's actions had created a moral framework of invulnerable simplicity for the Poles.

In Warsaw the narrative was grand, tragic and unequivocal. It was easy to put together a story of urbicide planned from the start of the occupation, or even earlier (on the basis of a rumour that Friedrich Pabst had been appointed as the future Chief Architect of Warsaw more than a month before the German invasion). The so-called Pabst plan made a compelling narrative element, although in reality it may have been little more than a vanity project for a peripheral regime functionary from Würzburg. Poles embraced the story that emerged from the capital's ruins, a sublime arc of victimhood and valour, as the story of the nation. Warsaw's tragedy was Poland's tragedy in its most concentrated form, reaching a peak of intensity in the Old Town's passion of resistance, devastation and martyrdom. As it rebuilt its capital city, the whole nation created an example to be followed throughout the country, in spirit if not necessarily in form. The reconstruction of each individual Polish town or city was understood to be part of the greater national project.[33]

No such understanding was available to Germans, for whom the very idea of a national story was fundamentally compromised. Jörg Arnold notes that *Der Brand* rarely even speaks of 'Germans' at all: 'the locality, not the nation, is the focal point of reference'. That was the position in which the people of German cities found themselves after Stunde Null. Each town had to work out a story of its own upon which to rebuild itself.[34]

Chapter 9
The U-Boat Cathedral Roof

After his stint in Warsaw, drawing up the plan for its replacement by a New German City, the architect Hubert Gross traversed Europe in command of a military construction battalion. Germany's conquests took him west to Holland and down to southern France, then back to the environs of Warsaw, where he was sent to build a fuel depot. The contrast with his previous assignment in the area serves as an apt symbol for the distance between the Nazis' visions for the lands they had seized in the east and the practical demands of being an occupying power. They still felt the urge to pursue their dreams in Germany itself, though. In January 1941, the leading Nazi architect Albert Speer expressed his hope that Gross would continue to develop the plans for Würzburg that had taken the Führer's fancy.[1]

Six months later, Gross was discharged from the army and returned to Würzburg, where he resumed work on the project. It was to be a local implementation of the standard Nazi requirements: monumental buildings to assert the Party's power, and assembly spaces in which its ability to mobilise the people could be demonstrated. These nazifying elements would be installed on the banks of the Main, claiming the riverside edge of the Old Town. They would, however, be restrained in scale by Nazi standards, out of respect for the city's elegant heart. Hitler himself was at pains to acknowledge the beauty of Würzburg, which he called a 'jewel among the cities'. Even so, Würzburg would be radically transformed. The Altstadt would lose not only its immediate connection to the river, but also a considerable amount of its prestige. With a new ensemble of power architecture erected alongside it, the Old Town would diminish in contemporary significance while gaining emphasis as a repository of heritage. It would be pushed back into history.[2]

The plan came no closer to realisation than the one for Warsaw, though. In 1943, Gross was sent east to Riga as a manager for Organisation Todt, the Reich's militarised engineering arm. As the Germans were pushed back west by the advancing Red Army, Gross was sent first to Danzig and then to Breslau, where he worked on Project Riese (Giant), a plan to build an underground complex in the mountains of Lower Silesia. The tunnels through the hard rock were dug by concentration camp prisoners, some of whom Gross brought from Auschwitz. Withdrawn from Breslau before its encirclement by the Red Army, he got himself back to Würzburg, reclaimed his old position as its chief planning officer in April 1945, and had proposals for the city's reconstruction ready by July. Hubert Gross, who had joined the National Socialist party a few months after Hitler seized power, was nothing if not adaptable.[3]

The circumstances to which he now had to adapt were both greatly reduced and politically adverse. There were just four people left in the planning office that had been able to send a team of twenty to Warsaw five years previously. Some were dead, some imprisoned, and some dismissed. Gross himself only retained his position until June 1946, when American-driven denazification caught up with him. But he continued to work for the city council as a private contractor, via a company that enabled the municipality to retain the services of people it had been obliged to let go, and he went on to practise as an architect in the city until his retirement. Würzburg found him essentially unproblematic.[4]

At Stunde Null, the first question that faced the planners was whether to reconstruct the city at all. Would it be better to leave the ruins as a memorial, and start again somewhere nearby, as one American occupation officer suggested? Similar thoughts were expressed about Warsaw – it would have been astonishing if they had not, when people ventured into that desert of rubble and human remains – but they were quickly replaced by the collective resolve to bring the city back to life. In Würzburg, practical considerations came to the fore. The firestorm had burned out the buildings, but the water, gas and sewage pipes had survived. A reconstruction on the same site would be spared the cost of laying new pipework, not to mention the difficulty of obtaining the pipes in the first place. Hubert Gross argued that a reconstruction in situ could also build upon other surviving elements, such as cellars, pavements and tramlines. Jan Zachwatowicz made much the same point as part of his case for rebuilding the Old Town in Warsaw, but there it was no more than a postscript to an argument that had already been decided by higher considerations.[5]

Gross's view prevailed. Although funding and supplies presented fewer challenges as time went on, the form of the reconstruction was conditioned by the Stunde Null period in which the economy was prostrate and looters carted building materials out of the city in farmers' wagons. The Altstadt street plan was retained – albeit with modifications – largely because of the pressure to make the most of the city's resources, rather than the desire to preserve the outline of its history.

Shortages also posed serious problems for the conservationists who strove to protect damaged historic buildings. The grandest of those was the Residenz, a baroque palace in its own grounds sited on the inner edge of the Altstadt, on the outside of the horseshoe-shaped Ringpark that had replaced the old city walls. It had been built as the seat of the local prince-bishops; Napoleon Bonaparte, who stayed there several times, is said to have described it as 'the most beautiful rectory in Europe'. Its centrepiece is one of the largest frescos in the world, Giovanni Battista Tiepolo's *Allegory of the Planets and Continents.* The raid of 16 March 1945 left the Residenz largely burned out and roofless; Tiepolo's work had survived, but was exposed to the elements. A group of volunteers led by a young art historian, Rudolf Edwin Kuhn, improvised some rudimentary protection in the first few weeks after the end of hostilities. They borrowed beer-tent tarpaulins from local breweries and hung them above the great stairwell on which the fresco was painted. Then the Monuments Man arrived to take on the task.

Lieutenant John Davis Skilton was an art historian who served in a US army medical detachment before becoming an officer of the Monuments, Fine Arts and Archives unit, dedicated to protecting cultural heritage in war zones. Despite his status as an agent of the occupation authorities, he faced as much of a struggle as the local volunteers to obtain the materials necessary for building a temporary roof. The tarpaulins were not enough to keep out the rain in heavy storms; at one point, Skilton had to hire some young locals to bail the water out in buckets. In search of timber, he found himself up against the US Army's powerful Corps of Engineers, which claimed a monopoly over all wood stocks and sawmills in the American occupation zone. The Corps guarded its wood jealously, and refused to allow any of it to be released for non-military uses.[6]

Skilton's qualifications for his post, a couple of art history degrees from Yale and a spell as a curator at the National Gallery in Washington, offered no hint of the remarkable skills he brought to 'organising' – the preferred German euphemism – the acquisition of resources from the rubble economy. He located a batch of logs floating in a river bay twenty kilometres downstream, stuck there because the Main was blocked by the wreckage of demolished bridges, and promised the owner that the Bavarian state would reimburse him for it. Next he got hold of a tug, and fuel to power it, but a series of obstacles still lay in his way. A detachment of Army engineers refused to let the timber barge move up the river, and started to load the logs onto their trucks; Skilton got the timber back and delivered it to a small sawmill that he figured the Corps of Engineers would overlook – but then the mayor of Würzburg commandeered both the wood and the mill. Skilton persuaded the mayor to return the wood, only for it then to be seized by another military engineering unit, who wanted it for repairing a bridge. Realising that they needed large logs, whereas he needed sawn timber, he did a deal with the commanding officer to exchange the former for the latter. Skilton subsequently relied upon the Germans to tell him about small caches of wood, which they brought him in their trucks using fuel that he provided.[7]

He also had to circumvent obstruction from the Army engineers in his efforts to obtain tar paper to stretch over the wood, and had to travel 100 kilometres to get the 2,000 square metres of it that he needed. When it came to the third essential haul of material, fifty tons of cement, he was finally blessed with some assistance from a fellow US soldier. A friendly sergeant who ran a supply depot assigned him a squadron of lorries with drivers who belonged to the French resistance forces, and they got twenty men from a displaced persons' camp to shift the bags. It struck Skilton as strange that Americans, Frenchmen and various Slavs were working together to preserve German cultural heritage. At that point, so soon after the war, it must have been hard to see that this was the peace taking shape. Looters were still at work, some of them carrying off objects from the Residenz. Skilton posted security guards at the palace – but withdrew them later in the year, after learning that they 'had a habit of using eighteenth-century door frames and furniture as firewood' to keep themselves warm on cold nights.[8]

When the roof frame was finished, he found himself having to cater a Richtfest, a traditional German builders' topping out ceremony, in which a tree is hoisted up to the roof. To provide refreshment for the sixty-five workers who had carried out the job, he bought a barrel of beer from a local brewery and went to a Benedictine monastery in search of food, coming away with bread and a small quantity of liverwurst, a rare delicacy at the time. The celebration marked the first stage in the reconstruction of the Residenz, which was eventually completed in 1987, at a cost in the region of €20 million.[9]

Skilton also helped to protect Würzburg's other most prestigious edifice, the Cathedral of St Kilian, built near the spot where the seventh-century Irish missionary was said to have been martyred. The cathedral's walls were left standing after the raid of 16 March, but it also needed a temporary roof. Instead of having to scour the surrounding region for scarce, costly and contested materials, Skilton found a source of roof beams only a couple of kilometres away from the site – in the wreckage of the factory where the U-boat hull sections had been built. Steel beams were not only cheaper than wooden ones, but lighter as well. Skilton obtained authorisation to use twenty-five beams that had been left over when the submarine construction had ceased in 1944, creating swords-into-ploughshares symbolism through a measure intended to solve a structural problem.

It was a solution that lasted less than two days, though. The works went on through the winter of 1945 and 1946, interrupted alternately by frosts and by flooding that inundated the nave below. Cracks began to appear in the pillars of the nave. On 18 February, the steel framework of the roof was completed. The next day, Rudolf Edwin Kuhn heard a crunching sound when he put his ear to a pillar. He ordered the craftsmen working under his direction to get out immediately, and locked the doors behind him as he left. Kuhn was only too aware of the hazards of post-bombing conservation, having been injured twice in falls when trying to hang the tarpaulins over the Residenz frescoes. His caution proved wise. A few hours later, one of the nave walls collapsed, and the cathedral ceased to be a symbol of survival for the city. The roof beams were later exonerated; the collapse was attributed to the water, which had fractured and undermined the masonry that had been weakened by the firestorm. Ten years later, the other wall was taken down because it was judged to be unsafe; the cathedral eventually underwent a full reconstruction, completed in 1967.[10]

Its surroundings came to reflect a compromise between modernisation and the care of heritage that bowed to internationally accepted conservation doctrines. Heritage preservation efforts concentrated on the Altstadt's key historical buildings, placing the emphasis on individual monuments rather than ensembles. There was no attempt to reconstruct the townhouses that had made the streets into baroque parades en masse: the city brought back the flagships, but not the fleet. German conservationists held to the principle that they should not create replicas. An ensemble reconstruction would have been unacceptable to them – not that it would have been a practical proposition in Würzburg's Altstadt, whose area is around 150 hectares, fifteen times the size of Warsaw's Starówka.

The two-dimensional form of the Altstadt had been preserved by the decision to rebuild on the old street-plan, and its proportions were maintained by limiting the height of the new buildings, but the replacements were otherwise largely indifferent to their setting. Nor were the old buildings' remains always respected. A number of eighteenth-century baroque facades that had survived the firestorm were demolished in order to widen streets for the benefit of motor traffic. And the oldest building to survive the war, the sixteenth-century Pleicher Handwerkerhaus (Craftsman's House), spent several decades falling into such disrepair that it was threatened with demolition until it was bought by a civic association in 1994. Unassuming and plain, it was easy to overlook, but it was the only house still standing that kept a channel open to the Altstadt's medieval origins. The belatedness of its recognition illustrates the uneven development of Old Towns, which rarely know themselves as well as they think they do.[11]

ROTHENBURG OB DER TAUBER

Chapter 10
A Wall Round the Whole Place

At half past three on a sunny afternoon in April 1945, Hermann Lichey set out from his battalion's command post in the back of a jeep, squeezed up against the spare tyre, holding a pole to which he had fixed half a bedsheet. There were three other American soldiers in the back with him, two lieutenants in the front with the driver, and two sappers lying flat on the jeep's bonnet, wielding a mine detector. They formed a truce party, sent to parley with the enemy under Lichey's improvised white flag.[1]

Lichey had been born and raised in Germany; now, approaching the age of forty, he was back in the land of his birth as part of a conquering army. As a native speaker of German, it fell to him to deliver his commanders' message. He was to inform the military commanders in the town of Rothenburg ob der Tauber, which lies about fifty kilometres south of Würzburg, that it would be spared bombardment if they agreed to surrender it. If they refused, and if the parley party was not back behind American lines within three hours, the town would be bombed and shelled to the ground.

Their schedule soon began to slip, when the jeep reached an impassable crater and had to turn back. The two officers and four privates continued on foot, approaching the enemy defences under their white flag, as parley parties in European wars had done since the Middle Ages. They fell silent as they marched along the road, until presently one of them asked, 'What the hell kind of place is Rothenburg?'

'It goes back to eleven hundred and something, and it has a wall around the whole place,' one of his comrades replied. 'Lots of art and ...' The soldier broke off, spotting German troops in a farmhouse up ahead. There were about forty of them, a tense mixture of ordinary soldiers and SS men. After more delay, as the lieutenant in charge of the post consulted his superiors, the Germans blindfolded the Americans and drove them to a former spa hotel by the river Tauber – putting them below the town and beyond radio contact with their base. With half an hour to go before the deadline, the parley party finally delivered the message. The senior German officer promised to withdraw, and the returning GIs just managed to reach their command post on the radio in time to call off the bombardment. When American soldiers entered Rothenburg the next day, the only German soldiers they encountered were fifty wounded men who had been left behind in the town square.

The blindfolds had prevented the parley party from seeing what kind of a place Rothenburg was. If they had been taken through the town, they would have seen towers, arched gateways, oriel windows and grandly spreading gables: the building blocks of a model medieval town, as imagined by generations of tourists before the war and since. But they would also have seen rubble, charred timbers and roofless houses, in a zone of destruction that covered some 40 per cent of the area within the town wall. Rothenburg had been attacked two weeks previously by a flight of American bombers; thirty-nine people were killed in the raid, and more than three hundred buildings were destroyed.[2]

Why did an American army take such trouble to avoid bombarding a town in mid-April that an American air force had bombed at the end of March? The air raid itself raised questions too. It was not as though the town had even been the planes' first choice of target: they had been sent to destroy an oil depot east of Würzburg, but were diverted because the site was hidden under thick fog. There were no depots, marshalling yards or any other such targets in Rothenburg, which contained nothing but heritage and picturesque views. The mission was recorded as an attack on the town area. It was remembered in the town as a wanton act of cruelty with no military justification, sacrilegiously perpetrated on Easter Saturday.[3]

An attack on the centre of a small town in Germany in the early spring of 1945, just three weeks before the Nazi regime surrendered, certainly seems gratuitous and punitive at first glance. It had been made by a flight of fifteen aircraft known as Marauders, led by a single plane of a type called the Invader. Perhaps the planes were living up to their names, marauding across the landscape and smiting any settlement that came within their reach, like all the other invaders that had ravaged swathes of Europe over the centuries before them. As the Allies bore down on Germany, restraints were shed in the headquarters where the directors of strategy planned their attacks, and in the cockpits where fliers fixed their targets in their sights.

To the invaders, however, the walled town above the river may have looked like a fortress that had to be neutralised. The raid was classified as tactical, not strategic, meaning that it was carried out in support of ground operations. That was the main role of the Ninth Air Force, to which the bombers belonged. In the early spring of 1945, it supported the offensive that the Allies' Sixth Army Group launched on 27 March. The Allied ground forces had not reached Rothenburg by the time of the attack, which took place on 31 March, but they were moving fast and getting close. A few days later, their front line straddled the Tauber about twenty kilometres upriver from Rothenburg. In the days before the raid, the townspeople could hear the sound of gunfire, borne on winds blowing from the west.[4]

Allied troops could have passed Rothenburg by and pressed on into Bavaria, but they might then have been vulnerable to attacks on their lines of supply and communication from German units holed up inside the town. The pattern of the attack certainly looks like what field commanders might request if they wanted air support for a ground assault. On its western side, Rothenburg sits atop a high scarp above the Tauber, giving defenders an overwhelming topographic advantage, but it can be approached from the east up a gentle slope. The bombers flew beyond the town and then turned back to attack it on its eastern side, damaging the length of the defensive wall that would have faced the Americans if they had been ordered to take the town by force.

The reason that their commanders never gave them the order was that, unbeknown to it, Rothenburg ob der Tauber had an American friend in high places. John J. McCloy's career came to include stints as President of the World Bank, Chairman of Chase Manhattan Bank, Chairman of the Council on Foreign Relations and, according to another high insider, the economist J.K. Galbraith, 'Chairman of the Establishment' in America. From 1941 to 1945, he was the US Assistant Secretary of State for War. On the day that Rothenburg was bombed he flew to Europe, where he embarked on a tour of American generals. One of them, Jacob Devers, was the commander of the Sixth Army Group. By chance, McCloy's meeting with Devers took place the day before the bombardment of Rothenburg was set to begin; by further chance, the general showed him the plan.[5]

McCloy was sorry to see it. Rothenburg had warm personal associations for him, the kind evoked by photos that fall loose from an old family album. As a child he had looked at etchings of the townscape that his mother had brought back from a visit there, and his own children's nursemaid had come from the town too. Having visited Rothenburg himself, in the 1920s, he knew what stood to be lost if the attack went ahead. He told Devers 'it was a shame at that late date in the war to destroy a city of such historical interest and beauty', and the general agreed to seek a negotiated surrender instead. That was how a party of GIs came to be sent off to Rothenburg with a radio, a white flag and an ultimatum.[6]

John McCloy's intervention recalls the story of how the banker Eric Warburg sought to save Lübeck from RAF attacks, by having a word with somebody in a position to take steps that might protect the city. It's even possible to imagine that McCloy had heard the story from Warburg himself, for the two men were good friends. In 1949, McCloy became the United States High Commissioner for Germany, overseeing the Federal Republic that had been established in the Western Allies' occupation zones. Warburg interceded with him in a bid to save part of the new Germany's heritage – not its historic buildings, but its industrial base. The Allies had decided to reduce Germany's manufacturing capacity by a programme of disassembly and demolition; the shipbuilding and aircraft manufacturing sectors were to be eliminated altogether. Over dinner in a villa near Frankfurt, Warburg argued that the Allies should stop dismantling German plants forthwith. McCloy retorted that the ancient German tribes had been obliged to break their swords after defeat, and grew increasingly angry as Warburg persisted. He came close to ordering his friend from the table, but ended up asking him to supply a list of facilities to be spared. McCloy still saw Germany's factories as an enemy asset, in contrast to his sympathetic view of its half-timbered houses.[7]

The American saviours' interventions on behalf of German heritage were appreciated for their symbolic significance and their underlying moral sentiments as well as for their physical results. John McCloy was made Honorary Patron of Rothenburg; John Davis Skilton was awarded the Federal Republic of Germany's Merit Cross – though he had to wait until 1976 for it. Their concerns for German heritage were early tokens of American willingness to start moving towards friendship with Germany as soon as the guns fell silent, or even before.[8]

They also represented the sense of common, border-transcending heritage that now suffuses Old Towns across Europe. Art and historic buildings constituted a unique domain, in which the Americans felt that German towns' losses were losses for them too. When Eric Warburg pleaded with McCloy to spare German industrial facilities, McCloy's immediate reaction was antagonistic, but when General Devers showed him the attack plan for Rothenburg, his reflex was protective. Turrets, arches and warm red tiles on steep-sloped roofs have a peculiarly captivating power, especially with an ancient defensive wall round them.

Rothenburg ob der Tauber is one of Middle Europe's oldest Old Towns, in the sense that it was among the first to embrace its antique character as its role. Like many ageing urban nuclei, it fell into disrepair and poverty as it found itself left behind by nineteenth-century industrialisation, but while other old towns deteriorated into slums, Rothenburg became part of the modern economy by reinventing itself as a tourist destination. Its industry was the provision of fantasies for travellers in search of escape from industrial society. By the early years of the twentieth century, they were making their way there over land, sea and ocean.

The early years of the previous century had been Rothenburg's last as a Reichsstadt, or Free Imperial City, a status conferring autonomy within the Holy Roman Empire that it had enjoyed since 1274. In 1802, as the Empire shuffled towards its final dissolution, the Kingdom of Bavaria took control of the town. By that stage Rothenburg was mired in its economic trough. The townsfolk became inclined to regard old structures as encumbrances rather than assets, demolishing a number of Gothic buildings and filling in the medieval moats. They left the main defensive walls, however. Those were protected by a royal decree: the new rulers valued the heritage they had acquired, but their subjects had yet to find a means of extracting value from it.

That possibility began to emerge from the 1860s onwards, as travellers made their way to the relict walled town in search of enchantment. Many were guided there by the writer Wilhelm Heinrich

Riehl, conservative and nostalgic in his outlook, who declared Rothenburg to be 'the most purely medieval' of all the old German towns he knew. His view of Rothenburg, as an uncannily preserved survival of the Middle Ages, has been resoundingly affirmed by its admirers ever since. It is now an illusion dependent on post-war reconstructions – and it bore only a superficial resemblance to the truth even when Riehl pronounced it, more than a hundred and fifty years ago. The walls dated back to the Middle Ages, but few of the buildings within them were actually medieval apart from the churches and the town hall, which gained a Renaissance frontage when it was rebuilt after being damaged by a fire in 1501. Most of the old houses dated back to Rothenburg's heyday in the second half of the sixteenth century, though they looked sufficiently like their medieval predecessors to satisfy the nostalgic imagination.[9]

Rothenburg took up its new role during the phase in which Germany's unification was completed, and the new state's citizens were faced with the question of what they had in common as a people. It became a beacon that drew Germans searching for their home town, their Heimatstadt, the idealised source-community that they could readily imagine flourishing beneath Rothenburg's benevolent gables. Home towns, their character built by looking after themselves, were a product of the balance of power within the Holy Roman Empire, which resulted in a mosaic of states that were strong enough to remain stable, but not to overwhelm smaller entities in their hinterlands. They formed symbolic containers for ideas of nationhood when Germany became a genuine empire, inaugurated in 1871, under Prussian leadership. Old towns affirmed that Germany was a Kulturnation, a nation formed by a shared culture, whose essential unity was now expressed in its political structure. Encircled by its protective walls, Rothenburg seemed like a vessel for an unpolluted wellspring of that culture.[10]

In order to function effectively as a portal into the imagined past, the town needed modern infrastructure. Most of all, it needed a railway connection. A branch from the main line between Würzburg and Nuremberg opened in 1873, sparing pioneer tourists a lengthy and tiresome coach ride. The stage was then set for Rothenburg to launch a transformative modern innovation of its own – not in the field of technology, but of marketing. The *Meistertrunk*, or *Master Drink*, was a masterstroke. Using the fabric of the town as scenery and a legend of Rothenburg's history as a scenario, it synthesised space and narrative to create a theatrical spectacle that looked for all the world like a centuries-old ritual. It has become an authentically seasoned tradition since its first performance in 1881, and is now listed in Germany's Nationwide Inventory of Intangible Cultural Heritage for UNESCO.

The play is set in 1631, during the decades of marauding and invasions known as the Thirty Years' War, when Rothenburg was seized by Catholic forces commanded by the Count of Tilly. It tells the celebrated local tale of how a heroic act of alcohol consumption saved the lives of the town's councillors. Tilly had resolved to execute them, the story goes, but his temper was improved by the local wine. He offered to spare the councillors if one of their number could drain the Pokal, a massive tankard that held more than three litres, in a single draught. A former mayor met the challenge and saved his colleagues. No contemporary sources recorded such a feat, however, and the story did not begin to take shape for more than a hundred years, attaining its familiar form in the early nineteenth century.[11]

The *Meistertrunk* tale told of a community so heroic in its solidarity that its leaders preferred to die together rather than to accept Tilly's initial offer, to hang only four of them, chosen by drawing lots. Its performance as a pageant by a mass cast of townsfolk affirmed the community's continuing vitality, to itself and to the visitors who came for reassurance that Heimat could still be found in the new German landscape. When bourgeois spectators looked at the re-enacted burghers, tricked out in knee-breeches and napkin collars, they saw their forebears and they saw themselves.

It helped that the old town was pretty much the whole town. There were some buildings beyond the wall, but Rothenburg did not begin any serious expansion beyond the limits it had set for itself in the Middle Ages until the second half of the twentieth century. It sat harmoniously with the countryside that surrounded it, unlike the old quarters of large cities, which were stifled and corrupted by the industrialised metropolises that held them under siege. Though small in scale by modern standards – the Baedeker guide of 1902 gives its population as 7,900 – it still had something of the character of a Free City.[12]

Baedeker's English-language edition informed its readers that 'In its wealth of architectural beauties and in its abundance of picturesque medieval streets Rothenburg is unapproached by any other town in Germany.' While Germans came in search of Heimat, foreigners were drawn by the lure of the picturesque. A stream of British artists made their way there and painted it (as did one notable Russian, Wassily Kandinsky, who subsequently moved through landscapes into abstraction). They universalised the scene, assimilating it into a dreamy romantic realm detached from any particular, exclusive culture or history.[13]

Another Briton impressed by the picturesque arrangement of buildings in Rothenburg was the architect Raymond Unwin, who offered them as an example in his celebrated book on town planning, and applied the lessons he drew from the town in the design of Hampstead Garden Suburb, an idealistic development in north London that sought to create organic harmony between the built and the grown. He alluded to Rothenburg forms in the silhouette of one block, and the arcade above the row of shops it framed. Unwin presented the town as a source of guidance for designing new settlements that would give people the space, light and greenery that they needed in order to live well and flourish, countering the pressures of mass industrial civilisation. Like the romantic landscape painters, he saw the German town as part of humanity's universal heritage. From an early stage in its career as a self-conscious Old Town, Rothenburg was claimed for the general as well as the particular. Foreign artists, urbanists and tourists all felt it to be somehow theirs.[14]

At the same time, it offered them the thrill of the exotic, a strangeness of time rather than place. They could fancy themselves to be explorers, their wanderings suddenly rewarded by walking through a gateway that seemed to usher them into the Middle Ages. The sensation of discovery was particularly heady for Americans of European descent. Confident that theirs was the nation of the future, they could take their ancestral continent's past as a measure of how far they had come. Robert Shackleton, author of a book called *Unvisited Places of Old Europe*, played the trope for all it was worth. 'You are the first American to enter the limits of Liechtenstein!', he has the statelet's governor tell him. 'We know of America, and letters come from America, for to your land some few of our people have gone, but never before has any one from America entered this principality.' Coming to Europe from the United States, Shackleton 'felt like a Columbus'. He included a chapter on Rothenburg – though by the time the book appeared, in 1913, the town conspicuously failed to fit its billing as an 'unvisited place'. Thousands of people were coming to stay each year, to say nothing of day trippers.[15]

By establishing its place on the tourist map of Europe, Rothenburg ob der Tauber connected itself to an international network through which it built up a stock of admiration and affection. Although that was an intangible kind of capital, it turned out to be the saving of the enterprise. If John McCloy's mother had not been one of the many foreigners who visited Rothenburg before the darkness closed over Europe in the 1930s, and took spell-casting pictures home with them, the whole of the town might have suffered the same fate that the American bombers visited on four-tenths of it.

One of the artists inspired by images of Rothenburg ob der Tauber was Adolf Hitler, who had initially hoped to pursue a career as a painter. On a visit there in 1934, a few weeks after adopting the title of Führer, he recalled how he had seen many pictures of Rothenburg in his youth, and had greatly enjoyed drawing the town himself. A few years later, he made funds available for the preservation of the town walls, stretches of which were in danger of collapse. His affection for Rothenburg was shared by the Nazi movement in general, for whom the 'Germanest' ('deutscheste') of towns became something of a pilgrimage destination.[16]

The feeling was mutual. Rothenburgers took to Nazism even before the party took power. At the election in July 1932, when the Nazis became the party with the most seats in the Reichstag with 37 per cent of the national vote, they took 60 per cent of the vote in Rothenburg. After Hitler became Chancellor the following year, Rothenburgers flocked to join his National Socialist German Workers' Party. Two-thirds of the town's population became members. Unlike Würzburg, whose Catholic traditions and associated political sympathies dampened enthusiasm for the radical new National Socialist movement, Rothenburg was a small Protestant town in a relatively poor part of Germany. In that respect it fitted the profile of Nazi-supporting localities, but it was more than merely typical. Rothenburg had a very special place in the landscape of the Third Reich.[17]

That place was inscribed principally through the activities of the Kraft durch Freude (Strength through Joy) organisation, which strove to instil National Socialist values in the German people through recreation and exercise. Kraft durch Freude – KdF for short – offered ideological tourist excursions to the town it described as 'an ever-lasting witness to the glorious German history of the Middle Ages, a shining monument to German community in olden times'. Rothenburg became a theatre in which Nazi illusionists conjured the spectacle of an ideal folk community magically preserved within its walls, where modern Germans would believe they were 'seeing a fairy tale of a long-gone golden age resurrected', as the Nazi party newspaper put it. Among the steps that the town took to enhance the magic was the institution of a Christmas market, without which the fairy tale would not have been complete.[18]

As well as providing affordable domestic holidays for Germans of modest means, KdF made a point of reaching out to members of the 'Volk' on the edge of the Reich or beyond its borders. The first contingents came from lands in the west. Under the peace settlements that followed the First World War, the Saar region had been placed under the control of the League of Nations. In 1935, voters in the territory opted to be reunified with Germany, by a majority of over 90 per cent. KdF transported Saarlanders to Rothenburg, where the organisation encouraged them to recharge their feelings of national pride and community. It also brought people from the Rhineland region, which was barred to military forces under international treaties. Hitler sent his troops into it the following year, to huge national acclaim.

From the opposite direction, a thousand Austrians came on a ceremonial day trip after their country was incorporated into the Reich in 1938, marching into the town from the railway station to be greeted by ranks of Nazis chanting 'Sieg Heil'. They departed in the same fashion after seeing the town's quintessentially Germanic sights, completing an occasion hailed by the local newspaper as the 'deepest expression of connection between people of the same tribe and same blood'. Germans from the Sudetenland made a similar procession after the Reich seized the region from Czechoslovakia later that year.

The Reich's revanchist ambitions further east were implicit in the organisation of visits from Danzig and the Memel territory. Danzig had been designated a Free City, kept separate from both Germany and Poland under the protection of the League of Nations, because it found itself in the corridor through Baltic Prussia that gave Poland access to the sea. Memelland was a strip of eastern Prussia that Germany had been obliged to give up under the Versailles Treaty in 1919; Hitler strong-armed the Lithuanian government into returning it in 1939. The symbolism of the trips was clear enough: the Reich had brought its people to the ideal German home town, and soon enough they would be living in the homeland as well, once its borders were extended to embrace them.

Rothenburg also offered the Nazi regime a means to project soft power abroad, in the form of the Shepherd Dancers, a group founded in 1911 to revive a local tradition on the basis of a historical claim dating back to 1517. They danced at the Albert Hall in London, and paraded through Hyde Park bearing the Third Reich's swastika flag. Back home, they performed in the market square for crowds on excursions from the huge Nazi rallies in Nuremberg, less than two hours away by train. Although there was no question of imposing the standard Nazi urban ensemble – a grand avenue, a vast assembly space, a massive Party building – as Hubert Gross had planned to do in Würzburg, there was no need. Rothenburg was homely, but on a scale that tended to the monumental. Its houses' proportions spoke of burgher prosperity; its main streets were straight and wide enough for marching columns. And if there was no space for the Nazi cohorts within the walls, they could always camp beneath them. The location was popular with the Hitler Youth, which at one point massed 1,400 of its members, drawn from more than 27 countries, in a tent city along the base of the town's fortified perimeter.

Enthralled as the Nazis were by Rothenburg, they did not regard it as perfect. Outside influences had started to appear even in this 'Germanest' of towns – as they necessarily would, in a place increasingly devoted to pleasing tourists. A drive was launched to remove hints of cosmopolitanism, such as foreign terms for hospitality establishments, and blots of modern commercialism, such as garish signs and pushy advertising. Hotels and restaurants were urged to rename themselves Germanically, labelling themselves as a 'Gasthaus' or 'Gaststätte', in Gothic letters on wooden or wrought-iron signboards.

Not all of the signboards offered hospitality. Four of them, placed at the town's gates, incited its opposite. They depicted caricatures of Jews in archaic garb, counting coins and toting sacks of money. One bore a verse, rendered in the appropriate Gothic script, accusing Jews in Rothenburg of 'profiteering and sharp cunning'. Another reproduced a municipal edict prohibiting the people of the towns from engaging in business transactions with Jews. Both texts dated from the sixteenth century, when Rothenburg expelled its Jewish residents. An article in the local paper explained that the tablets were set up 'to defend against everything un-German and foreign', and that the town had a special duty to warn the hundreds of thousands of people who visited it about 'the danger Jews pose to us'. The lesson of the reproduced historical texts, it claimed, was that 'national unity can only grow from the foundation of racial unity'. A local historian repeated the message in a book entitled *An Imperial City Defends Itself: Rothenburg ob der Tauber in the Struggle against Judaism*. Its cover featured another caricature of a hook-nosed Jew with a sack of money over his shoulder, drawn by the local artist who created the signboards, Ernst Unbehauen.

Eventually Rothenburg's Nazi activists followed up their propaganda of the word and image with propaganda of the deed. After the sixteenth-century expulsion Rothenburg had spent more than three hundred years without a Jewish community, until a new one began to form in the 1870s. Never large, it had dwindled to around twenty people by 1938, and they were gone by November that year. On a Shabbat in late October, Nazi thugs broke into their homes, drove them into the synagogue, and ordered them out of the town. New signs appeared on the city gates, hailing what they cast as Rothenburg's latest victory in its 'centuries of defensive struggle' against 'diabolical parasitism'. This was the culmination of the historical re-enactments that Rothenburg staged in its long Nazi carnival before the war. It turned out to be a curtain-raiser for the orchestrated unleashing of antisemitic violence across Germany, just over a fortnight later, that came to be known as Kristallnacht.[19]

While the Nazi pogromists were repeating the most shameful episodes of Rothenburg's history, Hollywood was working on the fairy tale. Walt Disney began developing his version of the Pinocchio story in 1937, and released it in 1940. He relocated the puppet's home from Tuscany to somewhere unspecified but definitely Germanic in character: if the mountains behind Jiminy Cricket's 'sleepy old town, pretty as a picture' are the Alps – Disney preferred not to say – they must surely be to the south.[20]

The film's visual concepts were developed by Gustaf Tenggren, an illustrator who grew up in Sweden and emigrated to the United States as a young man. Tenggren based Pinocchio's town on Rothenburg ob der Tauber, drawing his sketches from some of the many images of the place that had found their way across the Atlantic. He made it lower, softer, less regular and more intimate than its model, scaling it down towards a child's size. The houses leaned over the scampering characters like kindly old relatives in the sleepy European town that represented home – not for a community, and absolutely not for any kind of 'national community', but for the idealised family to which all Disney films were addressed.[21]

Disney evidently felt Middle Europe was the proper setting for fairy tales, a view doubtless conditioned by the efforts of the Grimm brothers, who emphasised what they saw as Germanic elements in the stories they compiled. Although the dominant region in this magical realm was German, it was disconnected from the real Germany and from the German nation, however conceived. A Germanic town in a fantasy movie signified an imaginary past, not an actual place. It was also easy to merge a country like Italy with one like Germany when contemplating Europe from across a continent and an ocean. Americans were ideally situated to see a town such as Rothenburg as a portal to a mythical age rather than to a mythical nation – and Rothenburg came to accept that a fairy tale was infinitely preferable to the story it had been telling itself.[22]

Chapter 11
Half-Timber Angst

In his travel book *Unvisited Places of Old Europe*, written before the First World War, the American author Robert Shackleton identified three German cities 'that are of especial interest from the standpoint of the picturesque': Nuremberg, Hildesheim, and the 'most picturesque' of the trio, Rothenburg ob der Tauber. By the end of the Second World War, Rothenburg was the only one left. A week before the American planes struck it, a raid by RAF bombers had devastated 70 per cent of Hildesheim. According to a Nuremberg periodical, the destruction of the Old Town area there was 'such that it is easier to report which historical buildings are still standing'.[1]

Rothenburg was lucky by comparison; not just because more than half of its fabric survived, but because almost all the bombs fell upon the less historically valuable half. The most important buildings are concentrated to the west of a street line that runs through the centre of the town from north to south, passing along the eastern side of the market square. A map of the bomb damage shows that only a handful of buildings west of the line were hit. They did include the town hall, which lost its Renaissance frontage, but the town's churches were spared.[2]

The prestige buildings were not really the point, though. Notable as some of them are – one standout is St James's church, which houses the

Holy Blood altarpiece carved by the Würzburg sculptor Tilman Riemenschneider in the early 1500s – they are not what makes the town what it is. Rothenburg was a jewel in itself, all of its buildings contributing facets, rather than a setting for individual gems. Unlike Würzburg, where the Residenz and the Dom church were raised up from the ruins but the townhouses only returned as shadows, Rothenburg had to be reconstructed as an entire ensemble. As the art historian Georg Dehio had declared in the 1900s, 'The whole town is a monument!'[3]

That was how the officials responsible for the care of heritage in Bavaria saw it too. 'Rothenburg as a Gesamtkunstwerk' – an artwork in its totality – 'must therefore be the first goal,' said Georg Lill, the director of the Bavarian State Office for Monument Preservation. But at the same time, the conservationists had been shaped by a professional culture in which Dehio's famous exhortation, 'Conserve, do not restore', continued to resound. They had to find a mode of reconstruction consistent with the principles of conservation, based upon respect for authenticity, that had become internationally accepted in the preceding decades.[4]

In the event, that proved surprisingly easy. The town and the State Office needed only a couple of meetings to agree on the way forward. Guidelines were drawn up by an architect in June 1945; Georg Lill readily endorsed them, emphasising that reconstruction should not be imitation. Replacement houses should be simple in design, traditional in their forms, proportions and materials, and draw upon the 'solidarity of traditional skilled labour'. They should not, however, be replicas of the buildings in whose place they stood. These precepts were developed further by Fritz Florin, a Munich architect, who oversaw the reconstruction. Florin sought to restore 'the former unity of the town image' by permitting facsimile reconstruction for a few key historical features, such as the town hall, while requiring new buildings to be recognisable as works of the current era on the one hand, and on the other to fit in with the surviving old buildings 'in a tactful manner'.[5]

In other towns, such stipulations would have encountered resistance from factions who regarded them as obstacles to progress, but Rothenburgers accepted them as the basis of a practical approach that addressed their most pressing needs: to replace lost housing – 741 families had been rendered homeless by the air raid – and to revive the town's sole industry, tourism. As in Würzburg, a policy of respecting previously existing property boundaries avoided legal entanglements. It also enabled builders to reuse foundations and walls that were still in place, saving labour as well as scarce materials. The plain and simple approach to design was economical too, since it maximised the use of locally available materials and minimised the need for specialist craft skills. Progress was rapid. As early as 1948, refugees were decanted from the Hotel Eisenhut, where Hitler had dined during a visit to the town in 1935, to make way for tourists.[6]

It would have been hard in the early post-war years to rebuild any other way than by using simple designs and traditional methods, for economically competitive modern techniques had yet to be developed, and the supply of the necessary materials had yet to be secured. The advent of steel and concrete did not come until after the initial phase of reconstruction, which was largely completed in Rothenburg by 1953. Also, the local architects would have had to learn new ways. There were only a few of them, their professional outlook shaped in the 1930s, and they were in the last place that an architect disposed to innovation would want to practise. Rothenburg had a tradition to uphold. In the 1900s, Robert Shackleton had reported that 'Every house is of ancient form; almost every house is in actuality ancient, and the few that fill gaps caused by fire or decay have been strictly built on ancient lines, for thus the city has consistently commanded ...' That was still broadly the picture, though by that point a scattering of nineteenth-century mansard windows and other additions had appeared across the townscape. Georg Lill, who had himself been in post as the director of the state monument preservation office since 1929, considered that such 'building-sins of the last generation should be ruthlessly removed'.[7]

The approach Lill set out encouraged the construction of buildings in the 'Heimat' style, rooted in local traditions, that had found
political favour in the 1930s. Rothenburg was rebuilt in a fashion
that would have met with Nazi approval, but the significance of the
style had changed with the downfall of the National Socialist regime.
The notion of Heimat, which had developed after modern Germany
came into being as the so-called Second Reich, found a new application after the demise of the Third Reich.[8]

In the Nazi period before the war, Rothenburg had been presented to
the German 'Volk' as a place where 'German spirit and the strength of
the nation are expressed through the splendid old buildings'. Its role as a
German home town was to demonstrate and sustain a national strength
that under the Third Reich had assumed a fundamentally militaristic
form. Now, after the Reich's total military defeat, the idea of Heimat was
disconnected from the state and fantasies of national ambition. It reverted
to an ideal of local homeliness, which Germans in search of an uncom-
promised and enduring basis for their collective identity found consoling
to imagine. The idea of Germany as a marching nation led by a Führer
was destroyed; the idea of Germany as a mosaic of homely communities
was still there in the ruins, offering hope for national renewal.[9]

As an especially evocative image of German community,
Rothenburg had a duty to the nation as well as to itself. A commen-
tary published in the local newspaper declared that Rothenburgers
should rebuild their town not for the sake of the tourist trade, 'but
rather to retain our nation's spiritual characteristics, its moral strength
and its creative talents; simply put, its cultural political mission'. A
sense of cultural purpose also underlay Georg Lill's efforts to keep
the light of the past shining in what was left of Bavaria's historic
urban centres. 'Germany does not have power politics or world trade
any more,' he reflected. 'One thing is left for us; not only the memory
that we were a cultured people . . . no, much more the fact that we
still are one.' Reconstructed, Rothenburg would embody both the
memory and the fact.[10]

The reconstruction of Rothenburg certainly embodied Lill's aesthetic ideals, to an impressive extent. Four-fifths of the new buildings complied with the guidelines endorsed by his office. A few architects, however, had other ideas. The main bone of contention was Fachwerk, or half-timbering, the feature that is to generic old German buildings what stripes are to zebras. It had become more prominent in Rothenburg as the town sought to cultivate tourists' expectations. Half-timbering was primarily a method of construction, and only secondarily a form of decoration; structural timbers were often covered over with plaster. As the tourist traffic swelled, building owners scraped off the plaster to expose the beams. The town's most popular photographic view, known as the Plönlein, features a gate-tower and adjacent houses. It was enhanced around the turn of the twentieth century by the removal of the plaster from the house in the foreground to reveal the timbers underneath, so that the scene combined the two stereotypical Old Town elements of half-timbering and medieval stonework.

Although decorative half-timbering had been part of the Rothenburg street scene before the town became self-consciously old, it had come to smack of twentieth-century commercialisation rather than authentic history. The overseers of the reconstruction from the State Office were set against it. Fritz Florin refused to countenance 'scenery-like imitations of medieval homes'. As the editor of an architectural magazine observed, however, people in the town itself were inclined to regard half-timbering as 'the embodiment of Rothenburg-ish', and were loath to forego it. Leonhard Kerndter, the leading local exponent of Fachwerk (and former leading light of the *Meistertrunk* play, having starred in the role of Count von Tilly), maintained that there was a place for 'simple, honest and clean' half-timbering in the reconstruction. He scored his greatest success with the Old Forge, previously a barn, which he rebuilt as an ornamental feature with a decorative frontage.[11]

The timber lattice that he applied to the face of the replacement building was not simple, and whether it was honest is open to

5. A postcard view of Rothenburg's Plönlein, sent in 1904.

question, but the Old Forge soon proved popular. In 1954 it featured on the cover of a German travel magazine, for an issue devoted to the 'Romantic Road', a tourist trail along a string of the region's picturesque old towns. Among the stops was Neuschwanstein, the castle purpose-built as a romantic fantasy, with Wagnerian operatic themes, for King Ludwig II of Bavaria in the 1870s and 1880s. It rapidly proved to be a road down which people were keen to go, taking themselves beyond recent history into fantasies of bygone ages. By 1955, Rothenburg was welcoming as many visitors as it had before the war. A fifth of its overnight guests were foreigners, most of whom must have been from countries that Nazi Germany had invaded or fought. The town was reclaiming its place in the world.

Meanwhile Leonhard Kerndter had become involved with a political party that had strong and unorthodox views about what Germany's place in the world should be. Kerndter had thrived in National Socialist Rothenburg, making his mark by setting a massive figure of an eagle holding a swastika on the town wall above the Hitler Youth camp site. After the war, he engaged in political as well as

161

architectural reconstruction. Along with Friedrich Schmidt, the town's former Nazi mayor, Kerndter was drawn to the resonantly named Deutsche Gemeinschaft, German Community, a political party which represented an attempt to find a viable framework for German nationalism after the defeat of National Socialism. The small right-wing group found a niche in Rothenburg thanks to Schmidt and Kerndter, who were elected on its ticket to the town council.[12]

One of Schmidt's initiatives as a councillor was an attempt to revive the Christmas market, which had lapsed since its inception during his term as mayor in the 1930s. He was assisted in the bid by Ernst Unbehauen, the artist who had made the antisemitic 'warning' plaques that had been installed at the town's gates. Unbehauen's return to Rothenburg's civic life had begun with a mis-step in 1950, when he was commissioned to paint murals for a new elementary school that had been established with the aim of instilling democratic values in the children of the town. He chose to illustrate the theme with a design he based upon a painting by Alfred Kampf, an artist favoured by the Nazis, called *Hitler Youth in Front of Ruins*. As the years went by, however, he managed to re-establish himself as an influential voice for heritage and the historic appearance of Rothenburg. In the 1960s he resumed the calls against intrusions of modern commercialism that he had first made in the 1920s. His authority was affirmed in 1966 by his appointment as the town's conservator, a position he held until 1974.[13]

A person would not have to be a fascist or an ultranationalist to agree with Unbehauen that brash modern advertisements should be kept off Rothenburg's streets. Conservation societies in historic towns all over Europe would sympathise with his view and applaud his efforts. But in Rothenburg ob der Tauber, denying the twentieth century had a subtext that went beyond Unbehauen's personal record as a Nazi and an antisemitic propagandist. A town that looked as though the twentieth century had not happened offered an enticing illusion to Germans who wanted to pretend that the century's fourth and fifth decades had not taken place. Joshua Hagen, the American historian who has examined Rothenburg's career as 'the most German of towns', observes that 'in the 1950s and beyond it came to represent opportunities for relatively untroubled engagement with Germany's past'. People could follow the town's history as far as the twentieth century 'and then fast-forward to 1950, because as the tourist guides will tell you, nothing happened. It was asleep, timeless, and nothing ever changed.'[14]

The illusion was a combination of unintended appearances and purposeful artifice. By and large, the architects who designed Rothenburg's reconstructions wanted them to be recognisably new, as a later Rothenburg architect, Hanns Berger, confirmed in a study of the reconstruction that he co-authored. But a difference that is clear to an architect may not be so apparent to an untrained eye, especially when the new building is designed to respect its elders 'in a tactful manner'. And the respectful, principled buildings found themselves mingling with new neighbours unashamedly designed to heighten the sense that Rothenburg enclosed a romantic medieval past within its walls. More half-timbering appeared as the years went by and the preservationists' early influence faded. It was what the public wanted, after all. Hanns Berger and his collaborator Tobias Lauterbach were standing in front of one of Leonhard Kerndter's retro-reconstructions one day, when a visitor told them to get out of the way because he wanted to 'take a picture of an old house, not two young guys'. Berger told the man that his and Lauterbach's combined ages were older than the building. 'Go away,' the tourist retorted, 'I don't care!'[15]

Sightseers not only don't care about whether a house is actually old or whether it just looks old. They are also active participants in the collective process of sustaining the spell, repeating the incantation 'fairy tale' and multiplying it endlessly across the internet. Their role does not require them to entirely believe the story: they may be well aware that a suspension of disbelief enhances their personal and collective experience. Rothenburg ob der Tauber is a consensual illusion, generated not only within its walls but in what the author William Gibson called the 'consensual hallucination' of cyberspace, as well as in Disney's studios and those of the artists whose paintings helped to make it the romantic vision that it became in the nineteenth century.[16]

When Disney's 'imagineers' considered how to represent Germany in the Disney World theme park, they took their inspiration from Rothenburg. As in Disney's *Pinocchio*, however, the romantic globalisation of the town tends to detach it from the nation. In fairy tales, princesses have names, but kingdoms do not. They have no place on any map, although the universe to which they belong is continually expanding. The modern world of fantasy is so extensively and richly developed, thanks to the power of computers to generate images, that places such as Rothenburg come to seem like projections of it, manifested by some anachronistic quirk in timber and stone. Inexorably, Rothenburg has moved from symbolising a nation to representing a period of time. Nowadays people don't come to Rothenburg in search of Germany. As Hanns Berger says, 'they want to see the Middle Ages'.[17]

Berger grew up in Rothenburg, in the latter stages of the twentieth century, without encountering the idea that the town might be seen to represent the German nation. He might have been told about it in school history lessons, he thinks, but not outside the classroom. By that time, it was becoming increasingly difficult for Rothenburgers themselves to distinguish buildings that were a few decades old from ones that had been built several hundred years before. As in the Old Town of Warsaw, the patina that had settled on the reconstructed buildings camouflaged their newness. The distinctions are blurred still further by the coats of paint applied to the old buildings, their timber grids emphasised in rich tones and bold contrast, broadcasting the signals of oldness as loudly as possible.

There are not nearly as many of them as there used to be. Some were demolished because their age was not sufficiently conspicuous, falling victim to the shift from valuing buildings because they are old to valuing buildings because they look old. That, Joshua Hagen observed, was Rothenburg's paradox: 'as Rothenburgers sought to capitalise on their town's medieval ambience, they destroyed much of its historical substance.' By Hagen's reckoning, it is likely that fewer than a quarter of the buildings within the town walls at the beginning of the twentieth century were still standing at the end of it – which implies that Rothenburgers probably destroyed as much of the town in the decades that followed the war as the American bombers did on that Easter Saturday in 1945. Rothenburg ob der Tauber has steadily become a new Old Town, getting younger in average age as it has grown older in appearance.[18]

VILNIUS

Chapter 12
What the Iron Wolf Meant

Unlike Warsaw and Würzburg and Rothenburg, the Old Town of Vilnius emerged from the war with nearly all of its buildings still standing, but almost none of its pre-war residents occupied them. Instead of reconstruction, it underwent the replacement of its population, along with the rest of the city. Vilnius's historic central district then spent more than forty years accumulating Soviet grime before Lithuania managed to struggle free of the USSR. After that, it took up a major supporting role in the exposition of the Lithuanian national story. The lead is taken by the castle complex beneath which it grew up, and which represents Lithuania's long history of statehood.

According to Vilnius's origin myth, the fourteenth-century Grand Duke Gediminas went hunting where a hill overlooks the confluence of the broad river Neris and its slender tributary the Vilnia. He spent the night in the valley below, and dreamed of a great wolf clad in iron. His adviser, a pagan seer said to have been rescued as an infant from an eagle's nest, told him it meant that a capital city would arise there, and its glory would resound across the world like the iron wolf's unearthly howl. Gediminas built a castle below the hill, set another on the top of it, and took Vilnius as his seat. By founding a capital, he turned his domain into a nation.

The development of the castle complex included turning the area into an island. Left to its own devices, the Vilnia had followed a meandering course to the Neris around the eastern apron of the hill. A second channel was dug for it along the western side, creating a moat around the castles. The site has continued to undergo physical, symbolic and mythological engineering ever since, in support of its function as the nucleus of Lithuanian nationhood.

Although Vilnius was already a settlement of some size by Gediminas's time, it is considered to have been founded in 1323, when the Grand Duke referred to it in correspondence as 'our city'. Gediminas's letters were pitches for human resources, inviting German cities to send him the merchants and craftsmen he needed to make his new capital a centre of economic as well as political power. To reassure them about migrating to a pagan state, he pointed out that there were a couple of Catholic churches in the city. He never converted to Christianity himself, though, and it fell to one of his grandsons, Jogaila, to make the decisive break with the old gods. Jogaila founded the link between the Lithuanian and Polish realms in 1386 by marrying Jadwiga, the King of Poland, a girl of 12 whose title signified that she was a monarch rather than a consort. The arrangement entailed Jogaila's baptism. It is said that he demonstrated the state's strategic change of faith by demolishing a sanctuary to the thunder-god Perkūnas that had stood at the foot of the hill on which Gediminas built his castle, and extinguishing the sacred flame that burned within it. In its place he built a cathedral.[1]

The narrative engineering began a hundred years later, in the first of a succession of unreliable chronicles that finished up with a suspected forgery in the nineteenth century. Their credibility gained a fillip in 1984, when a square outline was detected in the foundations of the cathedral and interpreted as the footprint of the pagan temple, but historians are divided about whether the masonry really is the remains of Jogaila's iconoclasm. On the other hand, the legend of the Iron Wolf does combine its mythological tropes with a certain down-to-earth plausibility. Nothing supernatural happens, and the pagan priest's interpretation of his lord's dream sounds like very much the kind of thing an ambitious medieval ruler would want to hear from his adviser.[2]

Development continued at the scene of Gediminas's dream, beneath the slope of the hill that came to be named after him. The lower castle complex extended around the base from the northern side, facing the Neris, to the west, enclosing the cathedral and facing the town that had grown up on the other side of the Vilnia's wandering stream. In the later part of the eighteenth century, the cathedral was remodelled in a classical style, long and colonnaded – 'like a Greek temple or a Polish municipal theatre', the German writer (and future author of the novel *Berlin Alexanderplatz*) Alfred Döblin cattily remarked. It was overlooked by its belfry, housed in a four-storey tower that had once been part of the castle's defences. By the end of the century the Vilnia's meander was gone, and the Grand Dukes' base was no longer an island.[3]

Their power had gone too, with the partition of the Polish–Lithuanian state and the advent of Russian rule. In the early 1800s, the imperial governor ordered the demolition of their old palace, which was situated between the cathedral and the hill. It had housed galleries and hosted operas in its heyday, but as the royalty of the dual state gravitated towards Kraków and Warsaw, it fell into disrepair, and was a ruin by the time the Russians took over the city. The space between the cathedral and the northern edge of the Old Town was opened up by the demolition of the Bishops' Palace and the Castle Gate. When a fortress was built around the castle area in 1831, as the Russian Empire battled with Polish rebel forces, a number of buildings were demolished in order to leave a clear field of fire in front of it. Eventually no structures were left in the space, which became filled with trees, and during rainy spells with mud. The Russian authorities did not regard it as a site to be accorded any great prestige, though in 1903 they did assert the supremacy of Russia's history over that of Lithuania by putting up a monument to Catherine the Great, which lasted until German forces captured the city in the First World War. Russian troops took it with them as they retreated before the German advance.[4]

A new phase of engineering began under Polish rule, in the late 1930s. Józef Piłsudski, the man who dominated Polish politics from the foundation of the new republic in 1918 until his death in 1935, was born on Lithuanian soil. Like many members of the Polish-Lithuanian noble class, he felt that he belonged to both nations, and his feelings underlay his hopes for a new federation between them – which came to worse than nothing, following his seizure of Vilnius and the consequent rupture between the two states. After his death it became literally true that his heart lay in Lithuania, for it was interred with his mother's remains in a Vilnius cemetery. (His brain also went to Vilnius, or Wilno as it was then, for anatomical study.) Polish architects drew up plans to remodel the space on the southern side of the cathedral, identifying the area in front of the former site of the Grand Dukes' Palace as the 'predestined' setting for a monument to the 'Great Son of the Wilno Region'. They highlighted the cathedral space's potential to accommodate crowds and celebrations.[5]

The initiative had an immediate political impact. For the Lithuanian government, based a hundred kilometres away in the city of Kaunas, the plan must have been a gross affront. After the legendary birthplace of Lithuanian nationhood had spent more than a century falling into neglect under Russian rule, the Poles were proposing to use it as a site on which to honour the man who had deprived the Lithuanian Republic of the city it claimed as its capital. Having built up a cult devoted to Vilnius, Lithuania's rulers were forced to look on as the Polish authorities laid their plans to profane its most sacred place. Against a background of increasing tension between the two states, the project was a matter of national significance on both sides of the border.[6]

The body charged with carrying it out, the City Bureau for Urban Development, assembled a cadre of alumni from Warsaw Polytechnic's

Faculty of Architecture. Some preparatory work began on the site, with a target date in August 1939 for the unveiling of the monument to Marshal Piłsudski, but little more than table-top models had been built by the time Poland was invaded from both sides the following month. The Soviets took Vilnius and then handed it over to Lithuania, on condition that the small Baltic state allowed the Soviet Union to set up military bases on its territory. 'Vilnius belongs to us,' Lithuanians joked mirthlessly, 'but we belong to the Russians.' That was confirmed in the summer of 1940, when the Soviet Union occupied their country and annexed it, incorporating Lithuania as one of the USSR's constituent Socialist Republics. A year after the Red Army marched in, Germany's forces drove it out, putting a Nazi occupation government in charge of Vilnius. The Red Army came back in vengeance three years after that, in July 1944, and re-established the Soviet order. Throughout all that time the Polish architects kept their jobs and continued to develop their plans for the cathedral area.[7]

They hardly had to make any changes, for the requirements of the successive regimes were all much the same. Poland and Lithuania were both authoritarian states that adopted fascist trappings. Lithuania's president, Antanas Smetona, styled himself 'Leader of the Nation' and based his party on the 'Leader-Principle', after Hitler's Führerprinzip. He also established a paramilitary organisation on the lines of Hitler's Brownshirts and Mussolini's Blackshirts – though he had to disband a more radical force, known as the Iron Wolf, elements of which later tried to stage a coup against him. For the colonels who ran the Polish regime, 'an authoritarian, highly militaristic, pseudo-fascist bureaucracy', the public theatre of mass mobilisation that they observed in Italy and Germany offered some hope of replacing the charisma that they had lost with the death of their Marshal. For the real totalitarian powers, Soviet and Nazi, that took control of Vilnius after extinguishing the two weaker states, a mass assembly space was an essential requirement. Occupying a city without one would be like occupying an apartment without a living room.[8]

When Lithuania was given control of Vilnius in October 1939, Lithuanians were reluctant to approach it. Most of its inhabitants were Poles, their hostility accumulated over twenty years of frozen conflict, and aggravated by the new authorities' moves to 'depolonise' the city, which ranged from changing street names to closing the university. The new head of the City Construction Directorate, Vytautas Landsbergis-Žemkalnis, found his fellow architects unwilling to move to Vilnius from their familiar surroundings in Kaunas, so he hired the Poles to perform roles similar to those they had undertaken for the previous administration. They themselves seem to have felt that they 'were working for the city, not the currently ruling power', according to Rasa Antanavičiūtė, director of the Vilnius Museum. Many of them expected to stay there, and perhaps entertained hopes that it would end up as Wilno again, after the fighting was finally over.[9]

Landsbergis-Žemkalnis also took up the Poles' plan for the Cathedral Square, though there would obviously no longer be a place in it for Marshal Piłsudski. Instead, the architect envisaged that the spot would be taken by a monument commemorating Vytautas the Great, Jogaila's successor as Grand Duke, in a space 'where the nation can express its joys and its sorrows'. (His own forename was itself a commemoration of the Grand Duke, and the second part of his surname was also a patriotic statement, being a Lithuanian version of the first part.) The new leadership resolved to build the square faster and better than the Poles had managed, but the work was still under way when the city yielded to Soviet control. Landsbergis-Žemkalnis had no difficulty fitting the concept into the new ideological framework. He was able to offer the new order a public space that by his estimate, calculated with a civil engineer's sense of precision, could accommodate gatherings of up to 9,100 people.[10]

The Germans had driven the Soviets out by the time the square was finished. Like their counterparts in Warsaw, the Nazi occupation

authorities found that they needed the services of the Polish architects who were already working in the city, so the project was
completed by the same team that had started it four regimes previously. Although the design was little changed, the Nazis did not
require a monument, and so a flowerbed was dug to fill the space. It
remained there until 1996, a few years after Lithuania regained independence, when it was replaced by a statue of the Grand Duke
Gediminas in armour, leading a horse.

That finally completed the suite of features that the Polish planners
had envisaged for the cathedral area in the late 1930s, and kept
faith with their subsequent director's vision of a monument to a
legendary Lithuanian ruler, albeit a different Grand Duke to the one
he had in mind. It was not enough, however, for some reconstruction
campaigners, who advocated rebuilding the Grand Dukes' Palace as
a way to help build the re-emerging nation. The most powerful calls
came from Algirdas Brazauskas, a politician who rose to be First
Secretary of the Lithuanian Communist Party and then became first
President of Lithuania after the end of Soviet rule. He may have looked
forward to living in the palace himself, for he proposed it as the presi-
dential residence. It was deemed too small for the purpose, though.[11]

The idea of rebuilding the Grand Dukes' Palace had been mooted
back in 1942 by Marian Morelowski, the art historian who went on
to furnish ideological arguments for the nationalistic reconstruction
of Wrocław. Morelowski was among the Polish experts recruited by
Vytautas Landsbergis-Žemkalnis to continue their planning work
for Vilnius, his principal task being to draw up a historical plan of
the city. For the palace he had little to go on, other than eighteenth-
century drawings of it falling picturesquely into ruin. Those,
Morelowski suggested, could serve as the basis for a creative reconstruction. Without proper documentation, a replica was out of the
question.[12]

Nobody would have especially wanted one, though, for the demolition was not regarded as any great loss to the city's architectural

heritage. The palace's significance was symbolic, not aesthetic. According to Brazauskas, 'The foot of the Gediminas hill is indescribably dear to us: it is not only the past, but also the future of our nation.' The palace rebuilt at the navel of the nation would give the modern republic depth and historic glory, manifesting its historical connection to the Grand Duchy. It was Brazauskas who laid the first brick, a relic from the original building, in 2004. He expressed his pleasure that he had confounded the sceptics who had criticised the project, and declared that the reconstruction would 'strengthen the state'. On 6 July 2009, when the country's annual Statehood Day fell in its Millennium Year, a symbolic opening ceremony was held at the still-unfinished palace, attended by presidents and monarchs of countries ranging from Iceland to Georgia.[13]

According to the National Museum that is now based in the Grand Dukes' Palace, the reconstruction is 'viewed by the public as important for national self-consciousness and historical memory, for the restitution of historical truths regarding Lithuania's independence and Vilnius as its historical capital, for the regeneration of the city's historic core, for illustrating Lithuania's historical and cultural roots in the Grand Duchy of Lithuania – a multinational state of Lithuanians, Poles, Belarusians, Ukrainians, Jews, Tatars, Karaims and other nationalities – and for showing the importance of Lithuania's European ties, historic and current'. Such a dense crowd of highly charged functions, jostling and pushing in different directions, certainly seems to demand a purpose-built palace to accommodate it. For a marketing slogan, the Museum described itself more simply as 'the heart of Vilnius'. A city that dates its foundation to the fourteenth century has been given an artificial heart that started to beat a decade into the twenty-first century.[14]

The National Museum's list of historical and contemporary roles for the Grand Dukes' Palace reads like part of the job description for a modern Old Town, packed into a single building. Yet the Old Town of Vilnius, Senamiestis in Lithuanian, has its own role to play in the exposition of Lithuania's nationhood. From up on the castle hill, its red-tiled roofs and church towers look like part of the composition – not just a background, but the hinterland that the castle complex needs in order to articulate the full range of claims it makes about the nation it represents. Like the Royal Castle and the Old Town in Warsaw, the castle zone and the town below it form a compound symbolic ensemble.

Whereas the castle complex asserts the historical depth of Lithuania's claims to statehood, the Old Town forms the basis for claims about Lithuania's historical development and its place in European civilisation. It is an exhibition of the Grand Duchy's cultural achievements, most of them churches, and many of them created not long before the state was terminated at the end of the eighteenth century. By then the city contained forty churches, for a population of 40,000 souls.[15]

Vilnius was nothing to boast about in the Middle Ages. According to a Flemish diplomat who visited it in 1413, during the reign of Vytautas the Great, it was little more than an assortment of wooden buildings scattered along the base of the castle area. It gained definition a century later when a defensive wall was raised, enclosing an area of 300 hectares; a main thoroughfare ran through it from its northern edge below the castle, past a marketplace and the town hall in the middle, to the wall's southernmost gate, known in Lithuanian as Aušros vartai: the Gate of Dawn. The medieval streets persisted, continuing to meander and disappear up alleys. In the eighteenth century, they provided a matrix for the spate of church-building, funded by wealthy patrons, that came to represent the city's cultural value. The poet Czesław Miłosz, who lived there between the two world wars, encapsulated the formula as 'Narrow cobblestone streets and an orgy of baroque'.[16]

Looking back decades later, from his eventual home in California, Miłosz saw the city of his youth as 'neither a provincial nor a capital city, although it was provincial above all'. As Miłosz observed, it was an 'oddity': its ambiguous state was a consequence of its historical position as a peripheral centre of that much larger oddity, the Polish-Lithuanian Republic. A more recent commentator, Laimonas Briedis, regards the Vilnius baroque as a product of the city's 'provincial' character, which allowed the local style to continue on an increasingly ornate trajectory decades after the major cultural metropolises of Europe had dropped it in favour of neo-classicism. That late efflorescence made it possible for Tomas Venclova, Miłosz's friend and fellow-poet, to present Vilnius as 'the largest baroque city north of the Alps, and the one furthest to the east'.[17]

In that light, Vilnius manifests as a significant European cultural actor; one that not only appreciated Italian aesthetic sophistication, but also transplanted it to another sector of the continent, and inflected the style with its own sensibility. Its Old Town is 'seen as proof that Lithuania is a European country,' says Rasa Antanavičiūtė.[18]

Chapter 13
Wilno, Vilna, Vilne, Vilnius

The transformation of pre-war Wilno into post-war Vilnius was effected by removing those of its inhabitants who called it Wilno, the Poles who had constituted the majority of its population. Their departure followed the removal by genocide of the second largest ethnic group in the city, the Jews, who called it Vilna or Vilne. The same sequence took place in the other borderland city that Poles had held dear, known today as Lviv, which had also been inhabited largely by ethnic Poles and Jews before the war.[1]

Vilnius's reconstruction was principally a population project and only secondarily a rebuilding programme, especially in the Old Town. Czesław Miłosz described the pre-war city as an enclave of negative ambiguity, 'neither Polish nor not-Polish, neither Lithuanian nor not-Lithuanian'. The aim of the reconstruction was to remove that ambiguity, remaking Vilnius as a city that was definitely Lithuanian and very definitely not Polish. It succeeded in establishing the city's Lithuanian identity, but had to make do with concealing the ambiguities endemic to the Old Town and the surrounding districts.[2]

Until the Nazi occupation, the heart of Vilnius's character as a multi-ethnic city was a triangular district adjoining the central space over which the town hall presides. The historic Jewish quarter was not beyond the walls – unlike in many European cities, such as Kraków, whose Jewish residents had been sent to live in the separate township of Kazimierz at the end of the fifteenth century – but right in the middle of the city. A larger Jewish neighbourhood spread out from it across the western side of the Old Town. By 1939, according to one estimate, the central district was home to 75,000 people, of whom 35,000 were Jewish.[3]

Many of that fraction were crammed into the overcrowded and insanitary alleys of the original quarter, which was an object of fascination for outsiders and a symbol of identity for Vilna's Jews. During the First World War, a boy named Moyshe Vorobeychik often happened upon German soldiers painting and sketching scenes in the quarter. Some of them were notable artists in civilian life. Vorobeychik himself became a photographer, under the name Moï Ver, and produced an avant-garde album based on one of the Jewish streets. The project represented a desire shared by other young Jewish artists in the city, to innovate and embrace modernity while retaining their cultural roots. They formed a group called Yung Vilne, whose emblem was a young tree growing above one of the old Jewish quarter's signature arches.[4]

Max Weinreich, an eminent linguist and scholar of Yiddish, felt similarly about the relationship between learning and place. He considered that modern Jewish research needed an environment like that of Vilna, where 'the houses and stones retain a memory' of its Jewish cultural heritage. Weinreich was a leading figure in the YIVO institute of Yiddish studies, which continued a tradition of intellectual enterprise that had made Vilna a centre of the Haskalah, or Jewish Enlightenment, in the nineteenth century. YIVO's headquarters opened in 1933 on a broad modern street at a distance from the city centre, but the emotional heart of Jewish Vilna was still embedded in the sclerotic alleys of the old quarter. The enclave retained its allure for outsiders too, despite the warning in a guidebook by a Polish professor about 'the typically eastern slovenliness of the inhabitants of this anti-hygienic district and its unbearable fug, which makes it impossible for a cultured European to visit these alleys, especially on hot summer days'.[5]

After the Germans took control of Vilnius in 1941, they confined its Jewish population to two ghettos, one in the old quarter and one in the newer neighbourhood. The former was the smaller of the two, holding 11,000 people. It was liquidated after a month, in October 1941, leaving 29,000 people in the larger one, which was maintained until September 1943 and used as a source of labour. The ghetto inmates' tasks included the construction of a model of Vilnius, which was produced by a team of thirty architects, engineers, draughtsmen and artists. They were forced to create a representation in miniature of the city from which they had been excluded, complete with the tiny zone where they were imprisoned in the middle of it. Four of them are known to have survived the war, but they were rare exceptions. The great majority of Vilnius's Jews perished in the Holocaust, many of them shot by squads of Lithuanian volunteers at a killing ground in woodland outside the city. Several hundred managed to stay alive until the end of the German occupation, and a few thousand escaped – many of them involuntarily, deported by the previous communist authorities – into the depths of the Soviet Union. Nearly all of the survivors subsequently emigrated to the United States, Israel and other distant lands. Vilna, the 'Jerusalem of Lithuania', became an exile memory.[6]

The dissolution of Wilno began with an attempt by Polish forces to recapture it. In July 1944, as the Red Army pushed westwards, the Polish underground state launched a nationwide operation to liberate cities and territories ahead of the Soviet advance. The battles of July were the overtures to the nine-week tragedy of the Warsaw Uprising, which began on the first day of August. Wilno's political and emotional importance to the Polish cause was expressed in the codename for the Armia Krajowa (AK) assault against the city's German occupiers: Ostra Brama, the Polish name for the

6. The shrine at the Gate of Dawn, Vilnius.

Gate of Dawn. A grand and reverent window is set above the arch on the inside of the gate; through it an image of the Virgin Mary, clad in gilded silver, presides over the street below. The site is one of the most intense foci of the Marian cult at the heart of Polish Catholicism, and therefore of Polishness as it is orthodoxly conceived, venerating Mary as 'Queen of Poland'. Thousands of silver votive offerings attest to its devotees' faith that the image has miraculous powers. It is said that the first of the offerings came from a Polish-Lithuanian commander who led his men through the gate in an assault on the Swedes who occupied the city in 1702.[7]

As a precedent, it was hardly auspicious. Instead of ejecting the occupiers with supernatural support from the Mother of God, the attackers were checked and forced to retreat. The assault in 1944 also lacked the miraculous intervention that would have been needed to achieve its double objective of driving out the Germans and keeping out the Soviets. After failing to overcome the German defences on the first day, and struggling to communicate with their comrades inside the city, Polish units operated alongside the Soviet forces. In the latter stages of the battle, AK troops fought their way through the Old Town to capture the city hall, and raised the Polish flag over the castle tower. It was quickly taken down by their inimical Soviet allies, who replaced it with a red one.[8]

After six days, the Germans were defeated, and on the day after that, the Soviet leadership ordered the disarming of the AK soldiers. The ensuing arrests of Polish officers heralded a programme of repression that saw thousands detained in Vilnius as the year went on. That sent an ominous message to the Poles who comprised most of the city's surviving population. In September, the Soviet and Polish authorities agreed terms for the removal of ethnic Poles from Lithuania to territory within Poland's new borders. It was to be a notionally voluntary exodus, not an expulsion. Lithuanian Poles were sent away from their homes and birthplaces in railway goods trucks, but they were not herded onto the trains at gunpoint. The official term was 'evacuation', which suggested that the Poles were being given aid – and that they were under threat.[9]

Many Wilno Poles held on for a time, hoping that the city would be restored to Poland. It had changed hands five times since 1939, after all; perhaps it might change hands once again. But in the absence of divine intervention from the quarrelling gods of geopolitics, they were forced to judge whether it would be better to go west into Poland, or to stay and risk being sent east to Siberia. Eventually they accepted that if the Soviet authorities wanted them out of Vilnius, it was unwise to try to hang on. Nearly 90,000 Poles left the Vilnius region by the end of 1946, even though most of them must have had little idea of where they were going or what they would find when they arrived.[10]

One couple, Wincenty and Pelagia Adamowicz, decided to take their family west after their son Ryszard became aware that the NKVD security force had its eyes on him. The Adamowiczes set out aboard a goods wagon which they shared with two other families, having provisioned themselves with food bought using money they got from selling their furniture. They spent two weeks being fitfully hauled across the weary post-war railway network before ending up in a barracks in Gdańsk, formerly Danzig, a city laid far lower by the war than the one they had left behind. Although they transplanted themselves successfully, they kept the lights of their old home town shining in their minds' eyes, and the image of the Ostra Brama Virgin Mary had pride of place on the wall in their new home. 'Every family celebration and religious holiday began and ended with stories about Wilno,' recalled Ryszard's son Paweł. 'Even before I went to Wilno, my imagination was filled with numerous images of the city of Gediminas.'[11]

The family made for Gdańsk because they had acquaintances among the faculty of Vilnius's university, for whom Wincenty had worked. A carpenter by trade, he gained employment at Gdańsk's new medical university, where the professors from Vilnius were redeployed. Their university still occupied its proud place in the Old Town, but it no longer bore the name of the King of Poland, Stefan Batory, who had founded it in 1579. As the city's pre-eminent intellectual institution, it was a key target of the drive to empty Vilnius of its Polish population. The authorities were not intent on cleansing every last Pole from Lithuanian soil. Their principal aim was to remove the Polish intelligentsia, which was almost entirely resident in Vilnius, and which they regarded as the section of the minority community most likely to be able to sustain opposition to them. The campaign was pursued far more intensively in the capital than in the rest of the country. More than four-fifths of those who registered for 'evacuation' from the Vilnius region were sent to Poland, but more than three-quarters of those who registered in other regions ended up staying in Lithuania. Although Vilnius had a minority Polish community, it was a replacement too. Few of the post-war Poles had lived there before the war; few had levels of education that could pose what the new authorities would consider a threat to the new order.[12]

Settling in the capital meant starting from scratch in a wrecked and unfamiliar city. As Tomas Venclova put it, 'Life in Vilnius at the beginning was an arduous sinking of roots into a new soil. In general, it was chaos.' He got lost after his first day at high school, a former Jesuit establishment that was 'an island amid the ruins' of the Old Town's Jewish quarter. Unable to ask for directions, because he met very few people and none who spoke Lithuanian, he took four hours to find his way home. It may have been a good thing that he encountered so few people, because in those days Vilnius 'was a city of outlaws, and it was dangerous'.[13]

Tomas had gone there with his father, a pro-communist poet whose readiness to colonise the capital was not generally shared by Lithuanian intellectuals. Replacing the Polish intelligentsia with a Lithuanian one proved to be a struggle. The city's new chief architect found that his colleagues were no more enthusiastic about leaving their comfortable apartments in Kaunas than they had been in 1939, when they were approached by his predecessor, Vytautas Landsbergis-Žemkalnis. 'We went and bowed down before them, trying to convince them to move to Vilnius,' he recalled, but his entreaties were fruitless. Unable to assemble a new team, he based his reconstruction plans on those drawn up by the Poles whom Landsbergis-Žemkalnis had been obliged to employ. Their concern for the silhouettes and cityscape of the Old Town was thereby sustained after they had gone.[14]

While urbanites remained reluctant to leave Kaunas, villagers became increasingly desperate to leave the countryside. They found themselves in the middle of a conflict waged against Soviet power by the partisans known as the 'Forest Brothers', in which the state's counter-insurgency strategy entailed mass deportations and the collectivisation of agriculture. Battered as it was, Vilnius offered them a haven, and in time a new intelligentsia emerged there, as young people who had spent their childhoods on farms gained city educations. A growing proportion of the city's inhabitants were ethnic Lithuanians, but that proportion grew very slowly. Lithuanians did not add up to more than half of Vilnius's population until 1989, and still formed less than two-thirds of it thirty years later.[15]

In the early 2000s, 58 per cent of the Old Town's residents spoke Lithuanian as their home language; 20 per cent spoke Russian, and 12 per cent spoke Polish. Despite the rupture brought about by the extermination of its second-largest ethnic group and the removal of its largest, Vilnius has continued its history as a city known to its inhabitants by a number of different names.[16]

The fabric of Vilnius was badly degraded in the battles to wrest it from the German occupiers, but it did not suffer annihilation on a scale comparable to that of Warsaw or carpet-bombed German cities. A survey of 525 buildings in the Old Town (compiled in part by the art historian Marian Morelowski, before his departure to Poland) found that two-thirds of them had escaped unscathed or needed only minor repairs. Of the 181 buildings that had sustained serious damage, only eleven were completely destroyed. More than that were lost in the post-war reconstruction, when houses were knocked down to create open spaces that satisfied prevailing doctrines of urban hygiene.[17]

From an orthodox Soviet point of view, however, those were little more than token gestures. In 1941, during the initial period of Soviet control that was terminated by the German invasion, the authorities sent a troika of experts to report on how the city should be improved. They complained about the terrain, the soil, and the dense stock of historic buildings in the Old Town that stood in the way of modernisation. The troika recommended cutting a swathe through those relics of 'lordly Poland' to make way for a grand thoroughfare that would run south to the railway station. There would be no place for the 'muddle' and 'semi-feudal character' of the Old Town in a 'well-built socialist city'.[18]

What they failed to recognise was that Vilnius was also to be a national capital, and it would therefore require a built history. As in Poland, the ruling powers developed a hybrid ideology that combined Soviet communism with local nationalism, maintaining ideological continuities with the era before the war. Communist media tirelessly reminded Lithuanians that the Soviet Union had delivered Vilnius to them: the ironies in that message would have become overwhelming if the city had then been bulldozed and replaced by a generic Soviet imposition. The cost of a full-scale 'socialist' reconstruction would also be hard to justify, after the economic devastation of the Great Patriotic War, in a city where most of the buildings remained usable. Instead, the new regime took up the interwar cult of Vilnius and encouraged florid verses about it to bloom in the Lithuanian Communist Party newspaper, *Tiesa* (*Truth*, or in Russian, *Pravda*). It was even acceptable to call Vilnius a 'holy city' – in tones evoking Lithuania's mythicised pagan past, so as to avoid lending any endorsement to its contemporary religions.[19]

Having acquiesced in the principle that the Old Town should be conserved, its new management faced the question of what to do about its celebrated fleet of churches. They were the crown jewels of the heritage below the castle hill, but such a concentration of religiosity ill befitted the capital of a Soviet republic. As in other Soviet cities, a number of religious edifices were desacralised and repurposed as vessels of secular culture. The cathedral became an art gallery, while the church of St Casimir was converted into a Museum of Atheism, complete with a stained-glass centrepiece devoted to a Polish-Lithuanian nobleman and martyr who was executed in the Market Square of Warsaw's Old Town in 1689, for writing a treatise called 'On the Non-Existence of God'.[20]

Vilnius's churches required new narratives as well as new purposes. Lithuanian scholars rose to the challenge, devising ingenious commentaries on the aesthetic qualities and historical significance of the city's architecture. One evaluation, published in 1948, provided a new ideological framework for the pre-war notion of the Vilnius baroque, identifying the style as an authentically national form. 'Lithuanian baroque is not that of a theatrical, artificial, cosmopolitan Jesuit style,' the art historian Vladas Drėma declared – 'it is a unique architecture of palaces and churches that speaks a different language compared to the baroque of other countries.' A few years later, however, another critic rejected the churches altogether: 'Baroque church architecture is full of anti-realist, reactionary moments, such as, for example, excessive splendour, refinement, illogical composition of architectural forms and symbols of religious character . . .' On the other hand, the Old Town's baroque houses had 'realist artistic qualities that are capable of being fully developed in our Soviet architecture'. They were not marred by the 'excessive splendour' that was the Vilnius baroque's defining quality.[21]

Although Vilnius's heritage scholars and professionals generally came to accept the local baroque, some continued to look askance at it. They regarded it as a Polish distortion of Lithuanian forms, not being minded to see it as a fruitful interaction between different cultural influences. The underlying truth, they argued, was that the Old Town was a Lithuanian town: to prove it, they stripped off baroque facades to expose the Gothic bricks that dated from before the creation of the Polish-Lithuanian Republic. For them, Gothic survivals were the material confirmation that Vilnius was fundamentally Lithuanian, not Polish – in the same way that their counterparts in post-war Wrocław had highlighted Gothic survivals as material confirmation that the Silesian city's true identity was Polish, not German.[22]

All these narrative exertions could have been avoided if the narrators had not been obliged to labour under the burden of past national glory. Their counterparts in the northernmost of the Baltic republics, Estonia, were freer to take their capital city's history as they found it. Tallinn, formerly known as Reval, boasts an exquisitely formed Old Town on a hill. At the top are the edifices of power, the castle and seat of government, surrounded by houses built for the aristocracy in classical and baroque styles. Down below is the medieval Old Town proper, richly vascularised with narrow alleys and winding lanes. Among its highlights is a pharmacy that dates back to 1422, and claims to be the oldest in Europe operating continuously in its original premises; nowadays it is a museum of itself as well as a shop that sells medicines. The Christmas trees set up each year in the square outside are claimed to represent a tradition started in 1441. They stand in front of a Gothic town hall that was there at the time; it was damaged but not destroyed by a Soviet air raid in 1944.[23]

More than 90 per cent of the Old Town's buildings survived the Soviet bombs, so its post-war care was more a matter of preservation than reconstruction. In the 1960s, a conservationist quartet – two architects, an art historian and an engineer – compiled an inventory of the Old Town's buildings that served as the basis for a protection order. It also provided the data for a notably inclusive account of the quarter's value, which was seen to lie in the unity of its ensemble. The later parts had grown out of the older ones, the art historian argued, and it was a mistake to pick them apart. In the northernmost Baltic capital, the Gothic, the baroque and their neighbouring styles were not to be divided, differently valued, or made to compete with each other.[24]

Like their Lithuanian counterparts, the Estonian conservationists were motivated by national sentiment. By drawing attention to the history of Tallinn's Old Town, they were discreetly developing a national theme that could run in the shadow of the grand Soviet narrative. It was a very different history to that of the Lithuanian capital, though. Tallinn had been ruled by Denmark, sold to the German military-monastic order of the Teutonic Knights, taken over by Sweden and absorbed into the Russian empire. It had flourished as a Hanseatic city, but its history as the capital of a sovereign state did not begin until 700 years after the Danish invaders seized the castle hill. There was no ancient national myth for the Old Town to sustain, nor any storyline of lost greatness, so the conservationists were able to value it as the product of its history instead of having to impress values into it. They could let the Old Town's history support national consciousness without turning it into a statement about ethnic identity.[25]

In Vilnius, it was not just the Polish storyline that was written out of the historical narrative. Jewish heritage in the Old Town was subjected to decades of attrition. The Great Synagogue at the centre of the old Jewish quarter was still standing at the end of the war, though it had lost its roof. It was left unrepaired, and in 1957 it was demolished. A kindergarten was built on the site, which was framed by characterless post-war housing blocks. The former main street of the quarter, with the town hall at one end of it, was widened to produce an abbreviated boulevard. Smaller streets were erased from the map altogether, along with names that were reminders of the area's former inhabitants. Žydų gatvė, Jewish Street, was made to adopt the name of an adjacent street, removing the most obvious public clue to the connection between the area's history and the state of neglect into which it was allowed to fall. Growing up in a flat nearby, Rasa Antanavičiūtė found it strange that there were still empty spaces in the neighbourhood, and that some of the streets seemed to end in the middle of nowhere, but she had no idea what had been there before. 'There was no information about that, absolutely no memory,' she says. 'It was very well erased.'[26]

The former Jewish quarter's disrepair became more conspicuous after the end of the Soviet era, as the prestigious parts of the Old Town were given their market economy facelifts. Conditions under communism had been more equal: soot, damp and greyness prevailed throughout the historic centre of the city. One consequence of the persisting neglect was that the monumental qualities of the Jewish quarter's surviving elements grew, their poignancy increasing as the buildings became more dilapidated. In the immediate aftermath of the war, people across Middle Europe had stared at the devastation in sublime despair and had been seized by the idea that it should be its own memorial. The ruins, monuments of the unintentional kind, should be intentionally preserved. Those counsels of trauma were almost never taken up, though a few isolated specimen ruins were permitted to stand as monuments, such as the gaunt tower of the St Nikolai church that remains as a memento mori by the side of a six-lane carriageway in Hamburg. In Vilnius, the buildings slowly made their own way towards a state of monumental ruin. The crumbling plaster told its own story unbidden.

Latterly, a new chapter began to unfold. During the war, the Ghetto Library had served as both a repository of knowledge and a base for resistance fighters, who hid weapons in its reading room. Among the partisans were Shmerke Kaczerginski and Abraham Sutzkever, writers who had been members of the Yung Vilne cultural group. Back then, they had had a vision of an artistic spring; now, as part of what became known as the Paper Brigade, they took on a rescue mission to keep rare Jewish books and manuscripts out of Nazi hands. They escaped from the ghetto in its last days; when they returned the following year, they set up a Jewish museum in the library building. It found itself on the wrong side of Soviet cultural policies, and was shut down in 1949 without ever having opened to the public.[27]

After spending the Soviet era in educational use, the building became derelict. In the new century, its dilapidation was turned to redemptive advantage. Employing a device previously used in Warsaw, its windows were filled with old photographic images that formed a portrait gallery commemorating the exterminated Jewish community. With its scarified render and exposed brick, the disintegrating facade that formed the backdrop evoked loss and suffering much more powerfully than polished marble. It also offered an implicit reproach to the city of Vilnius, which had restored Jewish Street's name but continued to neglect Jewish heritage in the back-streets of the Old Town. The images themselves announced that the

7. Images from photos found in ghetto ruins, placed in windows of the former Vilnius Ghetto Library.

situation was at long last being addressed: plans were in hand to turn the building into a memorial museum of the Holocaust in Lithuania and the Vilna Ghetto.[28]

Down the street, the faded Hebrew and Latin letters of shop signage in Yiddish and Polish above the entrance to a courtyard survive as a trace reminder of everyday life in the era when Vilne and Wilno co-existed. They might have been effaced if the property had been refurbished before such details came to be appreciated as period features. Neglect can sometimes preserve the past, by keeping it out of the present's way.

Precious few other Polish inscriptions can be seen in the Old Town. The survivors seem mostly to be on stone plaques solidly embedded in walls, defying deletion. They are left looking rather like tombstones. When Paweł Adamowicz first visited Vilnius, at the age of eleven, the erasure of its Polish heritage made a profound impression on him. He wandered around the places that his family's stories had already implanted in his imagination; in adulthood he testified that his most important encounter there was with diversity, which he both accepted and found that he liked. The young Adamowicz recognised that 'despite war and communism, Vilnius was still teeming with religious-cultural diversity'. Yet he was also left with the conviction that so far from acknowledging that diversity, let alone embracing it, the authorities had systematically erased and falsified the city's Polish history. His father pointed out where Polish inscriptions had been removed and Polish names changed to Lithuanian forms. It was an important lesson, Paweł averred, adding that it subsequently proved useful when, as mayor of Gdańsk, he was faced with decisions about restoring elements of the city's German or Jewish heritage.[29]

He had a long time in which to encounter such opportunities, and should have had more. Mayor Adamowicz was first elected in 1998 and won a sixth term in 2018, but he was fatally stabbed on stage at a charity event in January 2019. The attacker was a recently released convict who claimed the murder was revenge for his imprisonment.[30]

Adamowicz testified that his family's recollections of Wilno and its surrounding region 'immunised' him against 'dangerous diseases' such as nationalism. In his mind he treasured an image of the vanished republic of 'many nations, languages, flavours and smells', which he preferred to the official propaganda about an ethnically homogeneous state. Like Vilnius, the city in which he grew up had been re-founded with a new population after the war: by 1950, nearly 90 per cent of Gdańsk's residents had lived there for no more than five years at most.[31]

Attempts at polonisation by the new authorities included details such as the inclusion of arcades in reconstructed townhouse frontages on the main street of the city's historic zone, which had suffered destruction on a scale comparable to that of Warsaw's Old Town.

Absent from the pre-war streetscape, they were introduced to make the buildings look more Polish in style. The authorities were more concerned with appearances than with integrating the form and the content of the reconstructions, though. Whereas in Warsaw's Old Town the aim was to create modern flats within the walls of the reconstructed townhouses, the reconstructors in Gdańsk put up new apartment blocks behind the repro historic facades without aligning them, with the result that a single flat might stretch across three notional houses, and staircases might lie behind two frontages. It was not an approach calculated to connect the new residents with the history of where they lived. Children in the courtyards behind would say that they were from a particular staircase rather than a particular building, because their relationship to the staircases was clear, but their relationship to the historical facades was confused and awkward.[32]

After the end of communist party rule, a nostalgia for the history of others developed in both Gdańsk and Wrocław, as Poles grew curious about the Germans who had been there before them. Whether or not their interest in their predecessors was sympathetic, they were keen to read different stories than those they had heard from the Party. 'Suddenly, the inhabitants of Wrocław began to buy books about old Wrocław en masse. They were bestsellers,' recalled Marek Krajewski, whose own books, crime novels rooted in interwar Breslau, became bestsellers too. 'In the 1990s, there were framed photos of old Wrocław practically everywhere in the Market Square.' Book-buyers in Gdańsk snapped up an album featuring photos of the city's Danzig past; a series of volumes followed it in response to the unexpected popular demand. It was described as a 'sentimental journey' by one of its editors, Donald Tusk, who was then in the early stages of the political career that took him to the presidency of the European Council.[33]

The local embrace of Danzig contributes to a broad cultural and political project which finds expression in the idea of Gdańsk as a cosmopolitan European city. Donald Tusk suggested that it could serve as a symbol of Europe on the strength of its history, from the times when it prospered as a Hanseatic port to its spell as the interwar Free City, and its role as the birthplace of the Solidarity trade union that mobilised Poland's population in a movement for political change at the beginning of the 1980s. Its politicians, writers and academics formed a coherent, overlapping group that developed a distinctive vision of the city, based upon an inclusive approach to its past. Before the war, the Nazis had claimed it to be essentially German in history and character; afterwards, the communists argued that it was essentially Polish. After the communist regime came to an end, the new establishment hailed Gdańsk as a city shaped by diverse presences and influences.[34]

In Wrocław, cultural practitioners also took up the idea of uncovering the city's history – almost literally, in the case of a project entitled 'Breslau is still watching from under the plaster', which mapped old German signs exposed by dilapidation. The Polish intelligentsias that grew up in those post-German cities took up the German past as an underpinning for their sense of European identity, a sense that was widely shared across Poland and provided a popular base for the country's claim to a place at the heart of European institutions. They discarded the nationalist origin myths that the communists had devised, and replaced them with their own multicultural mythology. Paweł Adamowicz created his from the myth of multicultural Vilnius. It led him from a nostalgic vision of the old republic to a contemporary liberal understanding of diversity, affirmed unmistakably when he took his place at the front of 'Equality Marches' organised by LGBT+ activists in his city.[35]

Vilnius itself has not embraced its pre-war past in the same sort of way. Like their counterparts in any number of historic European towns, Vilnians are keen on scrolling through old photos of their city on Facebook, but they maintain a certain detachment. They have become readier to talk about Jewish Vilna, but not Polish Wilno.

One reason that they have not sought to appropriate pre-war heritage may be that they are satisfied with Vilnius's identity as the national capital, whereas people in Gdańsk and Wrocław had to find other distinctions for their cities.

Another reason may be that they were less radically alienated from their communist party. The populations of Vilnius, Gdańsk and Wrocław are all post-war replacements, whose roots in their home cities reach no deeper than two or three generations. But although all three were subjected to the Soviet command system, the chain of command was crucially different in Vilnius. Whereas Solidarity challenged the government in Warsaw, the Lithuanian struggle was against Moscow. The contest in Poland was framed as an internal matter – as it had to be, to avoid provoking the Kremlin – but the Lithuanian movement was explicitly a struggle for national independence. Lithuania's Communist Party claimed a place in the national movement. It had nurtured Lithuanian identity during the Soviet era, and it helped to end that era by declaring its independence from the Soviet Communist Party in 1989. Vilnians may subsequently have been less inclined than people in Gdańsk or Wrocław to question what the Party had told them about their city's history and its relationship to that of their nation.

They were told a great deal about the latter, but surprisingly little about the former. While an entire palace was built below the castle hill as a showcase for the exposition of Lithuanian history, the city did not manage to open a museum of itself until 2021 – and then only in temporary premises too small to accommodate permanent displays. According to its director, Rasa Antanavičiūtė, its purpose is to provide the city's residents with knowledge of its past that they lack through family memory, because the population only dates back to the 1940s, and because the city's history has been rewritten several times since then. Knowledge, it is hoped, will encourage a sense of belonging. The museum is intended to help Vilnians feel that the city is theirs, and thus to feel responsible for taking care of it.

The city's Old Town is certainly hers, for she grew up right in the middle of it, and lives there now. When she was a child, the district concealed a labyrinth that she and her friends made their playground. The architectural form that seems to represent the Old Town's character best is not the baroque but the courtyard, a mysterious space that may sometimes be glimpsed from the street through a gated archway, and in which private Vilnian life is led. During Soviet times many of the courtyards were open to each other – ideal for games of hide and seek, or for finding secret routes around the Old Town. Nowadays they are closed. From the outside, they make it look as though the Old Town wants to keep its stories to itself.

MIDDLE EUROPE

Chapter 14
Stumbling Stones

A few streets away from Rothenburg ob der Tauber's market square, and a couple of decades into the twenty-first century, the sight that numbers 10 and 12 Judengasse presented to the street told a similar story to the one that could be read on the wall of the Ghetto Library in Vilnius. The brickwork of number 10 was completely exposed. Amid Rothenburg's arrays of proudly furbished facades, the building looked as though it had been stripped of its citizenship. Next door, the frontage of number 12 was coated in a green algal bloom from the ground-floor windows up to the eaves: a picture of decay, but not the picturesque kind.

As in Vilnius, the story was one of neglect, followed by slow and belated recognition. A panel on a nearby wall told passers-by that the houses of Judengasse, Jews' Alley, the spine of Rothenburg's medieval Jewish quarter, had been undergoing 'careful and cautious renovation' since 1990. Yet number 10, its most historically significant building, was still a reconstruction site more than thirty years later. Its renovators, Kulturerbe Bayern (Bavarian Cultural Heritage), were urging the public to sponsor new roof tiles for the house, which was originally built around 1409.[1]

This was a reconstruction method based on a historical model: bricks in the town walls are inscribed with the names of donors who paid by the metre for the repair of damage the walls sustained in the 1945 air raid. The appeal was launched in 1950, nearly seventy years before the one for 10 Judengasse. Like Vilnius's Jewish Street, the Jews' Alley in Rothenburg was close to the heart of the old town, and likewise had to wait decades for recognition as an essential component of the district's heritage.[2]

Variations on the theme unfolded across Middle Europe. In Würzburg, the main synagogue had been located in the Altstadt, across the street from a Catholic seminary. It was destroyed by the air raid of 16 March 1945, as were the city's other synagogues, and its ruins were levelled in 1956; the trainee priests took over the space as a sports ground. A few dozen members of the city's former Jewish community, which had numbered over 2,000 before the Nazis took power, had returned after the war. Their attempts to establish a new synagogue did not meet with a generous response from the council. After considerable delay, it granted them permission to use a site outside the Altstadt, by the new ring road. The synagogue finally opened there in 1970, serving a congregation of around 150 people. In the 1990s, Jews began to immigrate from the former Soviet Union, increasing Würzburg's Jewish population to more than a thousand. A new community and cultural centre opened next to the synagogue in 2006, with the resonant name of Shalom Europa. Bavaria's Prime Minister hailed it as an 'outstanding symbol of German-Jewish reconciliation'.[3]

In Rothenburg, with its record as a most-favoured Nazi tourist destination, there were doubtless generational factors at play. If the town was prepared to have somebody like Ernst Unbehauen as its conservator, as it was from 1966 to 1974, it was probably not ready to engage with its Jewish history. After all, Unbehauen's own most notable engagement with that history was his use of sixteenth-century texts on the infamous antisemitic 'warning' plaques that he had placed at the town's gates. Whatever he or his surviving contemporaries subsequently felt about what they had done during the period of National Socialism, it did not encourage them to linger on Judengasse.

A nearby trace of Jewish presence, the name of the Judenkirchhof or Jewish Cemetery, was erased when it became a source of civic discomfort in the 1950s. The site had ceased to be used for Jewish burials after the expulsion of Rothenburg's Jewish community in 1520, and had become a general-purpose open space within the town walls. When tourists made complaints about its use for festivals, including the town's Cultural Days events, the dissonance between its origin and its contemporary uses was resolved by changing its name to Schrannenplatz (Granary Square). With its Jewish history discreetly removed from the street-map, it now serves as a car park.[4]

Complaints were voiced about the lamentable condition of Judengasse in the 1980s, but they were nothing new. Officials had filed reports about the poor state of the street's houses in the seventeenth century, and their successors sustained the theme into the twentieth century. These were homes for labourers, not burghers. In the tourist era they were pale by comparison with the grand gables and bold half-timbering around which Rothenburg created its visual spectacle. Their plain exteriors did not suggest that they had much potential as additions to the street scene, and their humble occupiers had little money to spend on them. Several of the houses were knocked down after the war, and the rest were left to deteriorate in what remained a backstreet, excluded from the investments in appearance that the surrounding area enjoyed.

Then a new generation of architects and conservationists discovered what neglect had saved from destruction in Judengasse. Historic interiors had survived thanks to the lack of investment, whereas they had succumbed to renovations at more prestigious addresses. Investigations in the cellar of number 10 revealed a mikveh, a Jewish ritual bath, that is thought to be one of the oldest in Germany. Eduard Knoll, a local architect, used the finds in Judengasse houses to mount a critique of Rothenburg's 'facade cosmetics', by which he meant an approach that treated the outward appearance of a building as everything and the interior as disposable.[5]

After stories sprang up about impending demolitions, his warnings about a threat to the medieval Jewish quarter exposed Rothenburg to criticisms in regional and national media. Judengasse became the focus for a change in the town's understanding of its built heritage. Rothenburg's principal historical society, the Verein Alt-Rothenburg (Old Rothenburg Association), had hitherto been largely concerned with the promotion of tourism, and therefore with facades. The society now took a more reflective turn, recognising the importance of interiors, and engaging with the Jewish strands of Rothenburg's history.[6]

Its engagement went beyond scholarly reflection, too. The Association bought houses in Judengasse, including numbers 12 and 10. It sold the latter on to Kulturerbe Bayern, which it thanked for turning the house back into what it long had been: 'a jewel and cultural object of German and European importance'. For its part, the Bavarian heritage body hailed its 'protégé' house as a symbol of the diversity of Rothenburg's history, in which 'the city and Jewish life were interwoven'. In Judengasse 10, Jewish and post-Jewish layers of the past had endured together as companions, and the caesura of the expulsion was invisible.[7]

Lateness in engaging with Jewish history, in its most recent and terrible chapters, was a phenomenon that extended beyond continental Europe. The United States and Britain were preoccupied with their own stories of the war for several decades after it ended: Americans dwelt upon their combatants' campaigns on the other side of the Atlantic and in the Pacific; Britons wove a collective narrative anchored in that phase of the conflict when their country 'stood alone' against Nazi Germany. Although the genocide of Europe's Jewish populations was regarded in the West as the most wicked of all the Third Reich's crimes, it had yet to attain its position as a historical object of unique and universal significance. Its time came in the 1970s and 1980s, when it became generally known as the Holocaust.[8]

In the East, recognition of the genocide was inhibited by the enduring Soviet reluctance to speak its victims' collective name. The preferred term was 'victims of fascism', or some other such formulation that covered all those who died through Nazi aggression. There were a number of possible reasons for this stance, including antisemitism among communists, antisemitism among populaces that deterred communists from appearing to be sympathetic to Jews, and the dominance of the Soviet war narrative, with satellite variations, that demanded a monopoly on memory. The effect extended beyond the commemoration of genocide, discouraging engagement with the deeper Jewish past.

Not everybody was discouraged, though. In Poland, the architects Maria and Kazimierz Piechotka took upon themselves the task of documenting Poland's old wooden synagogues, none of which had survived the war. Maria Piechotka had first seen photographs of such synagogues in one of Oskar Sosnowski's lectures as an undergraduate at Warsaw Polytechnic. They were, she recalled seventy-eight years later, an 'absolute revelation'. The buildings had been surveyed under the leadership of Szymon Zajczyk, a Jewish Pole who was arrested and murdered during the occupation of Warsaw. After the war, with the principal scholars dead and the synagogues reduced to ashes, all that remained were the photographs, and a set of drawings that had been saved from destruction in the archives of the Institute of Polish Architecture. The Piechotkas felt they had to conserve the memory of the synagogues, and to make their striking forms more generally known.[9]

They had the advantage of access to the archives, and their initiative enjoyed the patronage of Jan Zachwatowicz, who was then Poland's Conservator-General. On the other hand, they embarked on their project with the disadvantage of knowing nothing about Jewish history or religious culture, a state of affairs they felt they had to rectify in order to do their subject justice. An impulse rooted in their aesthetically and intellectually formative experiences at Warsaw Polytechnic's Faculty of Architecture, under a professor who valued historic provincial buildings regardless of which religion or ethnic group they represented, had led the Piechotkas to their engagement with Jewish cultural history. The knowledge they gathered went on a transatlantic return journey that arrived back in Warsaw to bear fruit there more than half a century later.

They completed a book on the subject in 1952, while Stalin was still alive. Even after the post-Stalinist 'thaw' was initiated in 1956, the book's theme did not sit comfortably with the Party's politics. The Piechotkas were led to think that it might not get past the censors, who were particularly uncomfortable with the material on synagogues that had stood at locations now on the far side of Poland's eastern borders.[10]

It was eventually issued in 1957, however, and an English-language version was published in 1959. Despite appearing in a modest edition with a prosaic title, *Wooden Synagogues* had a lasting impact in the United States. In 1970 the artist Frank Stella was given a copy to look at while he was in hospital. It inspired him to create more than a hundred artworks, brightly coloured and angular, known as the Polish Village series. After the end of the communist epoch, the Piechotkas produced new works about synagogues, this time rhapsodically entitled *Heaven's Gates*, and broadened their scope to encompass entire old Jewish towns.[11]

An American architectural historian, Thomas Hubka, drew on the Piechotkas' research for a study of a single vanished wooden synagogue. He chose one that had stood in a place called Gwoździec (in Polish; the town is now in Ukraine) and had been extensively documented before it was damaged by fire during the First World War. The resulting book, *Resplendent Synagogue*, introduced the

Piechotkas' work to Rick and Laura Brown, the founders of an educational organisation that promotes learning through the reconstruction of 'large historical objects'. They conceived the idea of reconstructing the synagogue, a notion about which the Piechotkas were 'both gracious and a little sceptical'. The Browns' vision fitted with that of POLIN the Museum of the History of Polish Jews, which was under construction in Muranów, the former Jewish district of Warsaw. They organised workshops across Poland in which 238 students, guided by 58 professionals, built and painted a replica of the Gwoździec synagogue roof. It was raised into position as the centrepiece of a POLIN gallery in April 2013. Maria Piechotka, then aged 92, helped to haul it up.[12]

It was a long way from its model's rural habitat, and its metropolitan setting was radically dislocated too. Few points of reference to the pre-war Jewish district had survived the destruction of the ghetto by the Nazis, and the area's post-war redevelopment by a regime that saw it as a space upon which to build socialism according to Soviet precepts. Large tracts of it had been reduced to rubble, without even the haggard frontages that were left lining streets throughout much of the devastated city. There was no question of restoring its previous form. It had arisen in the nineteenth century, so architects who had come of age after the First World War were not inclined to see anything of value in it – and the gloomy tenements that comprised much of its housing stock were the antithesis of what modern planners vowed to build. According to Bohdan Lachert, who shaped the reconstruction in the late 1940s, the old district had been the second most densely populated in the world, after Hong Kong.[13]

Lachert sought a form that would incorporate a representation of the area's history into the new residential district. He found his solution in the most immediate problem that the reconstruction faced. The volume of rubble piled up in Muranów was estimated to be three million cubic metres. An army of labourers ten thousand strong would take more than three and a half years to clear it, he cautioned.

It would be better to build on top of the rubble, and with it: the housing blocks were to be made from 'rubble-concrete', and would stand on terraces made of rubble, like monuments on plinths. The resemblance was not coincidental. Economic and historical considerations would combine harmoniously, building a future for the district that commemorated its past. Lachert's superiors found his vision too sombre by half, though. The walls were brightened up with stucco and decorative detail; columns and cornices created a generic socialist-realist look that effaced the estate's relationship to the memory of the place it occupied.[14]

South of Muranów, the Jewish district had extended as far as the smart downtown zone of the city. On one street, not far from the Palace of Culture and Science that rose above central Warsaw like the handle of a great rubber-stamp brought down by Stalin upon his satellite's metropolis, a few townhouses survived both the war and subsequent demolitions conducted in the area by the Bureau for the Reconstruction of the Capital. They endured into the twenty-first century, though their condition became increasingly parlous, and they eventually came to serve the commemorative role that had been attempted unsuccessfully in Muranów. Artists turned the tiny enclave into an improvised Old Town. In what became a template for the public representation of Jewish memory, windows were used as frames for photos of former members of Warsaw's Jewish community, ghosts summoned up in a pocket of forgotten urban space.

The project condemned the neglect of the buildings as the 'annihilation of memory', but as with its counterpart in Vilnius's former Ghetto Library, it was their dilapidation that gave them their historical eloquence. It was an Old Town that spoke not of the Middle Ages but of the middle of the previous century. The exposed bricks painted a picture of suffering and loss; the dark red hue brought burning to mind. Gradually, however, the image was dispelled by renovation: the bricks disappeared as the original facades were recreated by developers, who saw the potential of combining bygone bourgeois elegance with sleek modern interiors. They spliced the nineteenth and twenty-first centuries together, eliding everything that had happened in between.[15]

Round the back, space was found to represent the rupture of the Second World War and the Holocaust. The rear wall of one of the buildings is covered by a mural depicting images of the pre-war district. At the base is a skyline of buildings that still exist, including the only synagogue in the city that survived the war, glowing golden behind a row of churches – a reminder that the area was never a ghetto until the Nazis turned it into one. Above them, vanished buildings hang in the air against a backdrop of clouds, accompanied by shop signs in Polish and Yiddish, bearing surnames no longer found in Warsaw's civic registries: Grunberg, Goldstein, Rosenbaum. The artist behind it explains that the composition represents the transformation of the pre-war district, and the capital with it: the 'harmonious scene' disappears as 'the city crumbles to pieces, implodes, and rises above Warsaw only as a memory'. It is an Old Town rebuilt in the sky.[16]

On the pavement outside a Woolworth store in Lübeck's Altstadt, three small brass plaques commemorate three people who once lived above the clothes shop that used to be there. The inscriptions record that Carl, Lina and Elsa Camnitzer were deported from the city in 1941, and murdered in Riga. The memorial does not spell out that the Camnitzers were killed by the Nazi regime because they were Jewish: that is assumed to be understood. Among their neighbours were members of another Jewish family, the Schilds, to whom they were related. The Schilds remained in their own apartment, only to perish in the RAF's fire-raising attack at the end of March 1942.[17]

Similar plaques are embedded outside buildings in the Old Towns of Rothenburg ob der Tauber, Würzburg and Vilnius, as well as in two thousand other places around Europe. They are called Stolpersteine, stumbling stones, although that is not a literal description: they are laid flush with the pavement. The idea is that people may stumble upon them metaphorically, while shopping or sightseeing, and have their attention caught by a flash of historical memory. Each commemorates an individual victim of the Nazi regime, and is normally placed outside the person's last home. The first were installed during the 1990s, in Cologne. By 2020, 75,000 Stolpersteine had been placed at sites in two dozen European countries. Collectively, they comprise what the project behind them calls 'the largest decentralised memorial in the world'.[18]

The Stolpersteine are the invention of Gunter Demnig, a German artist, who made them himself until the demand became impossible for him to meet. Each is still made individually, as a practice that asserts opposition to the mass murder committed by the Nazis. Although the form is standard – a ten-centimetre concrete cube topped with brass – each is an individual artwork, which then combines with its installers to make up what the artist Joseph Beuys called a 'social sculpture'. Demnig presents the Stolpersteine as 'an art project for Europe'.[19]

His fellow social sculptors are typically relatives of victims, or local organisations that wish to accommodate elements of the dispersed memorial in their neighbourhoods. Their task is to gather basic details about the individual to be commemorated, and to seek permission from the local council to have the stone set in the pavement. Although the stones and their inscriptions have to adhere to a strict format, the original decision to place them on streets rather than the walls of buildings was pragmatic: Demnig realised that it would be much easier to get permission from local authorities than from private property owners. The result was a device that can insert a commemorative statement into a public space with a minimum of intrusion, making Stolpersteine particularly suitable for historic districts that have their own strict rules about their presentation. They also seem more chronologically appropriate than wall plaques for places like the Old Town of Würzburg, where nearly all the buildings are replacements for ones destroyed in the war. Several hundred stud the pavements of Würzburg's Altstadt.

Although the strategy has proved spectacularly successful, it leaves the project open to the objection that because such memorials can be trodden on, or soiled by street life, they do not uphold the dignity of the people they commemorate. Charlotte Knobloch, the President of the Jewish Community of Munich and Upper Bavaria, found the idea of underfoot memorials 'unbearable'. After years of controversy, Munich introduced small memorial plaques that follow the Stolpersteine inscription format, but are mounted on stainless steel posts. The design, which would look entirely at home in a contemporary art gallery, imposes municipal authority upon Demnig's civil society initiative. It performs a similar task of memory, but it is not a social sculpture.[20]

The defilement objection was also raised in Kraków, by the local branch of the Institute of National Remembrance's Office for Commemorating Struggle and Martyrdom. It reviewed an application by Nora Lerner, a Polish-born woman who wanted to place Stolpersteine for murdered members of her family at locations in the city's historic Jewish district, Kazimierz, and it delivered a decisively negative opinion. The head of the department assured Lerner that the Institute considered it a duty to commemorate Jewish victims of the Nazis, as Polish citizens. This was a significant affirmation on the part of a body whose full title identifies it as the Commission for the Prosecution of Crimes against the Polish Nation, since Poland is in the region of Europe where 'nationality' means ethnicity rather than citizenship. However, the Institute considered 'the German artist Gunter Demnig's Stolpersteine concept highly controversial and generally contrary to the accepted culture of remembrance in Poland'. It questioned whether pavements, trampled upon and exposed to pollution daily, were appropriate sites for respectful commemoration.[21]

Though the reference to Demnig's nationality seemed to suggest an incompatibility between German and Polish cultural traditions, his concept emerged from a movement that arose as a counter to accepted culture in Germany and many other countries. Demnig was born in 1947 and came artistically of age in the late 1960s. Stolpersteine were the product of an approach to art shaped by the oppositional currents of 1968, which in Germany were driven by an especially commanding historical imperative to devise new cultural forms. Meanwhile in Poland, a crackdown on student protests against censorship developed into an antisemitic purge, in which the communist leadership and a powerful nationalist faction within the party engaged in a contest for power at the expense of the country's Jewish minority. About half of Poland's remaining Jewish population, some 13,000 people, left the country as a result.[22]

The Stolpersteine concept could not itself be oppositional, for it depended on asking for permission from the relevant authorities. In Poland, however, it came up against the state's desire to shape the national culture of remembrance. Having expressed his organisation's lack of enthusiasm for Stolpersteine, the Kraków representative of the Institute for National Remembrance went on to present Nora Lerner with wordings for the inscriptions, should she want to go ahead anyway. She did, but the local authorities took their cue from the Institute and declined to approve her application.

Had they been inscribed according to the Institute's specifications, the plaques would have labelled Auschwitz as a German Nazi camp. Though Demnig did not consider such identifications necessary when he designed the project in Germany, persistent foreign references to 'Polish death camps', from President Obama downwards, have demonstrated that this is not the case when it comes to victims of Nazism who were murdered in German camps on occupied Polish territory. State-prescribed wording would have deformed the local character of a network that spans national borders and is the creation of social sculptors, but it would have supported the project's mission by preventing its message from being misinterpreted.[23]

The Institute's other specification was at odds with the project's aims, though. It wanted translatable words to be rendered in English, contrary to the Stolpersteine rule that inscriptions should be in the languages of the countries where they are located. The departmental head in Kraków told Nora Lerner that English-language plaques would be easy for her family's children and grandchildren to understand, living as they did in Israel and other countries. Local Poles would be able to understand the inscriptions – but they would also get the message that the plaques were for foreigners, not for them, and that Jewish memory was not part of their history. In Kazimierz, a township with a combined Jewish and Christian history, anglicised stumbling stones might be termed micro-ghettoisations.

Resistance such as that encountered by Nora Lerner left Poland with little more than a couple of dozen Stolpersteine as the international total headed towards six figures. There were none at all in Warsaw, which in 1939 had the largest Jewish population of any city in the world apart from New York, and now accommodates what must surely be the largest population of Second World War memorials in any metropolis. Their absence is a striking example of the unease about Jewish memory that continues to manifest itself, in varying forms and to varying degrees, in cultures of remembrance across Middle Europe. But their absence from another Polish city, Lublin, is not an effect of unease or ambivalence. A unique form of remembrance has been developed locally, at one of the gates of the city's Old Town. Treating Jewish memory as part of a common heritage, it has helped bring new life to the historic quarter.[24]

LUBLIN

Chapter 15
We Patiently Explain

Visiting Lublin during the autumn of 1924, Alfred Döblin took in the cathedral and ventured onwards through the Old Town, past crumbling tenement houses, until he found himself on a street called Grodzka. It pointed in the direction of Lublin's castle, which oversees the Old Town from a small hill nearby, and headed downwards into an under-zone of dark stalls, ramshackle huts and blind alleys. Döblin realised he was entering the city's Jewish quarter.

As in the previous stop on his tour of Poland, Wilno (or Vilnius, anachronistically), the eastern exit of the Old Town was an archway surmounted by a gatehouse. Döblin's eyes were drawn to the windows above the arch. What held his gaze there, however, was not an icon of the Virgin Mary like the one in Wilno's Ostra Brama, but the sight of the people who dwelt in the tenanted rooms above the gate: an image of human misery, not heavenly mercy. He railed against those who dared to talk about the gate's architectural beauty.[1]

In 1990, a theatre company called Teatr NN moved into the dilapidated rooms above the gateway. 'NN' stood for 'Nomen nescio', 'I do not know the name', a Latin expression used when a person's name is unknown or withheld. Seven years later, a woman walked into the gate building and declared 'I am the NN'. She explained that she had been

8. Lublin's Grodzka Gate around the turn of the twentieth century, looking much the same as when Alfred Döblin saw it in 1924.

brought to Lublin during the war, as a child of three or four years old. All she could remember was that she had been part of a group of children, one of whom was her brother, living on the streets of Lviv two hundred kilometres to the east. A woman saw her at the railway station, took her by the hand, hugged her, and brought her back to Lublin. As the train pulled out, she looked through the carriage window at her brother standing on the platform. She never saw him again.

In Lublin, her new foster mother gave her a home above the Grodzka Gate, in a flat occupying one of the rooms that had so dismayed Alfred Döblin. He had found it easy to imagine miserable conditions of life for the people living there and in the neighbouring houses, but he could not have begun to imagine the horror in which the street was trapped less than twenty years later, when it found itself on the edge of the ghetto imposed on the Jewish district by the Nazi occupation authorities. In the eastern territories conquered by the Third Reich, a child found without parents was likely to be Jewish, and at risk of being taken to be Jewish. When somebody told the Germans that there might be a little Jewish girl living in the rooms above the archway, she was concealed in a hiding place that had been prepared in case of searches. Brama Grodzka, the Grodzka Gate, was a place of safety in a world of merciless cruelty. There, an innocent child received the kind of protection that Catholics sought from the Mother of Mercy at the Gate of Dawn in Vilnius.

She was left with a recurring dream in which she saw a black curtain, and sensed that her parents were behind it. Every time she approached the curtain to draw it back, the dream ended. As Teatr NN's founder Tomasz Pietrasiewicz observed, she had survived 'not knowing to this day who she is, or who her parents were'.[2]

Pietrasiewicz and his colleagues turned Brama Grodzka into an 'ark of memory' for Lublin's Jewish communities, which were annihilated in the Holocaust. They wrote down the NN's story and presented it as the beginning of their narrative, on a large panel covering the wall of a room that had formerly been part of the dwelling; a plan of the flat, showing the positions of the furniture, is marked out on the floor. The panel can be drawn aside, like a page being turned, to reveal an aerial view of the Jewish quarter before the war. It is meant to suggest that the visitor is entering 'a Memorial (Yizkor) Book about life in the Jewish Town'.[3]

Lublin has a long history as a site for key moments in the formation of Polish states. A congress of nobles welcomed Grand Duke Jogaila of Lithuania there in 1386, as he made his way to his royal wedding in Kraków, and proclaimed him King Władysław II Jagiełło of Poland. Jogaila returned the favour by granting a range of privileges that enabled Lublin to develop as a centre of trade between the two countries he and Jadwiga had united through their marriage. The treaty of union that inaugurated the Polish-Lithuanian Republic was signed at Lublin's castle in 1569.

By that time, the urban kernel later known as the Old Town was taking shape on the high ground opposite, as a sturdy cluster of churches and townhouses arranged around a market square and an axis running from the Grodzka Gate on the eastern side to the western Kraków Gate. With an area of ten hectares, the walled town was the same size as its Warsaw counterpart. Meanwhile the space between the castle and the town was beginning to fill with buildings, as the Jewish quarter developed on the inferior land known as Podzamcze, meaning 'under the castle'. Jews had been prohibited from settling within the city walls in 1535, after Christian merchants objected to the competition they introduced.[4]

By the end of the sixteenth century, the district below the castle boasted one of the most important Hebrew printing houses in the country, and provided the base for the principal Jewish authority in Poland. Around the turn of the nineteenth century it became a major centre of Hasidic Judaism, after the legendary spiritual leader Yaakov Yitzhak haLevi Horowitz took up residence on Podzamcze's main street. He was known as the Seer of Lublin, because of his reputed ability to see into the future and across the world, and he bestowed a magical aura on the Jewish Town that remained as his posthumous legacy after his death there in 1815.[5]

As the century went on, however, many of Lublin's Jews were drawn to modernity instead of mysticism. Their local horizons were opened up in 1862, when they gained full citizenship and the city abolished restrictions on where they were permitted to live. 'Through Brama Grodzka, by which they had waited for so many years, they entered Lublin again,' wrote the historian Meir Balaban, 'renting and buying properties for shops and homes, first on Grodzka Street and later also on the Market Square.' The poorer incomers gradually found niches throughout almost the whole of the Old Town, which had fallen into decline after being abandoned by its wealthier residents. Those who could afford it made instead for the up and coming streets around the city's spacious central avenue. They resembled their Christian neighbours in their dress and lifestyle, while the old Jewish quarter became even more of a world apart.[6]

That world disappeared from the face of the earth during the Second World War. After the German invaders took control of Lublin in 1939, they ejected Jews from the townhouses around the central avenue, forcing them back to the old Jewish quarter. The Jews of the Old Town were sent there in April 1941, after the occupiers turned the former Jewish Town into a ghetto, which they liquidated a year later. Some 26,000 Jews from the Lublin region were killed at the Bełżec extermination camp, almost all of them upon arrival. Others were sent to a secondary ghetto on the outskirts of the city, Majdan Tatarski, and eventually to the nearby Majdanek camp. The Lublin extermination ended with Aktion Erntefest, Operation Harvest Festival, in November 1943. Over two days, SS squads and German police shot 42,000 Jews at Majdanek and two other camps in the region. At the outbreak of the war, some 43,000 Jews had been living in the city, out of a total population of around 120,000. Almost none of them were left alive by the war's end.[7]

Little was left of the Jewish Town either. The Germans razed much of it to the ground, as they did in Warsaw's Jewish district. There, the destruction had begun as a tactic used by the occupiers in their efforts to suppress the Ghetto Uprising. In Lublin, the Germans had already emptied the houses, which they condemned on the grounds of the buildings' poor construction standards and states of repair. Their underlying purpose was to erase the remains of Jewish presence, which in that locality dated back four hundred years.[8]

The main street disappeared altogether, and with it the form that the Jewish settlement had found in Lublin's topography. It had previously run along the base of the slope below the castle, its buildings jostling for space and concealing the lie of the land. Tumbledown shacks and solid edifices alike were gone, as was the warren of alleys into which Alfred Döblin had ventured. One unintended consequence was to give the Red Army a clear field of fire in front of the castle for its artillery when it fought its way into Lublin in July 1944.[9]

Three days after the Soviet forces captured the city, the new authorities installed the provisional body that became known as the Lublin Committee, and which formed the germ of the regime that eventually became the Polish People's Republic. This was the third key moment in Lublin's history as a site of state formation, initiating a drive to build socialism on Soviet lines that was led by a man with local roots. Bolesław Bierut was born near Lublin and went to school in the city. His early work experience there included a job as a bricklayer's assistant, and his presence was felt in the reconstruction of Lublin when he headed the country during its Stalinist period.

The site with the most obvious potential for symbolically loaded redevelopment was the barren plain, overlooked by the castle and the Old Town, that now lay where the main street of the Jewish district had previously been. A quadrant had been spared on the far side, where the tenement houses were in relatively good condition, and housed ethnic Poles who had been displaced by the creation of the Majdan Tartaski ghetto. Apart from that, the area formerly occupied by the Jewish Town was emptier than it had been since the Middle Ages.[10]

For nearly ten years, the authorities' efforts were concentrated up above, within the castle, and were devoted not to reconstruction but to the suppression of armed resistance. The castle had itself been rebuilt in the 1820s after a long twilight of ruin, its rectangular mass clad in a stern neo-Gothic facade appropriate to its function as a prison. Having served to incarcerate anti-czarist insurgents in the nineteenth century, communists between the wars and resistance fighters during the German occupation, it now held anti-communist partisans, many of whom had previously been anti-Nazi partisans. More than 30,000 prisoners were confined there during the new regime's first decade in power. Death sentences were carried out in the cellar of a building that stood by the castle's arched front entrance.[11]

The last execution took place in January 1954. On the following day, a new future was decreed for the castle, when ministers in Warsaw considered how the tenth anniversary of their regime should be celebrated in its birthplace. Three sites would form the setting for the events, and would serve thereafter as a symbolic complex that integrated the city's history with the ideology of the People's Republic. One was the Old Town, which had gaps in its teeth where tenement houses had been destroyed in the war, and was blighted by endemic dilapidation: it was to be repaired and given a facelift. The second was the castle, which was to be transformed into a cultural centre, and the third was the open area below its frontage, the obvious site for the public assembly space without which the Soviet-model ensemble would not have been complete.

With only six months until the anniversary, the plans demanded the kind of labour heroics that turned building socialism into a mass public performance. Teams of workers arrived from other cities to lend their hands and skills, an exercise staged as fraternal assistance with a note of friendly socialist competition. 'The best brigades of Warsaw plasterers are working for Lublin,' proclaimed a banner on scaffolding in front of an Old Town tenement building. Artists mounted scaffolding to paint decorations on tenement frontages; brigades of women were deployed to clear rubble from the slope below the castle. Julia Hartwig, a poet, described the workers' drive to finish the project as a season of heightened sensation, with bright lights burning late into the night on the scaffolding, and plasterers under starry skies, whistling beneath the roofs like night birds calling.[12]

The result was a spectacle of harmonious order that unified the city's two historic nuclei, the castle and the Old Town, with the socialist-realist statement arena below. The oval People's Gathering Place was framed on the opposite side to the castle by an elliptical terrace of apartment dwellings, with frontages styled in reference to Renaissance merchants' townhouses. An elevated pathway swept out from Brama Grodzka, over a gap excavated to evoke the drawbridge that had once stood there.[13] It headed up and around to the castle entrance, from which a monumental staircase descended to the Gathering Place below. The stairs were said to have been Bierut's idea.[14]

Among the measures taken to perfect the geometry of the new townscape was the demolition of the building that had stood by the entrance of the castle, hosting administration above ground and executions below it. This was an instance of 'disencumbering', a practice favoured by planners who followed the grand reshaper of Paris, Baron Haussmann, in believing that cities should boast expansive vistas and monuments displayed in splendid isolation. Monuments in more cluttered environments could be seen to better advantage by disencumbering them of the humbler structures that crowded in on them.[15]

In Podzamcze, most of that had already been done by the German occupiers after they liquidated the ghetto, though as a postscript to genocide rather than as an improvement to the city's skyline. They failed, however, to raze one of the Jewish quarter's most physically and symbolically substantial buildings, the Maharszal synagogue, which stood below the northern side of the castle. Its ruins were still standing after the war, but the city authorities eventually demolished them to make way for a new crosstown throughway. Lublin's castle now had uninterrupted views from all sides, rendering it clearly visible as a monument, with a hill for a plinth. The landscaping raised the Old Town's profile to similar effect.[16]

A single structure from the heart of the Jewish Town survived intact: a well that had stood at the end of the main street, and had served the residents of the district in the absence of a piped water supply. The solitary relic was far removed from the new focus below the front of the castle, stranded on the other side of the new throughway, and ended up on the edge of a bus station. Meanwhile the People's Gathering Place bore no reminders of the main street that had run through the area, although its benches were styled to resemble those found in the Old Town. It was as if the Jewish quarter had never existed.[17]

The rushed epic that transformed Lublin's historic centre in 1954 bore numerous resemblances to Warsaw's reconstruction projects. As well as the shared deadline of the 22 July anniversary, there was the decorative painting of townhouse frontages, the trumpeted support from other parts of the country, and the propaganda treatment of the work itself as a kind of festival. The crescent of houses on the People's Gathering Place was known as the 'Lublin Mariensztat', in reference to the model socialist-realist housing estate built below the Royal Castle scarp in Warsaw, and the adjacent throughway was called the East–West Route, just like its counterpart in the capital.

In the Old Town, however, the resemblances were superficial. The quarter had suffered in the war: German bombs had damaged the cathedral in 1939, and left the townhouses on one side of the Market Square in ruins. But unlike Warsaw's Old Town, it had not been devastated, and so there was no need to rebuild it all from the ruins. There was no need to think the project through as there had been in Warsaw, where the requirement to integrate national form with socialist content was satisfied by conceiving the new Old Town as a model housing estate that looked like a historic replica from the front.

So did Lublin's Old Town. A short film about the quarter, made in 1956, shows renovated facades gleaming as if suffused with the radiance of a new era. As the voice-over remarks, Poland now has 'new Old Towns'. Schoolchildren gather in the Market Square, rapt expressions on their faces. A low-slung modern car pulls up; a smiling woman leans out and takes off her sunglasses. Lublin's Old Town is helping usher the country into an era of leisure and consumption. With the castle behind her, a woman writes on the back of a card showing Old Town tenement houses. 'How nice the greetings from such an enchanting place will be,' the narrator comments.[18]

And then the spell is broken. The camera takes off its newsreel blinkers and turns away from the parade of restored exteriors by the Market Square to reveal what lies behind the facades. Children play in a courtyard littered with rubbish. A little girl clambers up rickety wooden stairs, smiling just as brightly as the schoolchildren in the square. A hole gapes in the boards of a deck that gives access to homes stacked upon each other in the ancient tenements. A young boy eats at a table inside one of the rooms, protected from a crack-veined ceiling only by an ominously bending timber frame. Viewers must have wondered not just whether the children would have to grow up in these squalid and perilous conditions, but whether they would survive the hazards to grow up at all. All the while, the voice-over continues without the slightest change in tone, praising the 'authentic historic character' of the crumbling houses: 'Here is a real work of art!' With heavy but controlled irony, the Old Town of Lublin is telling a trenchant new story, and not just about itself.

The film was an early entry in what became known as the 'black series' of documentaries, a genre that appeared during the so-called 'thaw' following the political upheavals of 1956, when the communist party adjusted its style of rule under Władysław Gomułka's leadership. Filmmakers turned their cameras away from the model housing estates to show scenes of squalor and degradation, refuting the newsreel propaganda about socialist progress in the new Poland. By parodying the newsreel style, the Lublin film challenged not just the content but also the form of the propaganda. Gomułka himself singled it out as an example of cultural irresponsibility.[19]

Its central trope, implicitly condemning those who delighted in the Old Town's external beauty while ignoring the conditions in which the quarter's residents lived, was much the same as Alfred Döblin's reaction to the sight of Brama Grodzka in 1924. Its central charge, that exteriors had been decorated but interiors neglected, echoed the criticisms that had been made when artists painted the facades of houses on the Market Square of Warsaw's Old Town in 1928, to celebrate the tenth anniversary of the new Polish Republic, and latterly following the reconstruction of the Market Square in the capital. But those criticisms had been confined to the buildings on the site. They had no deeper or broader resonances. In its indictment of the work done to celebrate the tenth anniversary of the communist regime, *The Old Town of Lublin* indicted both the Party's approach to progress and its relationship with truth. After its tour of the slums, it warns that there are 'barbarians' who would like to make the interiors of the buildings resemble the facades: 'They don't understand that with us, facades and interiors play completely different roles.' There it was, spoken out loud: a statement that summarised the defining characteristic of life in the Polish People's Republic, split between what was said in public and what was believed in private.

There were few developments in the story of the Old Town itself. The quarter was still in a 'technically and morally degraded' state in the 1970s, according to an architect who worked on revitalisation plans for the area. Behind the frontages, the walls were still crumbling, the stairs were still falling apart, the roofs were still leaking, and the residents still had to share communal outside toilets. More than 4,700 people lived there, a population denser than that of Warsaw's Old Town district in the late 1930s. Under the plans, the

Old Town would be reconfigured as a nucleus of heritage content and tourist facilities. Most of its residents would be decanted elsewhere, reducing the population to just 1,600 (a target that was not attained; at the start of the 2020s the figure stood at 2,200). The planners considered the quarter unsuitable for large families, recommending that in future it should be inhabited by small families and single people. They also proposed that it should offer workshop space for creative and professional people – such as architects.[20]

That idea was beyond the reach of the country's hapless economic system. Instead of gentrifying, the Old Town continued to decline – as did the economy, and the ideological edifice it supported. Tomasz Pietrasiewicz and his theatre company staged their first performance at Brama Grodzka as the moribund regime was being dismantled. By then, the quarter was in as bad a state as the economy. 'Everything was falling to pieces,' Pietrasiewicz recalls. 'The Old Town was this kind of ghetto where people from the margins of society were visible. People were afraid of spending any time at all there.'[21]

Brama Grodzka itself was in such a poor state of repair that the Teatr NN company moved out for a time, but Pietrasiewicz decided to return. 'Poland was starting from zero, starting something new – the new world I'd dreamed of, that I'd fought for,' he says. 'A free, independent Poland. I thought, this is the last chance I'll have in my life to create something new in a normal country, a free country.' He wanted to build the theatre 'from zero' too.[22]

Although he grew up in Lublin – and had lived close to the former Majdanek camp for eight years of his childhood – he had acquired only a minimal awareness that the city had a Jewish history. To him, the People's Gathering Place – which had long since functioned mainly as a car park – was a relic of the communist regime that he detested. He had no curiosity about what lay beneath it, or what had been there before. 'When I began to come here, I knew nothing at all,' he recalls. 'I completely lacked interest in the history of this place, Jewish or any other. All that mattered to me was that I'd come to

Brama Grodzka, we had the space there, and we could do our theatre.' Then, at that crucial zero moment in his life, he learned about the history of the place he had occupied. 'Somebody told me about the Jews, that they lived there, behind Brama Grodzka; that it was a highly symbolic place; that the Jewish Town was on one side and the Christian one on the other.' He suddenly began to feel responsible for the place, and he underwent a transformation catalysed by empathy for the suffering of the people who had been there before – 'a kind of second birth'.[23]

Brama Grodzka underwent a transformation too, into a 'Theatre of Memory': a museum, archive, visual installation and remembrance centre, presented in scenes and conducted as performances. The latter are known as mysteries, after the mystery plays of the Middle Ages, and they include the centre's archive work as well as its staged outdoor ceremonies. There are 43,000 folders in the archive, one for each of the individuals who comprised Lublin's Jewish population on the eve of the war. The people working on the documents carry out their research in front of the centre's visitors, as part of the exhibition; the visitors are invited to participate in the 'mystery of memory' themselves, by writing down the names of individuals recorded in the files, or sending letters to them. Pietrasiewicz emphasises that anybody can take part in the *Lublin. 43 Thousand* project: 'Our research is done in many parts of the world by hundreds of people. People working with us become co-creators and participants of the mystery.' Gunter Demnig, the creator of the Stolpersteine memorial plaques, would call it a social sculpture.[24]

The Brama Grodzka centre's most spatially expansive and symbolically intensive mystery, *One Land – Two Temples*, took the form of a human chain that linked the sites of two vanished places of worship, the church of St Michael, which stood in the Old Town until its demolition in the nineteenth century, and the Maharszal synagogue on the far side of the castle hill. On an October night in 2000, the Chief Rabbi of Poland dug up some soil from the site of

the synagogue, and placed it in a clay pot. Among the ribbed foundations of St Michael's, the Archbishop of Lublin knelt down and did
the same. The pots were passed from hand to hand along the chain,
several hundred metres long. On the side of the Jewish Town stood
Holocaust survivors; on the Old Town side were Righteous among
the Nations, non-Jewish Poles who helped save their Jewish neighbours and compatriots from the Holocaust. They told their stories as
the pots were passed to them.[25]

In a subsequent mystery, Lubliners' recollections of the Jewish
Town issued from under the ground, where the cellars and foundations of the quarter lie buried. Manholes around the area were fitted
with floodlights and loudspeakers, creating spectral manifestations
designed 'to demonstrate that the forgotten or hidden past always
finds ways to come back'. The mystery was concluded by switching
on an old streetlight set below the path from Brama Grodzka to the
castle; it remains permanently lit as a 'Lamp of Memory'.[26]

Oral history, memory recorded not long before it ceases to be
living, forms an essential element in the Brama Grodzka centre's
mission to integrate Lublin's Jewish and non-Jewish historical narratives. Yet the stories that Brama Grodzka's interviewers heard from
elderly Lubliners, recalling their memories of the Jewish quarter
between the wars, spoke more vividly of the distance between the
communities than of what they might have had in common.

The witnesses remembered the district much as Alfred Döblin
had described it: a place of tumult, noise, noisome smells (arising
from the absence of water and sewage pipes), dilapidated shacks and
muddy streets. It probably came as even more of a culture shock to
Döblin than it did to the local people, for he was a modern middle-
class German Jew seeing for the first time what traditional Jewish life
looked like. As a child, he had 'heard that my parents were of Jewish
origin', and gained a passing acquaintance with the Jewish calendar,
notably the holidays that enabled him to get off school – but apart
from that, he was reminded that he was Jewish mainly by the everyday

antisemitism he encountered. When he passed through Brama Grodzka's archway, the future author of *Berlin Alexanderplatz* found that he had stumbled into a world dramatically foreign to him.[27]

For Christian children from surrounding parts of Lublin, the foreignness of the district made it an exciting place to visit, with its myriad shops and mysterious nooks, its strange tongues and customs, such as haggling over prices instead of just paying them, and its everyday carnival of difference. But where children saw adventure, adults saw danger. Some parents warned their children that if they ventured into the Jewish quarter alone, they might be abducted and murdered for their blood, which Jews would use in the ritual preparation of matzos. It was not a new accusation. In 1636, several Jews were tried on charges of ritual murder at the court building in Lublin's Market Square, after torture that included burning with red-hot irons; one was sentenced to death by quartering. Although he alone was convicted, the prosecutor's indictment extended to the entire Jewish community of Lublin.[28]

The blood libel persisted as a latent accusation against Jews as a whole, believed by adults as well as the children they used it to scare. It sprang up in town after town during the social and psychological state of war that continued, along with partisan armed conflict, after the defeat of Nazi Germany. Rumours that Jews had kidnapped Christian children for their blood helped to incite the Kielce mob that killed forty-two Jews, with the help of soldiers and policemen, in July 1946. Shortly after the pogrom, a Jewish delegation met the Bishop of Lublin, Stefan Wyszyński. The future primate of Poland told them that 'the question of the use of blood by Jews has not been decisively resolved.'[29]

His words were echoed more than seventy years later, when a panel of academics at the Catholic University of Lublin considered remarks made by one of their fellow professors, a priest who argued that Jewish ritual murders were facts that 'cannot be erased from history', on the grounds that they are recorded in old legal documents. Explaining their support for the decision to discontinue proceedings against their colleague, the university's disciplinary commission, which included professors of philosophy, history and theology, described the question of Jewish ritual murder as 'a problem that, it should be emphasised, still remains unresolved'.[30]

The cleric's faith in the veracity of legal judgments based on torture suggests a radical refusal to read historical documents historically. A controversy which played out in the town of Sandomierz, on the old 'Jagiellonian Way' between Lublin and Kraków, suggests that works of art may be treated as historical documents in a similarly uncritical fashion. Sandomierz boasts a particularly well-preserved Old Town; and the blood libel is also strikingly well preserved in a painting of a ritual murder scene that hangs in the cathedral at the edge of the historic town centre. Dating from the first half of the eighteenth century, it depicts Jews killing local Christian children, using a spiked barrel to drain blood from one of their victims. The painting was covered by a curtain in 2006, and then revealed again in 2015. A plaque now stated that the scene 'controverts historical truth', and that Jews did not carry out ritual murders. It added that from the thirteenth century onwards, popes had forbidden the spreading of such accusations. But it did not explain why, in that case, the cathedral had served as a gallery for the painting since the eighteenth century.[31]

One of the artist's depictions of murdered Sandomierz children was presented as a document of real events during a trial held at Lublin's court building in 1710, when Jews accused of murdering a Christian child were shown the image before they were tortured. Three hundred years later, after the cathedral painting finally aroused controversy, teams of researchers interviewed Sandomierz residents about their views of the matter. One of the most consistent themes in the local people's comments was that since it was hanging in a church, there must be some truth in it. The painting was a visual depiction of the blood libel stories they had all heard by word of mouth, and they took its presence in the cathedral as an affirmation of the tales' likely veracity.[32]

Most considered that it should remain there, and some reacted combatively to the possibility of its removal. 'When they come to take that painting down, I'll go there myself with a hoe and rake,' promised an eighty-year-old woman of gentry stock. Another woman of similar age claimed that she had already rushed to the painting's defence: 'A few Jews came and staged a protest . . . Well, we ran there because the word went out that the Jews wanted to take the cathedral, and we wanted to defend it! And we chased the Jews away.' Their reflexes anticipated the scenes in England fifteen years or so later, when bands of 'statue defenders' arranged themselves in front of monuments (including, to widespread amusement, a statue of the novelist George Eliot) which they claimed were threatened by activists whose historical narratives were at odds with their own.[33]

Those performances were amateurish versions of a script written in the United States, where historic monuments had become hotspots of political contestation. As with many other nationalist and populist irruptions, what happened in an eastern European town foreshadowed what was to come in the West. The object at issue was significantly different, though. Whereas a statue of a Confederate general is a symbol, the Sandomierz blood libel painting is a narrative instrument. As a component of an Old Town ensemble – albeit a fitting rather than a fixture or a part of the structure – it has made use of its setting to tell a story that helps a noxious myth to persist in the locality.

The local people who served as guides in the cathedral told the story too. 'If the guide explains that it was the Jews who murdered . . . those children,' observed one of the interviewees, 'well, it creates feelings of disgust towards those Jews.'[34]

In Lublin, the oral history testimonies revealed no such revulsion, malign fantasies or jealously guarded animosities. What they left above all, however, was a sense of the strangeness and otherness that the speakers had felt in the Jewish district. 'It was another world,' recalled one of them, Romuald Dylewski, who went to school in Lublin in the 1930s. 'Those children, those people who sat out on the streets, like in Arab countries . . .' 'I never went down Broad Street,' said another, referring to the main street that had formed the axis of the district. 'What was I afraid of? The alleys, like in Marrakesh.'[35]

Such references to the world beyond Europe were a recurrent feature of outsiders' observations about Jewish quarters. A German guidebook published in Vilnius during the First World War, presumably for members of the occupying forces and administration that controlled the city at the time, told its readers that 'on a warm summer day, the crooked, cramped street with its narrow sidewalks and impassable pavement turns into a stage. This local scenography is familiar to everyone who has travelled to the Orient.' In 1887, when plans were made to demolish the former ghetto in Prague, a local magazine welcomed the prospect of an end to 'the repulsive labyrinth of twisting, narrow streets filled with foul-smelling odours from gutters, smoke gushing forth from low chimneys, and animated figures and scenes, which look as if they were carried to Prague straight from the Orient, from somewhere in Baghdad.'[36]

Romuald Dylewski likewise compared the Jewish quarter of Lublin to Baghdad – with the advantage of speaking from experience. Qualified as an architect, he worked as an urban planner in both cities. Thanks to the Polish state's efforts to export its planners' and architects' skills to the Middle East, he became acquainted with a number of cities in the Arab world, and became fascinated by the 'exotic' culture he encountered in them. When he visited the old quarters of Cairo, Damascus, Beirut and Baghdad, the smells of spices and garlic reminded him of the vanished Jewish neighbourhoods he had known as a child in Lublin and the surrounding towns. He came to see deeper resemblances, too. The irregularities in the form of Lublin's Jewish district arose, he argued, from Oriental building practices, in which street lines were defined by the position of buildings rather than the other way around. In how they built, they cooked and how they lived, Jewish communities had preserved and cultivated the atmosphere of the Orient.[37]

Dylewski's view of the vanished Jewish districts as an 'essentially Oriental world' enabled him to argue that their features were the product of a culture that was different to that of their surroundings, but not inferior to it. He had been drawn to those quarters as a child, and he regarded their destruction as a loss to the country. At the same time, he deepened the sense that their histories were separate from those of their neighbours. His argument implied that even if the Jewish quarter had been able to rise up out of its poverty, it would still have remained radically different from the rest of the city, thanks to an Oriental view of urban space that had been sustained within it for hundreds of years. The story that emerged from his recollections, and those of the other non-Jewish Lubliners who contributed their memories to Brama Grodzka's archives, was of a place that had always been a long way away.

The idea that Jewish and non-Jewish Lubliners have a shared history was the fundamental premise for the Brama Grodzka project, but it was ahead of public opinion. Only a minority of people fully endorsed that view in a survey conducted in 2010 – after twenty years of Teatr NN activity at the Grodzka Gate – while a majority regarded the histories as separate, but with common elements. The latter position is arguably a more objective view of a history in which the spatial, administrative and cultural separateness of Jewish communities is so marked. It may be a better account of how things were. But to simply accept the history as shared, without qualification, is to take a moral stance about the role of memory in the present. It is a statement about how things should be.[38]

Teatr NN's task has thus been to reconstruct the Jewish Town as memory, and to construct that memory as shared. Bringing together multiple voices, a host of photographic images and a rich seam of municipal records, it organises them into a narrative based upon a sense of common humanity, produced by evoking empathy among its visitors for the Jewish people of Lublin who were murdered in the Holocaust. Against that background, the idea of treating what came before as a common history resonates with Christian ideas about redemptive acts, and Jewish ones about healing the world. The narratives of separateness look different in that light too. Instead of simply saying 'that was how it was', they acquire an undertone of regret: 'but it could have been different'.

The custodians of memory at Brama Grodzka still have to 'explain patiently that it is our common, Polish-Jewish history', as the panel at the start of the exhibition tells visitors. After thirty-odd years, however, Tomasz Pietrasiewicz feels that their patience is being rewarded. 'I think it's starting to get through to people,' he says.[39]

By reconstructing the destroyed Jewish Town in its theatre of memory, Teatr NN revitalised the surviving Old Town. 'We started bringing life back to it,' says Tomasz Pietrasiewicz. 'Step by step, the Town began to revive.' Having dared to set up its base there, despite the quarter's sorry state and its reputation as a place to avoid, the company put the area on the map as the site of a major new cultural initiative. Commercial enterprises followed the trail Teatr NN had blazed, and the Old Town finally became the magnet for tourists that the plans of the 1970s had proposed.[40]

It was a remarkable instance of what in local government circles is known as culture-led regeneration. A centre based on the remembrance of genocide encouraged investment that turned the Old Town's axis, from the Grodzka Gate to the Kraków Gate, into a promenade of lively bars and restaurants. Teatr NN's meditative immersion in the evacuated space on one side of the gate conjured up a ribbon of conviviality on the other. Under the weathered brows of the townhouses, some of them inked with historically themed tattoos, the place looked like a modern European Old Town at last.

Among the businesses that took advantage of the opportunities Teatr NN created are ones with views of history very different to

9. Regeneration at a sixteenth-century tenement house on the Market Square in Lublin's Old Town.

those that inspire the activities at Brama Grodzka. Overlooking the remains of St Michael's church, a 'Patriotic Shop' offers a range of products emblazoned with the national colours, red and white, from air-fresheners to polo shirts. Clothing is the core business of the patriotic retail trade, a prominent market sector in Poland. Its most notable characteristics are its strong design sensibilities and its iconographic vision of Polish history as a succession of armed conflicts, from the medieval battles against the Teutonic Knights, through the campaigns fought during the heyday of the Polish-Lithuanian Republic by hussars with feathered crests rising high above their heads, to the partisan resistance against the German occupation and the communist regime that followed it. In this exclusively militaristic picture, Poland's history is its combatants, their weapons and their insignia.[41]

Hussars also feature on the Facebook banner of another patriotic enterprise with a branch in the Old Town, a restaurant offering 'a Real Kebab at a Real Pole's' establishment. One of the cavalrymen is impaling a turbaned Turk with his lance, from which a red and white pennant flies. The scene alludes to the narrative that Poland saved Europe from Turkish conquest, and consequent Islamisation, by defeating the Ottoman army outside Vienna in 1683. Like the patriotic apparel, the banner picture on the Facebook page suggests a deep insecurity – as if the Real Pole fears that his embrace of kebabs may cast doubt on his Polishness, and seeks to face down any such suspicions by splashing an image of a Pole killing a representative of the culture from which the kebabs derive. He has specified that his employees must be of Polish descent, and if they have a political outlook, it must be right-wing.[42]

A more elegant and visible statement about identity is made by a restaurant on the Market Square that shares Teatr NN's feelings about the history of Lublin. Mandragora describes itself as a Jewish restaurant, meaning that it serves Jewish cuisine, but not that it is owned or staffed by Jewish people. Unlike the patriotic retailers, among whom the Lord is largely invisible except on sweatshirts bearing the slogan 'God – Honour – Fatherland', Mandragora roots its narrative in religious tradition. It highlights the symbolic significance of dishes it serves, noting their roles in the celebration of Jewish holidays and the Sabbath. The restaurant's website assures visitors that although it does not have a kosher certificate, it does everything else it can to comply with the Torah's rules about the preparation of food. A visit to Mandragora is 'not only a culinary experience but also a cultural one'.[43]

The experience is also shaped by decor designed to evoke the 'rich cultural tradition of the pre-war Jewish Lublin'. Mandragora is not intended to be a replica or simulacrum of a pre-war townhouse. It is a modern space dressed like a stage set, with rugs, lace tablecloths and similar props that evoke images of a bourgeois family dwelling from before the war. Like the set of a period drama, it has a fundamentally reassuring quality. It represents the imagined comforts of past times, not the conflicts, and seeks to evoke the idealised warmth of family life. 'When you come into the restaurant, you immediately feel that it's like a home, and not just a room with dining tables in it,' says Mandragora's proprietor, Izabela Kozłowska-Dechnik. 'The heart of Jewish celebration is the home,' declares the menu, 'and cooking plays an important role in it.'[44]

That statement would be equally true if the word 'Jewish' were changed to 'Polish' – and therein lies the basis of the offer that Mandragora makes to its guests: that the ideas of home and family at its heart are ones they will recognise as their own. A sense of deep commonality between Jewish and Christian Polish traditions pervades the restaurant's account of itself. Its name comes from the Song of Songs in the Old Testament, a text sacred to both faiths. 'Lublin is a multicultural city, and that's what gives our Lublin cuisine its character,' Kozłowska-Dechnik says. Families from different cultural communities – Jewish, Catholic, Orthodox – were often neighbours, she observes; dishes from different traditions sat side by side on their tables and intermingled. The cooking in her own family home was Jewish as well as Polish, but she didn't realise that until she was grown up.

Whereas other representations of Lublin before the war tend to emphasise the separateness of the Jewish community, Mandragora's speaks of a neighbourly shared life. 'Many Polish and Jewish families were friends before the war. It was a very strong relationship,' Kozłowska-Dechnik says. 'For me, it's extremely important to preserve and show that symbiosis, that friendship and togetherness, from before the war.'[45]

She is talking about a different place from the Jewish quarter below the castle. Although the space between the castle and the Old Town is necessarily the zone where memory must be concentrated, the city centre on the other side of the Old Town has its own special significance for Lublin's common Polish-Jewish history. It is where the Jewish and Christian families were neighbours; where the distinctions began to blur, and the possibility of a shared community became conceivable. But it lacks focus in memory precisely because it is not marked out by clear distinctions, and that leaves empty space on the map.

The effect is symbolised by a poem painted, as a Teatr NN initiative, on a wall at the bottom of a flight of steps leading up into the Old Town from a street that used to be part of the Jewish district. It is located by the line of the wartime ghetto boundary: the closest that non-Jews could approach. The site seems to dictate the theme of separation. 'Classmates' reflects upon it with exquisitely measured understatement, describing the two girls whom the teacher would never address by their first names, who left the classroom before religion lessons, and whom the poet last encountered at the border of the ghetto nearby. The poem is haunting not just because of its poignancy, but also because it tells of the small things, the everyday distinctions and discriminations that kept Jewish children apart from their peers even when they were in the same classes at school. Such details resemble experiences that are common and familiar, unlike the girls' fate, and are thus impossible not to imagine. They undermine confidence in the quality of co-existence before the war.[46]

Although the poem rings all too true – and the girls it depicts were indeed classmates of the poet, Julia Hartwig – it does not condense the whole story of the pre-war relationships between Jewish and non-Jewish Lubliners. There has to be a place for a narrative that asserts the possibility of friendship, and Mandragora is clearly such a place. A restaurant is a site for the celebration of life and companionability, where memory is illuminated with a kindly light. 'These places may represent what people wish that the Jewish world had really been once upon a time,' observes Ruth Ellen Gruber, a long-time explorer of what she calls 'virtually Jewish' culture in Europe.[47]

Mandragora stages a different kind of theatre to the one in Brama Grodzka, for which it provides a necessary complement. Although Teatr NN's documentation of Lublin's history is encyclopaedic, its vision is inevitably dominated by death, and set in the quarter that was destroyed. Without Mandragora's image of the past, idealised and atmospheric as it is, the picture would not be complete. Mandragora does not present evidence of convivial neighbourly relations between Lublin's Christian and Jewish residents – an aspect of the picture that feels in need of documentary support – but a restaurant's task is to serve meals, not to conduct historical research.

The scene that the restaurant's decor suggests, a well-to-do Jewish family's home, belongs to the city centre rather than the Old Town. It certainly does not belong to the later pre-war history of the building that accommodates the restaurant. The three-storey townhouse, which dates from 1521, passed into the ownership of a Jewish family, the Mandelsbergs, towards the end of the nineteenth century. By the 1930s it had become a typically dilapidated Old Town tenement, divided into more than twenty flats, and its condition triggered a series of repair orders from the municipal building inspectorate. The owner appealed against one of them on the grounds that he had no money for renovations because of the prevailing economic crisis.[48]

Among the residents was another member of the Mandelsberg family, Bela, a historian who taught the subject in Jewish secondary schools. In the evenings she gave lectures for workers in Yiddish, under the auspices of the left-wing Zionist party to which she belonged, and on free days she led tours of local historic Jewish sites.

She prepared a history of Lublin's Jews in manuscript, and also a guidebook to the city in Polish and Yiddish, but the war came before either could be published. She remained in the house, which by the spring of 1940 provided a roof over the heads of 104 Jews, and which was denied to Jewish occupants a year later, after the establishment of the ghetto on the other side of the Old Town. In 1942 Mandelsberg was sent to the concentration camp at Majdanek, and thence to her death by shooting. Some of her articles were published abroad many years later, including one about the 1636 blood libel trial. By then, the history she told had been brought to an end. It was eventually taken up again in Brama Grodzka, and remembered in the house where she had lived.

As an enterprise in which non-Jews channel Jewish culture, Mandragora is an example of a phenomenon that developed in Kazimierz, the historic Jewish district of Kraków. A major Jewish settlement for nearly five hundred years, it escaped demolition by the Nazis in the Second World War. Hans Frank, the Nazi Governor-General, had installed himself in Wawel Castle, the traditional seat of Polish monarchs, and adopted a monarchical attitude to the city he supervised. Regarding Kazimierz as a historically important part of Kraków, he had its Jewish population expelled to another suburb, where he established a ghetto. After the war Kazimierz was left a place of ghosts and dereliction, a neighbourhood that the authorities neglected and people avoided after dark, until its rediscovery in the late 1980s.[49]

Since then it has become the scene of a Jewish cultural revival, driven and sustained by Poles who are not themselves Jewish. There are restaurants, of course, and klezmer music, and ambivalent encounters. Jewish visitors often regard Jewish-themed tourist enterprises with distaste. They sometimes express indignation that non-Jewish Poles run these businesses, making money out of the memory of an exterminated population. It sounds bad to people abroad, too. Geneviève Zubrzycki, a professor of sociology based in the United

States, reports that when she talks about Kazimierz and its Jewish Culture Festival in North America, audiences sometimes liken these activities to 'playing Indian' or 'blackface'. Such remarks 'reflect a mix of disbelief, skepticism and discomfort at the cultural phenomenon, with a hint of outrage'.[50]

Zubrzycki herself sees much more in it than commodification, appropriation or kitsch. It is part of a broader effort, she suggests, to 'soften, stretch and reshape symbolic boundaries of Polishness that the Right has sought to harden and shrink using a conservative, nationalist version of Catholicism'. Other observers also see possibilities in the Poles' use of memory for a 'future-oriented project of enlightenment', which puts reflection upon history to work in the service of pluralism and democracy. To the Right, reflections that complicate or question the master-narrative of Polish heroism, victimhood and sacrifice look unpatriotic, a quality considered to border on treason. The nationalist-conservative stance insists that the story must be kept simple, dramatic and devoid of nuance.[51]

Mandragora certainly seems like a softened, stretched and reshaped representation of Lublin's Old Town and its cultural space, in contrast to the hard, shrunken effigy endorsed by the Patriotic Shop and the Real Pole's kebab restaurant. After all, its name 'symbolises love, fertility, happiness'. The atmosphere contrasts with that of Brama Grodzka too, but Mandragora and Teatr NN share a sense of duty. 'I certainly feel obliged to talk about history,' says Izabela Kozłowska-Dechnik, 'and I feel obliged to tell it through cooking, through dishes, through Mandragora's hospitality. I feel obliged to talk about our city and the community that lived here in great numbers before the war.'[52]

Erica Lehrer, an anthropologist based in Canada, has found a similar sense of duty among the proprietors of Jewish-themed establishments in Kazimierz. They regard themselves as custodians of a heritage that they have a duty to look after, in the absence of people from the culture that produced the heritage. Kazimierz turned into a sink estate for the city's underclass after the war because the communist authorities did not consider they had any such duty, having assimilated the pre-war nationalist vision of an ethnically homogeneous Poland.[53]

The restaurant and the 'theatre of memory' both illustrate that historical reconstruction is a reiterative process rather than a project with a fixed term, because memory fades unless it is constantly regenerated. For Izabela Kozłowska-Dechnik, the reiterative regeneration is the hospitality work that her staff undertake from day to day, cooking and serving the dishes through which she talks about Lublin's history. For Tomasz Pietrasiewicz, it is a nightly practice of reflection at Brama Grodzka. He began to go there late at night in order to work without distractions, and gradually became a 'nightwatchman' at the gate. It is his own personal mystery of memory, conducted in the building where the NN child was hidden and Alfred Döblin glimpsed some other nameless human beings for whom he felt a pang of empathy. 'This is my place in the universe,' the nightwatchman says.[54]

PRAGUE

Chapter 16
If the Twentieth Century Had
Not Happened

In the summer of 1933, Europe's leading modern architects went to sea, holding their fourth annual congress on a cruise ship that sailed across the Mediterranean from Marseille to Athens and back. They struggled afterwards to summarise their conclusions, which included a section on the historic heritage of cities that the Italian participants had insisted on including. The Swiss architect Le Corbusier took it upon himself to write the findings up in his own words, which eventually appeared as a book entitled *The Athens Charter* in 1943.[1]

By then, of course, the mass destruction of historic urban heritage in the heart of Europe was under way. The comments in the Charter prompt the question that hangs over the story of Middle Europe's Old Towns in the twentieth century: how would they have fared if they had not been destroyed by bombs and shells? Modern urban planning was essentially a demand for space: space for motor traffic to move freely; space to let in light, and give urban dwellers room to breathe. An old quarter folded round narrow winding streets represented the exact opposite of what the modern planners were striving to achieve – especially if it was densely packed with overcrowded, insanitary and degraded tenements, as so many old quarters were. On both structural and humanitarian grounds, their continued existence was placed in question.

Although the Charter acknowledged that old urban clusters could be 'precious witnesses of the past', it indicated a number of conditions they should meet in order to be allowed to remain standing. They would be protected if they represented a former culture and were of universal interest – which was the kind of cosmopolitan attitude that made the totalitarians and nationalists of the period view modern architects with distaste. Care should be taken in deciding what to keep; duplicate examples could be dispensed with if they stood in the way of progress, which suggested a bias towards preserving specimens rather than maintaining ensembles. The principle that old buildings should only be kept 'if their preservation does not entail the sacrifice of keeping people in unhealthy conditions' implied that it was a choice between one or the other, heritage or health, rather than a practical problem that might be solved by overhauling houses instead of demolishing them. 'Certain people, more concerned for aestheticism than social solidarity, militate for the preservation of certain picturesque old districts unmindful of the poverty, promiscuity, and diseases that these districts harbour,' Le Corbusier commented sternly, like Alfred Döblin decrying the aesthetes who praised the beauty of the Grodzka Gate in Lublin while disregarding the misery of life inside it.

The Charter went on to observe that 'The destruction of the slums around historic monuments will provide an opportunity to create verdant areas', revealing its preference for disencumbered monuments that could be appreciated from a distance, as if in an expansive open-air gallery. All in all, it showed little sympathy for huddles of old buildings in city centres, nor any sense that their intimacy might have qualities that should be valued.[2]

Although the modernists proposed more radical approaches to urban organisation than other schools of architectural thought, all of them faced the same basic challenges. Cities were burgeoning; they had to accommodate motorised traffic; and their housing stock was in dire need of improvement. Old districts embodied the problems in particularly concentrated forms. It is easy to imagine that many of them would have been partly or completely destroyed even if there had been no war in the middle of the century, as the drive to modernise Europe's cities gathered momentum.

Prague, that most central of Middle European cities, was ahead of the field. One of its historic districts was demolished around the turn of the twentieth century, falling to explosives set by municipal engineers rather than bombardment by enemy forces. What happened in Prague suggests what would have happened in Old Towns across the continent if Europe had somehow managed to meet the challenges of modernity without tearing itself apart.

Touring Middle Europe in 1858, the English novelist George Eliot arrived in Prague and set out after breakfast to do the 'grand old city' in a day. Her explorations took her into the Jewish quarter, Josefov, which occupied the area between the central Old Town Square and the river Vltava. 'The most interesting things we saw were the Jewish burial-ground (the Alter Friedhof) and the old synagogue,' she reported. 'The Friedhof is unique – with a wild growth of grass and shrubs and trees, and a multitude of quaint tombs in all sorts of positions, looking like the fragments of a great building, or as if they had been shaken by an earthquake.' Their skewed attitudes were in fact the product of crowding: extra layers of earth had been added over the years to accommodate more graves, and the older tombstones were raised up to the new levels.[3]

Like many visitors of the time, Eliot was captivated by the Romantic melancholy of the Old Jewish Cemetery. It conjured up the same kind of spell in the middle of the Bohemian city that the ruins of a monastery might cast in some reach of the English countryside, though here the stones were overgrown by lilac rather than ivy. According to the scholar Peter Demetz, a son of Prague himself, the graveyard held a particular attraction for English, German and American writers, whose path to it 'followed literary convention; ever since the later eighteenth century, cemeteries had been sweet places of melancholy reflections about frail life and sublime death, and Prague's Jewish cemetery exerted a strong pull on minds shaped by Christian tradition'. Today, the tombs remain much as Eliot found them, still standing at their rakish angles, but their surroundings have been transformed by processes that were already underway by the time of her visit. Prague's historic Jewish quarter was beginning a decline that by the end of the century would become a fall.[4]

Eliot visited Prague ten years after the revolutionary convulsions of 1848, which fractured the old order of the Habsburg Empire. Serfdom was abolished, freeing Czech peasants to converge on the metropolis in search of new livelihoods. Jews were released from restrictions that had confined them to ghettos, and then from a ban on owning property; by the end of the 1850s, they were allowed to own land. Wealthier Jews began to move out of Josefov, which in its enforced confinement was becoming choked with blind alleys and overcrowded housing. Their exit accelerated Josefov's decline into a slum district: poor people moved in, many of them immigrants from the countryside, and became poorer still. In 1885, the city's Municipal Health Commission reported that rates of illness and mortality from infectious diseases in Josefov were more than twice as high as those in Prague's other four wards. It recommended that the district should be cleared and rebuilt. The city authorities held a contest for plans to redevelop the quarter: the winning proposal was called Finis Ghetto.[5]

By that time, most of Josefov's inhabitants were Christian, and Czech Jewish leaders who had long since finished with the 'ghetto' supported its demolition, because they aspired to live assimilated lives in a modern city. Their German Jewish counterparts also favoured the plan. If it had been confined to Josefov, it might have commanded general support, but Finis Ghetto also took in substantial adjacent tracts of the core Old Town, Prague's First Quarter. It formed the basis of an urban renewal plan that threatened 324 houses in the First Quarter, more than there were in the whole of Josefov. The scale of the proposed demolitions provoked a reaction among Czech architects, artists and other layers of the cultural intelligentsia, who feared a loss of national heritage that would weaken their national identity.[6]

Their protests were galvanised by the start of the demolitions towards the end of 1896, which included the destruction of baroque houses on the north side of the Old Town Square. A novelist wrote a pamphlet called *Bestia Triumphans* (*The Beast Triumphant*) in which he denounced the city council, claiming 'it is clear as daylight that they hate not only us but also the old buildings that we are protecting. They are disgusted at the sight of old streets and the dirty roofs of old towns.' The movement gained political strength in 1898 when candidates supporting its aims did well in municipal elections. At a protest meeting called in the wake of the poll successes, the director of Prague's Museum of Decorative Arts argued that 'if the great nations and great countries, with their vast historic monuments, carefully protect every single item, all the more urgently should a small nation with its modest heritage do likewise! With every monument torn down, we are deprived of part of our own essence and are heading towards a nondescript lack of form ...' The kind of monuments he had in mind presumably did not include the tombstones torn out to make way for his new museum building, which took a strip from one side of the Old Jewish Cemetery.[7]

The plan's most salient feature, a straight avenue forming an axis through the middle of the district, was clearly inspired by the boulevards that Baron Haussmann drove through Paris. An alternative vision of urban planning was beginning to emerge at just that moment, however, with the publication of the Austrian architect Camillo Sitte's book *City Planning According to Artistic Principles*. Presenting a careful appreciation of the aesthetic benefits that urban development within medieval town walls had produced, it encouraged preservationists to think in terms of historic ensembles rather than single structures, creating a conceptual basis for the care of Old Towns. Sitte's work catalysed the formation of two opposing urbanist camps, one advocating straight streets and the other keeping faith with crooked ones. In his own view, both kinds had their place. As he observed, 'the meandering line is more picturesque, the straight one is more monumental.' But straight boulevards and streets became boring, he chided, if they were allowed to go on for too long. Sitte's principles guided the final design of Josefov's new street layout, in the 1900s, though the central avenue remained.[8]

Monotony was the least of the charges levelled against linear thoroughfares. Beyond the fringes of the professional debates, the straight street was demonised by an antisemitic Prague newspaper in a polemic against the Finis Ghetto plan headlined 'The Fanaticism of the Straight Line'. The diatribe was calculated to inflame the resentments of its lower middle-class target audience, the artisans and shopkeepers who felt themselves to be victims of modernisation, and who were extensively represented among the residents facing eviction from the condemned quarter. It extolled the 'intimate charm' of medieval city lanes, and claimed that modern straight streets were 'an aesthetic manifestation of the needs of accumulating Jewry', designed to serve Jewish businesses by channelling the maximum number of 'consumers of Jewish goods'.[9]

Although it must have been a challenge for even the most dedicated antisemites in the newspaper's readership to keep up with all the charges about alleged Jewish machinations that appeared in its columns, it would have been impossible not to grasp that they all supported a grand conspiracist theme of profit and influence. It was not the first time that story had been set in Josefov's cemetery, either. The newspaper agitation at the end of the century claimed that Jews were making money out of the activities in Josefov by controlling networks of power in the city government, and singled out the boulevard at the centre of the Finis Ghetto plan as an exemplar of what it portrayed as malign Jewish influence on the form of cities. Thirty years earlier, the cemetery at the centre of the former ghetto had featured as the setting for a fictional scene that depicted Jews meeting to discuss their strategy for controlling the entire world. Parts of that narrative have persisted and replicated ever since.

The story first took the form of a chapter in a book by Hermann Goedsche, who left the Prussian postal service under a cloud after he was implicated in forging material to discredit a reformist politician. Evidently feeling assured that sensational fiction was his métier, he wrote a string of novels under the pseudonym of Sir John Retcliffe. The Prague cemetery episode featured as a set piece in a volume of his *Biarritz* series, which began to appear in the late 1860s. It describes a midnight gathering, held once every hundred years, at which representatives of the tribes of Israel report on the previous century's progress towards achieving 'power and supremacy over all other nations on Earth'. The tombs overgrown by thickets that had induced feelings of sweet melancholy in the likes of George Eliot were recast as a lair of plotters and sorcerers. A blue flame issued from a grave to illuminate the proceedings, which closed with the apparition of a golden animal – an image of the golden calf idol that Moses destroyed, according to the biblical Book of Exodus.[10]

Around the turn of the century, parts of the dialogue were rewritten and presented as records of actual discussions in the *Protocols of the Elders of Zion*, the notorious forgery that purported to document Jewish plans for global domination. It spread far and wide in the decades between the world wars and is now endemic in the conspira-sphere of the internet: a virus whose first host was a malevolently imagined locus in Prague's old Jewish quarter.[11]

While the antisemitic payload of Goedsche's episode was stripped of its fantastical packaging in its translation to the *Protocols*, the cult of 'Magic Prague' was boosted by the demolition of old Josefov. When the clearances came to an end in 1912, 260 stone buildings had been knocked down. Fewer than a dozen were left standing; among them were six synagogues, including the thirteenth-century Old-New Synagogue (originally known as the New Synagogue, until newer ones were built) and the Jewish Town Hall, which dates back to the sixteenth century. Josefov was transformed into a showpiece contemporary quarter of avenues, upmarket shops and art nouveau

10. Leaning tombstones in Prague's Old Jewish Cemetery.

apartment blocks. Finely traced perpendicular detailing on the facades of the old cemetery's new neighbours provided a visual measure of how far the tombstones in the throng below, weathered fossils of the old ghetto, had lurched from the vertical. The cemetery was a refuge for the last vestiges of irregularity and disorder left in the district.[12]

Those were qualities missed in certain circles. Two main currents developed in reaction to the municipal redevelopment plans of the late nineteenth century. One was an early manifestation of the twentieth-century urban conservation movement, emerging from the architects and their sympathisers who had opposed the plans. They continued their activities in the Club for Old Prague, founded in 1900 and still active today. The other emerged from the allied chorus of literary protests against the disappearance of the 'mystical Ghetto', and manifested in a plethora of creative productions that immersed themselves deliriously in the eerily glowing ghetto of their authors' fantasies. The works cast their aura over Prague as a whole. In 1935, the surrealist artist André Breton hailed the city as 'the magic capital of old Europe', which 'carefully incubates all the delights of the past for the imagination'.[13]

The figure that towers over this magic capital is that of the Golem, a being said to have been fashioned from clay by the revered Rabbi Loew, who died in 1609, and whose tomb is now a landmark in the Old Jewish Cemetery. To animate the Golem, the Rabbi placed in its mouth a piece of paper bearing letters that formed one of the names of God. According to a version of the story that encapsulates the core of the legend, he used his creation as a servant during the week and removed the piece of paper on Friday afternoons, so that the Golem would be inert on the Sabbath. One Friday he forgot to deactivate the creature; fearing that it would uncomprehendingly violate the Sabbath by doing work, he pursued it through the streets of the ghetto. He caught up with it outside the Old-New Synagogue and pulled the paper out of its mouth, whereupon it disintegrated. Its remains are said to be secreted in the attic of the synagogue.[14]

The Golem was reanimated as a supernatural presence that makes intermittent and indistinct appearances in the novel of the same name by Gustav Meyrink, a banker and occultist who spent many years in Prague. Meyrink's book sold copiously when it appeared in 1915, the year in which the German director Paul Wegener made the first of his three Golem films. The novel's mood reflected the notorious image of the zone in which it was set: claustrophobic, disorienting and ominous. It generated new and haunting images of Josefov in the benighted condition that led to the district's erasure.

The films added depth by contributing images of the ghetto's mythical past. In *The Golem: How He Came Into The World*, the last of the films and the only one that still survives, the expressionist sets depict a town that seems to be the product of nature rather than the work of masons and carpenters. Timbers bend like living boughs and lanes meander like streams. Everything is leaning and crooked, as if the design has taken the tombstones in the cemetery for its model. There is not a straight line or right angle in the place. Roofs settle upon houses like hats, anticipating Disney.

Josefov thrived as a ghost town, making itself useful to the other historic portions of the city by pumping its magical emanations into the atmosphere around them. It had also helped to protect them from suffering similar fates, by mobilising its mourners into the conservation movement that made its voice heard in the debates about how to develop twentieth-century Prague. In the 1920s, planners eyed Josefov's new central boulevard keenly as they strove to modernise what was now the capital of independent Czechoslovakia. It could serve as the first stretch of a cross-river route running north from Wenceslas Square, a space that was symbolically important – the new state's independence had been declared there in 1918 – as well as being a hotspot for commerce and leisure. The Old Town was in the way, though, and so were the conservationists. According to one architect, 'sentimental art historians' were imposing a 'reign of terror ... not only over architects with modern views and sensibility ... but also over the population of the city, by forcing their lives into a tangle of old narrow streets'. In the end, the authorities opted to maintain the Old Town's integrity, and sent the traffic the long way round.[15]

The Old Town survived the Second World War too, though Prague was bombed several times – once in error, on 14 February 1945, by American aircraft whose crews mistook it for Dresden. Czech insurgents mounted an uprising a few days before Germany surrendered to the Allies, seizing the Town Hall on the Old Town Square as one of their bases. Enemy shells set the building ablaze and damaged the astronomical clock, the mechanism that had ordered the Old Town's time since the early fifteenth century. The clock was repaired and the medieval part of the Town Hall restored, though a wing added in the nineteenth century was demolished. Now the crowds gather below the clock to be hypnotised by its hourly cavalcade of apostles and allegorical figures, while the exuberant rocketry of the multiply-spired Týn church presides over the far side of the square.[16]

Prague's Old Town stands as a lovely and poignant symbol of what might have been, if the twentieth century had not happened. Although it is impossible to know how much of it would have been left standing if the conservation movement had not been mobilised by the plan that finished the 'Ghetto' of Josefov, the case of the city's former Jewish quarter has lessons for counterfactual histories of Old Towns in Middle Europe. It shows how historic districts became vulnerable to demolition if they were regarded as hazards to public health, if they were not considered by those in power to have unassailable symbolic value, and if they were seen to be standing in the way of progress. Though elite Old Towns in national capitals and ancient cities would have been safe, many historic quarters in the lower leagues might have fallen victim to those criteria.

It also illustrates how the loss of historic substance sensitises people to the possibility of further losses, stimulating not just the establishment of formal conservation bodies but also the growth of a more diffuse public consciousness, that evokes nostalgia for what has been lost and affection for what remains. And to the south of the Old Town Square, Wenceslas Square offers a reminder that Old Towns continue to form as time goes by. Romantic explorers will nowadays find what they are looking for in the arcade passages that are the twentieth-century equivalent of medieval alleys on the periphery of the market square. Faded art deco is as sweetly melancholic as ivy-clad ruins, being a vestige of that magical bygone age before the Second World War.

FRANKFURT AM MAIN

Chapter 17
The New Old Town

L ike Frankenstein's monster, its Germanic cousin, Josefov's Golem was frightening and dangerous but not wicked. The Golem was also imaginary, and confined even in legend to an attic. In the 1920s, Hannover gained an Old Town monster too, but unlike the Golem, this one was real, human and predatory: a serial murderer who claimed that his urge to kill was triggered by his sexual lusts. The attic room he occupied in an old half-timbered house was the chamber in which he murdered many of his victims and dismembered their bodies. He was eventually convicted of killing twenty-four boys and young men, for which he met his own death under the guillotine in 1925. The tales that circulated about Fritz Haarmann were as irresistible as they were macabre, and they shone a ghastly light over discussions about what should be done with Hannover's Old Town.[1]

Haarmann's crimes and their setting were discussed at length by Theodor Lessing, a philosopher and controversial public intellectual who was himself murdered, by Nazi assassins, in 1933. Lessing depicted the Altstadt as a sink of indigence and depravity, populated by wretchedly impoverished families, thieves, pimps and brutalised Great War veterans, with an economy based on the sale of sex and stolen goods. He included the Old Town's gathering-places for lesbians and 'so-called homosexuals' in his portrayal of the district as a den of 'vice', picking out the Gay Crowd (Zur Schwulen Guste) dance hall, located in 'one of the oldest and most notorious streets in the Altstadt', and the Ballhof, originally built in the seventeenth century at a duke's behest.

The themes all came together in the person of Fritz Haarmann, who literally sold flesh. Meat of unclear origins was one of the principal commodities in the black markets of the Altstadt; Haarmann was among those who traded in it. The understanding in such transactions is that the customer does not ask where the goods come from, but after Haarmann's arrest, nobody could help but wonder how he had sourced his supplies. Rumours about the abduction of children and the sale of human flesh in the market had already been going around, and people vented their inflamed emotions when Haarmann came to trial. They scuffled with police and broke windows – but it could have been a lot worse. As Lessing observed, if the killer had been Jewish, there would have been pogroms amid cries of ritual murder.[2]

By the 1920s, many city authorities had come to regard their Old Towns as lesions of morbid decay, but it was only in Hannover that the public was confronted with a single monstrous individual who seemed to represent all the Altstadt's pathologies: criminal, psychological, social and, in respect of the meat, hygienic. When the Nazis came to power, they funded a redevelopment scheme that imposed their new moral order on a section of the Old Town. Inevitably, it was centred on the creation of a public assembly ground. Half-timbered houses were demolished around the Ballhof, which became a home for the Hitler Youth, with a newly cleared space in front of it on which they could parade. A city official noted that 'All prostitutes, who lived in large numbers in this area, were removed because of the proximity of the Hitler Youth Home.'[3]

The Nazis' limited incursion fell far short of a comprehensive clearance, but that was effected by bombs during the war. Much of the city centre was destroyed on the night of 8–9 October 1943, when the RAF set it ablaze with a quarter of a million incendiaries; more than 1,200 people died. With only around thirty half-timbered houses left standing at the end of the war, the reconstruction planners (who included Hans Stosberg, the architect responsible for the nazification of the town of Auschwitz) consolidated the survivors. They created a 'traditional island' along two streets near the Ballhof, filling the gaps in the rows with facades that they took from buildings that had escaped destruction elsewhere in the district. One that they left in situ was the house where Fritz Haarman had his attic eyrie. It was among the 2 per cent of Hannover's half-timbered houses that escaped the bombing, though it was eventually knocked down in a postscript clearance.[4]

By concentrating and containing the remnant half-timbered houses within the 'traditional island', Hannover's rebuilders created a display of the city's past in a compact form that was big enough to make a splash, but too small to get in the way of their plans for the future. Under the circumstances and given the extent of the destruction, it was a satisfactory post-war settlement between the city's heritage and its contemporary aspirations. Other German cities failed to strike similar balances, and came to regret it.

Kassel, in central Germany, turned its back on its past more firmly than many cities were prepared to do. During the war, forty air raids were visited on it. As a target for area bombing, it had a fateful combination of military industries – its products included the feared Tiger tanks and V-1 cruise missiles – and a highly flammable historic kernel. The RAF's assessment highlighted the Old Town's 'narrow winding streets' and the absence of firewall parapets between its buildings. Two weeks after the climactic raid on Hannover, Bomber Command dispatched a force of more than 500 aircraft to Kassel. Their aiming point was St Martin's church, the Old Town's central landmark. Little was left of the Old Town after the attack and the firestorm it raised. Much of the rest of the city was destroyed too, and thousands of people lost their lives – estimates ranged from around 6,000 to 8,500; the number the city itself remembers is 10,000.[5]

The story of Kassel's Old Town in the decades before its destruction was a typical one. By the turn of the twentieth century it had declined into poverty, but like other neglected historic quarters across Middle Europe, it was then taken up by local representatives of the nascent conservation movement. Extolling the delights of wandering through those narrow winding streets, the conservationists regarded the Old Town as a reservoir of Heimat, notwithstanding the unhappy conditions endured by many of those for whom it actually was home. In the National Socialist 1930s, it was seen as a manifestation of the 'German spirit', like Rothenburg ob der Tauber. Even so, the district was modernised as well as conserved during those years before the war. On the one hand, the Altstadt's half-timbering was exposed after having been concealed under plaster since the eighteenth century, when it was covered up in order to make the quarter's appearance consistent with that of a new district built in stone. On the other, houses were knocked down to open up a straight route through the winding streets.[6]

After the war, the city authorities expanded on the theme. In 1946, Kassel's chief planner declared that the devastation had created a 'unique opportunity' to build 'a new and healthy organism, extensively re-organised'. The reorganisation eventually included an urban throughway that powered across the terrain of the former Old Town, in which a solitary surviving medieval tower was crowded round by indifferent modern buildings, pressing brusquely against it.[7]

The idea of the Old Town remained, though. In the words of the historian Jörg Arnold, it 'served as a foil and a point of comparison with the real world of everyday experience ... Old Kassel became a site of longing for all those who were dissatisfied with the reality of the new town.' It was a ghost that told stories, underlining that an Old Town can perform its narrative function even if it does not actually exist.[8]

With almost nothing left to be conserved, the pre-war conservationists had no basis on which to argue for an alternative to modernisation, and lapsed into nostalgia for the lost Old Kassel. By and large, people accepted the course that the authorities chose. When residents' views were surveyed in 1964, 90 per cent of respondents expressed their approval of the way that the city had been redeveloped. A book about Kassel by Manfred Haussmann, a poet and veteran of both world wars, was published the same year. In it he reflected that the raid of October 1943 'looked like the end at the time, but in the following years it proved to be the start of a new flowering'.

Thirteen years later, however, he sounded a melancholic and regretful note. 'Anyone who knew the historic town centre . . . will mourn the magic of the half-timbering, the little alleys and squares, the shops and the fountains, the oriels and the gables as long as they live,' he wrote. 'Life in Kassel, and in the world, is the poorer for their loss.' The mood had changed, and unhappiness with the new Kassel was no longer confined to the old conservative intelligentsia. Now the most vocal complaints came from left-wing intellectuals, the generation of 1968, who condemned the reconstruction as a dull and alienating capitalist failure. Kassel, they said, was still kaputt.

Unlike many of their criticisms of capitalism, their feelings about modernist reconstruction were in tune with broad and growing swathes of public opinion across Europe. Now that concrete had become the dominant substance of redeveloped city centres, the shock of the new was turning to disappointment, which naturally led to unfavourable comparisons with how things had been done before. As the past became a point of reference, it presented itself as a model for the future. And it was embraced most ambitiously by the German city that had forged the most determined and ambitious course into the future, the only one with a skyscraper skyline: Frankfurt am Main, the internationally prominent financial centre and air transport hub.

Allied bombing had created a ruin zone that included almost the whole of Frankfurt's Old Town area, hitherto one of the greatest forests of half-timber in urban Middle Europe. After the most devastating air raid, which took place on 22 March 1944, all but one of the half-timbered houses were gone. Just like Kassel's post-war planning chief, the architect who became Frankfurt's chief planner in 1949 saw the losses as 'a unique opportunity that should not be missed'. The vision of a fresh start was also supported by a strong undercurrent of moral opposition to the idea of restoring the Altstadt's previous forms, as a campaign to reconstruct one of the historic district's buildings revealed. Among the old houses lost was the one in which Johann Wolfgang von Goethe had been born in 1749; it was destroyed in the raid of 22 March, which was the anniversary of the poet's death. Its furniture and contents survived, having been removed for safety by the director of the adjoining Goethe Museum, who also documented the house and engaged students to draw it during the war years – actions that echoed those taken, at immensely greater risk, by the defenders of architectural heritage in Nazi-occupied Warsaw. The Association of Active Old Town Friends, set up in the 1920s to support the neglected district and its residents, organised similar surveys for 400 of the area's other houses.[9]

After the war, the preserved materials and plans gave credibility to calls for the reconstruction of the Goethe House in its previous image, enabling its advocates to argue that the form would be historically accurate, and the structure would be filled with authentic objects. It would also be filled to overflowing with symbolism. The historian Rudy Koshar observes that to its would-be resurrectors, the Goethe House represented not only the 'proud civic and domestic traditions' of the eighteenth-century bourgeoisie, but also 'German cosmopolitanism and liberty'. Support from abroad, such as that of the writers André Gide and Thornton Wilder, offered encouragement that a peaceful Germany could be reintegrated into the Western culture from which it had excluded itself by its actions.[10]

The moral counter-argument was articulated most trenchantly by Walter Dirks, a Catholic socialist, who saw 'connections between the spirit of the Goethe House and its destruction'. Moral opponents of reconstruction considered that Goethe was not innocent, because he had encouraged the bourgeoisie to look inwards and avoid their responsibilities as citizens. There was 'justice' in the ruin of Goethe's house, Dirks declared, and so the last chapter of the house's history should not be erased.[11]

Antipathy towards historical reconstruction was also prevalent among the city's planners, while enthusiasm for the return of the Goethe House ran high in literary circles. Poets were pitted against architects – and as the literary critic Max Richter approvingly remarked, the poets prevailed. The reconstruction went ahead, and the new Goethe House was opened in 1951.[12]

Among the dignitaries at the ceremony was John J. McCloy, who had intervened to save Rothenburg ob der Tauber in 1945 and was now the US High Commissioner in Germany. McCloy, who had donated 150,000 Deutschmarks to the project from High Commission funds, made a speech in which he highlighted Goethe's record of public service as a political administrator, not unlike himself. His main message, which he presented as an expression of the sentiments of the Allies 'and with them all the civilized nations of the world', was that Goethe's 'cosmopolitanism and his internationalism' represented values that should guide the nations as they strove to build a better world by transcending nationalism. 'May all of those who seek the unification of Europe and who from far and near will make pilgrimages to this building, achieve in his spirit a universal form of thinking and acting,' he concluded.[13]

McCloy also spoke of Goethe's dedication to the ideal of freedom, which made it impossible for totalitarians 'in his own country or elsewhere' to succeed in appropriating his name. The American High Commissioner thus projected an internationalist and anti-communist narrative onto an Old Town house in Germany during a period in which a communist regime built nationalist narratives into the Old Towns it reconstructed in Poland. He also invested it with a theme of universality that prefigured UNESCO's concept of World Heritage, a designation to which Old Towns everywhere would aspire.

Although Goethe was considered universal, however, the houses surrounding his were not. The surveys conducted by the Old Town Friends on the other 400 houses were not put to use. A few other historic buildings would be retained, but the Altstadt as a whole would be cleared and rebuilt as a new district with modern housing – which the Friends' founder, Fried Lübbecke, denounced as 'Bolshevik'. An empty space remained at its heart, though. On one side was the cathedral, which was still standing after the war, and on the other was the town hall, known as the Römer, which was rebuilt behind the gable frontage that had withstood the bombing. In the cityscape narrative that unfolded after the war, the three gables of the Römer formed an asterisk marking the footnote to which Frankfurt's history was relegated. Another city might have put a historical monument in the space between the cathedral and the town hall, but Frankfurt chose to fill it with a statement of monumental indifference to history, in the massively overbearing form of the brutalist Technical Town Hall, eventually completed in 1973.[14]

It was too much even for Frankfurt. Within a year the city's mayor, Rudi Arndt, signalled a municipal change of heart. Arndt had acquired the nickname 'Dynamite Rudi' ten years previously, after suggesting that the city's opera house, which had stood in ruins since the war, should be blown up instead of being rebuilt. Now, like many other people in both West and East Germany, the mayor looked to Poland for lessons in reconstruction, proposing the Old Towns of Warsaw and Gdańsk as models for reconciling his city's contemporary needs with its heritage. What excited him was not the reproduced historic facades, but the modern organisation they concealed. He saw mismatches of the kind found in the main street of Gdańsk's historic centre, where the house boundaries described by the frontages do not correspond to the boundaries of the flats behind them, as creative uses of space rather than historical travesties.[15]

Arndt had found a lesson for his capitalist West German city in a strategy developed twenty years previously as a way to meet the ideological requirements of the new Soviet order, when dwellings for workers formed the socialist content that complemented and validated the historical narratives lining the streets. When he solicited the public's views, the responses showed that plenty of people seemed to like the way he was thinking. A sea-change in the city's approach to its heritage was under way, and it became irreversible once Arndt's Social Democratic party lost power to the conservative Christian Democrats in 1977. In the first half of the 1980s, a row of half-timbered houses was reconstructed along the eastern side of the space overlooked by the town hall, the Römerberg.[16]

The sight was applauded locally, but the structure soon proved to be unsound. Cracks appeared in walls, plaster fell from ceilings and floors sagged; repairs cost two million Deutschmarks. The head of the city building department blamed the damage on the use of timber beams that had not been allowed to dry properly, and had shrunk after installation. Builders in the Middle Ages had used freshly felled timber too, countered the architect who had led the East Side project, but in those days houses didn't have central heating. Modern standards of comfort, with their unnaturally high and sustained temperatures, had dried the beams out too rapidly.

As expensive as they proved to be, the defects in the new-old houses were not judged to be as fundamental and intractable as those of the Technical Town Hall. By 2001, the Social Democrats' mayoral candidate was talking about blowing it up, and in 2005 a competition was held for designs to replace it. The winner proposed flat-roofed modern buildings on a narrow medieval street plan, which included several passages that had been erased in the post-war redevelopment.[17]

By that stage, though, there was insufficient appetite for such a compromise with history. The principle of reconstruction with a replica appearance had already been established on the east side of the Römerberg, the Ostzeile, and it had helped to launch a wave of historical rebuilding. In one art historian's jaundiced view, it was a 'breach in the dam' that advanced the cause of 'pseudo-historical architecture' in German cities. A survey published in 2014 estimated that about a hundred such plans had been proposed since the Römerberg one was first mooted; of those completed or under way, half were replica reconstructions. In Frankfurt a local association with a representative on the city council called for more replicas in the historic centre, and amid lively public debate the city's political parties pivoted towards history, creating a dynamic that resulted in the project to build a new Old Town between the Römerberg and the Domplatz, the cathedral square. The 'Neue-Altstadt' opened in 2018, with celebrations that included a ballet performed by 110 drones above the river Main, during the course of which the machines traced an outline of Goethe's head.[18]

The DomRömer Quarter eventually cost €200 million, double the original estimate. As a bill of €17.8 million for upgrading the 1980s Ostzeile houses to twenty-first-century standards also underlined, new old buildings do not come cheap. In Rothenburg ob der Tauber, the post-war rebuilders had been able to work much as their forebears had, using materials and techniques similar to those that had been used to build the originals. There was no question of that in the heart of the Frankfurt metropolis, where buildings had to be modern even if they looked old on the outside. In the House of the Golden Scales, a reconstruction based on a seventeenth-century prototype, a framework of timber made from 500-year-old oak stands on a concrete base. All the buildings in the DomRömer development have reinforced concrete stairwells, some of which descend below the ground, giving occupants of the quarter's eighty flats access to their parking spaces in the huge subterranean garage that lies underneath their homes. It was the base of the 1970s development, and could not be removed. 'We had the task of founding the chaotic Middle Ages on a well-structured underground car park,' the

DomRömer's project manager remarked. That car park had been the future once, and now fantasias of the past sat on top of it.[19] The House of the Golden Scales revels in its exuberant exterior, richly coloured and gilded, with geometrically patterned details on the timber and a swirling frieze around the silhouette of the gable. Next door the facade is unpainted, subtle in its detailing and monochromatic in its colour, the red of the sandstone from which it is made. Between them, the two buildings represent the range of styles crammed into the seven-hectare quarter. Of the development's thirty-five houses, fifteen are classed as reconstructions and the rest as new buildings, which work creative variations upon historical motifs. Some stick to the basic geometry of the houses, outlining their antecedents with triangles and rectangles. Others are more venturesome, such as the one faced with capes of slate tiling that make it look like a downtown pied-à-terre for Batman.

Unlike the Old Towns rebuilt under the direction of the communist regime in Poland, which edited out styles deemed to be inconsistent with the desired national narrative, Frankfurt's new Altstadt is conspicuously inclusive in its attitude to different historical periods. One of its buildings has a concrete facade that refers to its art nouveau predecessor, built in 1913; another reconstructs a house originally built in 1292. Combined with the variety of the new designs, crammed together like a permanent display of entries in an architecture competition, and the irregular layout of the narrow streets, the quarter's historical eclecticism makes it simultaneously arresting and confusing. There are stories being told here, but they are difficult to follow because all the characters are talking loudly at the same time.

For Stephan Trüby, a professor of architecture at the University of Stuttgart, the medley of the new Altstadt was the kind of historical spectacle that obscured the shameful passages in German history. In a newspaper article that became the focus for the debate about the DomRömer Quarter as the district neared completion, Trüby warned that reconstruction architecture 'is currently developing into a key medium for the authoritarian, völkisch, historical revisionist right in Germany'.[20]

The story of Frankfurt's new Old Town certainly illustrates how rightists can gain influence and political leverage by taking up an idea that appears non-political and is popular with the public at large. As Trüby pointed out, the proposal that eventually led to the building of the DomRömer Quarter was the idea of a right-wing essayist, Claus Wolfschlag, and was put on the political table by a councillor of similar ideological sympathies, Wolfgang Hübner (who for a time belonged to the conspicuously right-wing Alternative for Germany party). Pro Altstadt, a group set up to campaign for the reconstruction, calls Wolfschlag and Hübner the 'two fathers' of the initiative. They succeeded in winning support for their project from parties across the political spectrum, though Pro Altstadt was frustrated by the outnumbering of reconstructions by buildings with new designs.[21]

Whether historical replicas will actually function as a medium for the völkisch German right is another matter. They may stimulate broader conversations and critical reflections, according to the urban theorists Grischa Bertram and Friedhelm Fischer. 'What was once perceived as a reluctance of Germans to talk about the war seems to have turned into a fervent eagerness in German cities to apply localised preservation and re-construction efforts toward an exploration of the themes of war, history, and national identity,' they observe. And although the criticism from the left cast the DomRömer Quarter as a beacon for nativist movements, the district could prove to be an unexpectedly rich medium for nurturing a sense of multicultural identity. In a city where more than half the residents have a background of migration, either personal or family, the new Altstadt may tell stories that help to create a new sense of belonging. Peter Feldmann, the city's mayor, suggested that it could act as an 'identity anchor for the people of Frankfurt'.[22]

If so, it would be a top-of-the-range device. People in Gdańsk and Wrocław, lacking roots in the formerly German cities that went any

11. Crowds at the Christmas market in Frankfurt's Old Town district. The buildings overlooking them date from the 1980s.

deeper into history than 1945, anchored themselves by adopting the cities' pre-war history as their own. They could not say 'This is the history of the city my ancestors built', but instead they could say 'This is the history of my city'. Images and vestiges of the old urban fabric served them as points of attachment; by and large they made do with books of old photos. In Vilnius, also repopulated since 1945, residents can now visit a modest city museum set up with the same aim. Should the DomRömer Quarter turn out to perform a similar function, Frankfurt's communities of recent origin will have an entire prestige urban development as an anchor for their identities, lodged fast in an underground car park.

Frankfurters of all backgrounds certainly seem to have embraced the DomRömer Quarter enthusiastically, unperturbed by its free-wheeling attitude towards historical authenticity. It is a tourist attraction for them, like central quarters in many cities where metropolitan populations nowadays live almost entirely in suburbs, and as the director of Frankfurt's German Architecture Museum suggests, for foreign tourists, particularly Chinese ones, arriving at Frankfurt's great hub airport. Peter Cachola Schmal argues that having 'ur-cities' of western civilisation that tourists can walk around gives Europe, and especially Germany, a unique selling point. 'In the end,' he remarks, 'it doesn't matter whether the Old Town is authentic or reconstructed.'[23]

Meanwhile, purists can make a pilgrimage to a site surrounded by forest in the south of the country, where they can don coarse linen garb and set to work with axes, helping to build a 'Carolingian Monastery Town' that will be lucky if it is completed within fifty years. The aim of the Campus Galli project is to create a walled complex, which at eight hectares will be a fraction larger than the DomRömer Quarter, according to a plan that was drawn up in the ninth century but was not used to build the monastery for which it was prepared. The Old Town with the oldest form in Middle Europe will thus be an entirely new construction, modelling a history that never happened.[24]

MIDDLE EUROPE

Chapter 18
What Stories They Could Tell

Outside the railway station, a tableau of sculpted luggage commemorates the wartime deportations of Jews from Würzburg's Hauptbahnhof. Across the road, on the perimeter of the Old Town, there in the pavement are the first stumbling stones, overlooked by the frontage of a tourist hostel. They have more than a dozen close neighbours, remembrances of Jewish Würzburgers who were taken away and murdered in lands far from their homes. The station itself was built to replace the one destroyed by American bombers in an attack that killed more than 170 people. Memorials of violent death set the scene for the Altstadt.[1]

Inside the historic centre, ghosts are evoked not just by the hundreds of Stolpersteine but also by the prosaic post-war buildings that replaced the baroque townhouses consumed in the firestorm of March 1945. By keeping to the same height as their predecessors, they cast the melancholy shadows of the vanished buildings over the quarter's preserved medieval layout. The sense of loss is deepened because the reconstruction is neither the one thing, a replica ensemble, nor the other, an uncompromisingly modern fresh start.

There's a different sense of absence in Warsaw's Starówka, the most fully realised historical reconstruction among Middle Europe's

Old Towns. Up one solid street and down another, into the centre-piece Market Square and out again, everything seems to be here – the portals, the cobbles, the parasols, the tourists and the ice creams – but something always seems to be missing. The conviviality is subdued in comparison with, say, Kraków, where the grandly scaled Old Town is the centre of the city. Unlike many of the tourist parties that descend on Kraków, visitors enjoy themselves respectfully, conscious that they are strolling round a monument. The quarter is an enclave isolated from the larger metropolis, a sidebar to the city's growing contemporary attractions.

Given its history and its significance, that is perhaps as it should be. Behind its restored wall, it has attained composure and peace. In front of the wall, an unsettling figure stands guard: the Little Insurgent, a statue of a young boy in boots and a helmet far too large for him, a submachine gun hung around his neck. It commemorates the many children and adolescents who served in the Warsaw Uprising, though it does not portray a typical one – mostly they carried messages; few carried guns. The prototype for it was fashioned by a sculptor during the aftermath of the war, modelling clay after his day's labours clearing rubble. Nowadays it is a shrine, and a conundrum for foreign onlookers who are used to regarding children in war simply as victims. A promenade round an Old Town can raise challenging questions about the present as well as the past.[2]

In Frankfurt's new Altstadt, however, the most challenging questions are about contemporary tastes. The new designs based on historic forms seem concerned to distance themselves from their source material, asserting the modernity of their architects' sensibilities. Boasting creativity as well as craft, they cast aesthetic aspersions on their historical-replica neighbours. They also make the simulacra look fake, by reminding the neighbourhood of its artificiality. What's missing from the DomRömer quarter is any sense that the past is present in it. Although it is a lavish exercise in staging, it discourages spectators from suspending their disbelief. The replicas look like full-size models, not buildings that might perhaps be genuinely old, and they probably always will. But there's no doubt that the conviviality it hosts is authentic. At Christmas and other festive times, its ground level is occupied by cabins with imitation half-timbering, bratwurst stalls, antique-style street lamps and all the fun of the fair, cheerfully indifferent to considerations of good taste like those that hang over the surrounding buildings.

After the long period of eclipse in which urban planners regarded them as problems, Old Towns now look like solutions. As cities turn back from cars to people, and themed recreational locations become magnets for residents as well as tourists, Old Town spaces are recovering the roles as central urban foci that they had been losing since the nineteenth century. Picturesque streetscapes and pedestrianisation are a winning combination. Old Towns are always works in progress, and they are never finally resolved or finished. Without constant care, they crack, fade and flake. Alfred Döblin noted a street of crumbling houses when he passed through Lublin's Old Town in 1924: nearly a hundred years later, there were buildings crumbling in the same street again. Dilapidated tenements in the backstreets of the quarter are a reminder of the long eclipse that so many of Middle Europe's Old Towns went through before they were reappraised. They also make the place feel like a real neighbourhood, rather than an open-air museum.

At one corner of the Market Square, flaking plaster is used to the same effect as in Vilnius's Ghetto Library, forming a backdrop for old portrait photos set in window frames. This is not a derelict building like the Library or the houses in Warsaw's former Jewish district that presented similar displays, though. It houses part of the Mandragora Jewish restaurant enterprise. The lowest storey is smoothly plastered; the people in the portraits above it look as though they would have been at home in the bourgeois comfort that the restaurant's interior is designed to evoke. Mandragora's proprietor picked out the photos from one of her family's collections. Though the design formula is the same as that applied in Warsaw and Vilnius, the symbolism is different. The images are there to represent a community's existence in former times, rather than to commemorate the annihilation of that community. Subtly, they draw the past away from death and towards life.

A handsome basilica, Gothic in origin, stands at the end of the street that leads out of the Market Square from Mandragora's corner. It still boasts fragments of the Holy Cross, credited with saving the city from Cossacks in the seventeenth century, fire in the eighteenth century and cholera in the nineteenth, though most of the sacred wood was stolen in 1991. One of the church's highlights is a painting that depicts the miracle of 1719. Fire has broken out in the wooden buildings of the Jewish neighbourhood outside the city walls, and threatens what is now known as the Old Town. Dominican friars bring out the relic, claimed to be the largest piece of the Holy Cross in Catholic Christendom, through the Grodzka Gate. As they carry the reliquary in a procession below the walls, the flames die down and the Christian upper levels are saved. It is said that the wood was carried in a similar procession around the Tribunal courthouse building, which fills most of the Market Square, during a German air raid in 1939.[3]

The scene representing the Fire of Lublin is animated underground, at the end of a route that starts at the Tribunal and weaves its way through the labyrinth of cellars beneath the townhouses, emerging at the open space where St Michael's church used to stand. Created by the Brama Grodzka centre, the trail draws on the organisation's theatrical background for its finale, bringing the painting to life with sound, light and moving parts that recall old-fashioned mechanical scenery. Hearing voices speaking a medley of different tongues, visitors 'discover the multicultural character of the city'. Then they climb up out into the light and find themselves next door to the 'Patriotic Shop', where no such character is to be found.[4]

Back at the Dominican church, a panel on the wall hails the Union of Lublin between Poland and Lithuania as a major step forward in

Europe's progress towards democratic integration, which 'led to the peaceful and inclusive coexistence of people of different ethnic and religious backgrounds'. The European Union awarded the Union of Lublin one of its European Heritage Labels, intended to develop its citizens' sense of shared European identity and promote what it sees as European values. Hailing the award, the city called the Polish-Lithuanian dual state a 'prefiguration of the European Union'. The church is the Old Town's representative of the Union of Lublin because a thanksgiving mass was held there after the swearing of the act at the castle. EUROPE STARTS HERE! exclaims the panel.[5]

As across much of the continent and its offshore islands, however, Europe also threatens to stop here. On the one side, Brama Grodzka and Mandragora are telling their inclusive stories; on the other, the 'Patriotic Shop' is telling stories about an exclusively defined nation – and then there is the 'Real Pole' with his kebab restaurant, cele-brating old battles against the Turks. Amid the angry cacophony that has replaced anything that might reasonably be called public conver-sation, there is scant chance that the storytellers on different sides will talk to each other. That is what is missing in Lublin's Old Town, and most other places too. But it is unwarranted to assume that the current state of the world will be permanent, and there will be plenty to converse about if the climate becomes less polarised. It is perfectly possible to embrace both a mainstream national story and storylines that have been excluded or disconnected from it. Tomasz Pietrasiewicz sounds like any other patriotic Pole when he recalls his hopes for a 'free, independent Poland' around the time he brought his theatre group to Brama Grodzka.

Like the fabric of Old Towns, Europe's historical fabric requires constant care and renewal. It needs to be woven together, a task that requires imagination and thought as well as good intentions. With their symbolic significance and their experience of being renewed, the Old Towns are natural hubs for such activity – especially in coun-tries where conservative ideologies enjoy ascendancy in national politics. Cities are more inclined to openness; they have their own senses of themselves, and they want to tell their stories their own way. At the end of the path Alfred Döblin took through Lublin's historic kernel, the Brama Grodzka building now offers inspiration instead of the hopelessness that Döblin saw behind its windows. It shows how creativity and contemplation can enable Old Towns to tell enriched, transformative stories – and how a solemn remembrance of loss can help bring cheerful new life to an old quarter.

Among the lessons it offers, one of the most valuable is about how to make multiculturalism meaningful. Waving in the direction of a city's multicultural history is not sufficient to claim a tradition of tolerance or productive diversity, for the fact that different communities co-existed in the past does not necessarily mean that they respected or valued each other. That, however, is beside the point. What matters is that people nowadays respect and value the various cultures that were once to be found in their cities, which is the basis on which the Brama Grodzka centre has developed its relationship with the community that no longer neighbours its building. They can make use of the past to promote the values they cherish and pursue the future they seek – which is exactly what the past is there for.

Nativists, illiberal democrats and dictators can do that too, though, typically with passion and sometimes with steel. The need to put the past to good use is starkly silhouetted against the thunder-clouds raised by Vladimir Putin's onslaught against Ukraine, driven by a tyrannical narrative that denied the country's nationhood and cast it as a land populated by Russians awaiting liberation. European cities were bombarded once again; historic monuments were swaddled with sandbags. The fear of war hovered over Middle Europe and beyond – as Kraków's hospitality trade testified, counting the cost of cancelled tourist bookings, 400 kilometres from Lviv and more than 250 kilometres from the Ukrainian border. Even at that range, the assault broke the Old Town's spell and triggered a moment of doubt, in which strangers ceased to see Kraków's grand Market Square as a place in which conflict was no longer imaginable.[6]

Russia opened a new phase of history by reprising an old one, with armoured columns and grandiose myths of national destiny. For all the contradictions and selectivity that can be found within them, Europe's Old Towns represent a historical storyline that transcends what Putin brought back to the continent. The return of war underlines that Old Towns are precious not only as assemblages of historic objects, but also as zones of peace where people can intermingle freely and happily, leaving the conflicts of the past behind. We must look after them, and never take them for granted.

Acknowledgements

I'm immensely grateful to the people who generously shared their thoughts and stories with me in conversation: Tomasz Pietrasiewicz of the Brama Grodzka – Teatr NN centre and Izabela Kozłowska-Dechnik of the Mandragora restaurant in Lublin; Rasa Antanavičiūtė and Violeta Davoliūtė in Vilnius; Roland Flade in Würzburg; Hanns Berger in Rothenburg ob der Tauber and Joshua Hagen on his research there. I'm also grateful to Marija Drėmaitė, Hellmuth Möhring of the Rothenburg Museum and Anne Thomas of the Stolpersteine project for providing information and comments.

I have Tomasz Kitliński and Paweł Leszkowicz to thank for introducing me to Lublin, which turned out to be every bit as important as they said it was, and more than justified its marketing as a 'city of inspiration'. Thanks also for help and guidance to Joanna Zętar of the Brama Grodzka centre, Markus Hundemer of the Bayerisches Landesamt für Denkmalpflege, Ammon Cheskin, Vytautas Petronis, Eugene Michail, Lisa Redlinski, Malcolm Wolf, Richard Grayson and Suzanne Treister. I'm grateful to Julian Loose and Frazer Martin for their editorial support, to Eve Leckey for her sympathetic copy-editing, and to the anonymous reviewers whose comments helped make the advanced stages of the project a highly fruitful exercise.

Some parts of the book benefited from particular sources to such an extent that I feel acknowledgement over and above endnote citation is due, to Andrzej Skalimowski's biography of Józef Sigalin, Gregor Thum's book on Wrocław, and Joshua Hagen's publications about Rothenburg ob der Tauber. I'd also like to salute the commitment of the Brama Grodzka centre and a network of other Polish institutions to making historical archive material available online. And in London during the pandemic restrictions I was grateful for the British Library's efforts to admit readers, via a meticulous chain of protocols stretching from street entrance to desk. Before the lockdowns, I was able to make a tour of Old Towns across Europe by train, thanks in no small measure to the Man in Seat Sixty-One (seat61.com).

As memory is one of this book's main themes, it feels appropriate to remember two late family friends. One was Zbigniew Dembiński, who worked on the construction of the East–West Route in Warsaw as a young man, and who sent me a package of materials to help me with my research shortly before his death. The other was Karol Kwiatkowski, a veteran of the Warsaw Uprising, whose perspective on the memory and commemoration of the Uprising made a lasting impression on me.

My deepest thanks are to my wife, Sue Matthias Kohn, and our son, Teo Kohn, for their love, their support and their editorial evaluations. Sue toured the Old Towns with me, and Teo also accompanied me on a field trip. Both of them read draft texts, offered guidance and provided encouragement. I'm glad as well as grateful that they have been part of these journeys.

Notes

Introduction: Seven Symbolic Quarters

1. Conversation #14: Marek Kohn, 28 August 2017, https://conversationswitheurope. wordpress.com/2017/08/28/conversation-14-marek-kohn/
2. Aleja Herbów Miast Hanzeatyckich i Handlowych, http://www.turystyka.torun.pl/ art/210/aleja-herbow-miast-hanzeatyckich-i-handlowych.html
3. Remarks by President Biden on the United Efforts of the Free World to Support the People of Ukraine, 26 March 2022, https://www.whitehouse.gov/briefing-room/ speeches-remarks/2022/03/26/remarks-by-president-biden-on-the-united-efforts-of-the-free-world-to-support-the-people-of-ukraine/
4. Daniel Tilles, Destroyed Russian weapons put on display in Warsaw to "prove Russia can be defeated", 28 June 2022, https://notesfrompoland.com/2022/06/28/destroyed-russian-weapons-put-on-display-in-warsaw-to-prove-russia-can-be-defeated/; Jakub Borowski, M. Dworczyk: zniszczony rosyjski sprzęt wojskowy pokazuje, że Rosję można pokonać, 28 June 2022, https://dzieje.pl/wiadomosci/m-dworczyk-zniszczony-rosyjski-sprzet-wojskowy-pokazuje-ze-rosje-mozna-pokonac
5. Maria Wilczek, EU justice commissioner tells Poland to abide by European court rulings to defuse conflict, 19 November 2021, https://notesfrompoland. com/2021/11/19/eu-justice-commissioner-tells-poland-to-abide-by-european-court-rulings-to-defuse-conflict/
6. Nora 1996 vol. 1, 21.
7. Van Wyck Brooks, On Creating a Usable Past, *The Dial*, 11 April 1918, 337–41.
8. Présentation du projet de loi complétant la législation sur la protection du patrimoine historique et esthétique de la France et tendant à faciliter la restauration 23 juillet 1962, https:// www.assemblee-nationale.fr/histoire/andre-malraux/discours/malraux_23juil1962.asp

Warsaw

Chapter 1. Market to Monument

1. Koczorowska-Pielińska 1958.
2. The Idea of the Republic in Poland-Lithuania: A Conversation with Robert Frost, https://www.youtube.com/watch?v=qsYlvY443vs; Gieysztor 1979, 157–8.

3. Zwierz 2014.
4. Zwierz 2014; Oppmann 1931.
5. Rothschild 1974, 36.
6. T. Snyder 2004, 62.
7. Dmowski 2014 (originally published 1902); Michlic 2006, 63–9; Wapiński 2018.
8. In 1921 the recorded figure was 33.1 per cent. The percentage subsequently decreased, falling to 29.1 in 1938. *Warszawa w liczbach 1939*, 14.
9. Zwierz 2014; Popiołek 2016, 43, 51; Adam Wolmar, W trosce o rynek staromiejski, *Kurjer Warszawski* 152, 3 June 1928, 13–14; Popiolek 2016, 27.
10. Lorentz 1970 vol. 1, 40.

Chapter 2: Soldier-Architects

1. Maria Piechotka „Marianna", https://www.1944.pl/archiwum-historii-mowionej/maria-piechotka,354.html; Maria Piechotka – o okresie przedwojennym, o wojnie, o powrocie do Polski, Dom Spotkań z Historią, https://www.facebook.com/84072659617/videos/2886389184816493
2. Zachwatowicz 1946a; Prof. Oskar Sosnowski – audycja z cyklu 'Biografia dzwiękowa', 22 September 2002, https://www.polskieradio.pl/39/156/Artykul/1540879,Oskar-Sosnowski-architekt-na-posterunku
3. Zachwatowicz in Lorentz 1970, 112–13; Prof. Jan Zachwatowicz - twórca polskiej szkoły konserwatorskiej. Audycja Jana Owsińskiego z cyklu 'Radiowe portrety Polaków', https://www.polskieradio.pl/39/156/Artykul/909950,Jan-Zachwatowicz-udaremnil-zamach-Niemcow-na-kulture-polska (1980 audio); Anna Legierska, Obrońcy skarbów: Estreicher, Lorentz i inni, 22 September 2017, https://culture.pl/pl/artykul/obroncy-skarbow-estreicher-lorentz-i-inni; Jozefacka 2011, 160.
4. Guerquin 1984; *Jan Zachwatowicz 1900–1983*, 2000, dir. Antoni Krauze, https://www.youtube.com/watch?v=H-usZEnQhZs
5. Prof. Oskar Sosnowski – audycja z cyklu 'Biografia dzwiękowa', Polskie Radio 22 September 2002, https://www.polskieradio.pl/39/156/Artykul/1540879,Oskar-Sosnowski-architekt-na-posterunku; Kazimierz Maciej Piechotka „Jacek", https://www.1944.pl/archiwum-historii-mowionej/kazimierz-maciej-piechotka,558.html
6. Prof. Oskar Sosnowski – audycja z cyklu 'Biografia dzwiękowa', Polskie Radio 22 September 2002,https://www.polskieradio.pl/39/156/Artykul/1540879,Oskar-Sosnowski-architekt-na-posterunku; Kazimierz Maciej Piechotka „Jacek", https://www.1944.pl/archiwum-historii-mowionej/kazimierz-maciej-piechotka,558.html; Jozefacka 2011, 159.
7. Kazimierz Maciej Piechotka „Jacek", https://www.1944.pl/archiwum-historii-mowionej/kazimierz-maciej-piechotka,558.html
8. Jankowski 1996 vol. 2, 81; Jankowski 1996 vol. 2, 79; Jankowski 1996 vol. 2, 83.
9. Jankowski 1996 vol.1, 67; Jankowski 1996 vol.1, 76-96; Jankowski 1996 vol.1, 158–9.
10. Jankowski 1996 vol.1, 224–7; Jankowski 1996 vol.1, 237–42.
11. Jankowski 1996 vol.1, ch.11.
12. Jankowski 1996 vol.2, 73; Czapska 1988; *Jan Zachwatowicz 1900–1983*, 2000, dir. Antoni Krauze, https://www.youtube.com/watch?v=H-usZEnQhZs.
13. Jan Zachwatowicz, Chronicles of Terror, https://zapisyterroru.pl/dlibra/show-content?id=435; Němec 2018; Atlas zum Wiederaufbau: Würzburg, https://www.bavariathek.bayern/wiederaufbau/orte/detail/wuerzburg/65; Gerken 2004, 363.
14. Sosnowski 1930; Jozefacka 2011, 154–6; Gawryszewski 2010.
15. Steinbacher 2005, 68–71.
16. Władysław Czerny, Chronicles of Terror, https://zapisyterroru.pl/dlibra/show-content?id=392
17. Němec 2018; Lorentz 1970 vol. 1, 42.

18. Popiołek 2016, 71, 83; Lorentz 1970 vol. 1, 42; Popiołek 2016, 75, 79; Lorentz 1970 vol. 1, 40–1; Lorentz 1970 vol. 1, 42. Two songs Lorentz mentions as particularly popular, 'Dnia pierwszego września' and 'Siekiera, motyka', feature in a celebrated film about musical resistance in the streets and courtyards of occupied Warsaw, *Zakazane piosenki (Forbidden Songs)*, 1946, dir. Leonard Buczkowski, https://35mm.online/vod/fabula/zakazane-piosenki; Lorentz 1970 vol. 1, 50.

19. Lorentz 1970 vol. 1, 50–1; Lorentz 1970 vol. 1, 42.

20. Wółkowski 2021.

21. Fałkowski et al. 2004; Zyblikiewicz et al. 2022, 276–8, 432; https://mobile.twitter.com/Maciej_Swirski/status/1565336900872781824

22. Władysław Czerny, Chronicles of Terror, https://zapisyterroru.pl/dlibra/show-content?id=392; Jozefacka 2011, 157–8; Zamek Królewski długo przypominał o dramacie wojny, https://www.polskieradio24.pl/39/156/Artykul/891177,Zamek-Krolewski-dlugo-przypominal-o-dramacie-wojny

23. Execution announcement including Bryła's name: https://upload.wikimedia.org/wikipedia/commons/d/d3/Bekanntmachung_Warschau_1943.jpg

24. Krzysztof Jóźwiak, Akcja Braun, https://historia.uwazamrze.pl/artykul/1149259/akcja-braun

25. Maria Piechotka – o okresie przedwojennym, o wojnie, o powrocie do Polski, Dom Spotkań z Historią, https://www.facebook.com/84072659617/videos/2886389184816493

26. Kazimierz Maciej Piechotka „Jacek", https://www.1944.pl/archiwum-historii-mowionej/kazimierz-maciej-piechotka,558.html; Jankowski 1996 vol. 2, 430; Maria Piechotka „Marianna", https://www.1944.pl/archiwum-historii-mowionej/maria-piechotka,354.html

27. Jankowski 1996 vol. 2, 276.

28. Jankowski 1996 vol. 2, 281, 294. Other photos of 'Agaton' and his men, including scenes from the cemetery deployment, can be seen at https://www.1944.pl/szukaj-zdjec,strona,1,7791.html/szukaj/Agaton

29. Maria Piechotka „Marianna", https://www.1944.pl/archiwum-historii-mowionej/maria-piechotka,354.html

30. J. Majewski 2017, 38; Richie 2013, 417–19.

31. Hanson 2004, 105; Kazimierz Maciej Piechotka „Jacek", https://www.1944.pl/archiwum-historii-mowionej/kazimierz-maciej-piechotka,558.html

32. Jankowski 1996 vol. 2, 382–3.

33. Jankowski 1996 vol. 2, 419–20; Hanson 2004, 113.

34. Kazimierz Maciej Piechotka, https://www.1944.pl/powstancze-biogramy/kazimierz-piechotka,34310.html

35. Kazimierz Maciej Piechotka „Jacek", https://www.1944.pl/archiwum-historii-mowionej/kazimierz-maciej-piechotka,558.html; Jankowski 1996 vol. 2, 430–1.

36. *Jan Zachwatowicz 1900–1983*, 2000, dir. Antoni Krauze, https://www.youtube.com/watch?v=H-usZEnQhZs; P. Majewski 2009, 376–7.

37. Lorentz 1970 vol. 1 44–5, 50; 1951.

38. Ewa Faryaszewska, https://www.1944.pl/powstancze-biogramy/ewa-faryasze-wska,9807.html; Ewa Faryaszewska. Bohaterska łączniczka ze Starego Miasta. Poległa ratując zabytki i dzieła sztuki, Wojciech Rodak, 20 August 2019, https://warszawa.naszemiasto.pl/ewa-faryaszewska-bohaterska-laczniczka-ze-starego-miasta/ar/c15-7295705; Janina Gruszczyńska-Jasiak *ps. Porzęcka, Janka*, https://lekarzepowstania.pl/osoba/janina-gruszczynska-jasiak-ps-janka/; Janina Gruszczyńska-Jasiak, Ostatnie dni Starego Miasta, http://www.sppw1944.org/index.html?http://www.sppw1944.org/relacje/relacja49e.html; Kazimiera Elżbieta Świderska, https://www.1944.pl/powstancze-biogramy/kazimiera-swiderska,45341.html; Stanisław Konarski, Zygmunt Michał Miechowski 1913–09–25 – 1944–09–25, https://www.ipsb.nina.gov.pl/a/

biografia/zygmunt-michal-miechowski-1913-1944-historyk-sztuki; Popiołek 2016, 89–93; P. Majewski 2017.
39. Jankowski 1996 vol. 2, 493; Jankowski 1996 vol. 2, 457, 460.
40. Thum 2003, xxiv–xxv.
41. Klaudia Kamieniarz, Tak burzyli Zamek Królewski. Zdjęcia pozwoliły ustalić datę, 8 September 2019, https://tvn24.pl/tvnwarszawa/najnowsze/tak-burzyli-zamek-krolewski-brzdjecia-pozwolily-ustalic-date-292311; Trial of the Major War Criminals before the International Military Tribunal, Nuremberg, 14 November 1945 – 1 October 1946, Vol. XXXIX, 1949, 380 (German text); Trials of War Criminals before the Nuernberg Military Tribunals Under Control Council Law No. 10, Nuremberg, October 1946 – April 1949, Vol. XII, 1949, 1081 (English translation); Ciborowski 1964, 58-9 (photo of document; also reproduced in Główna Komisja Badania Zbrodni Niemieckich w Polsce 1946).
42. Jerzy Putrament, Warszawa w lutym, Odrodzenie 13, 25 February 1945; Jan Zachwatowicz, Chronicles of Terror, https://zapisyterroru.pl/dlibra/show-content?id=435
43. Kołodziejczyk 1995; Czapska 2006, 1988; Zachwatowicz in Lorentz 1970, 123–9; Jan Zachwatowicz 1900–1983, 2000, dir. Antoni Krauze, https://www.youtube.com/watch?v=H-usZEnQhZs; Hillmann 2001; Pruszak 2014; Jan Zachwatowicz, Chronicles of Terror, https://zapisyterroru.pl/dlibra/show-content?id=435
44. Archiwum Historii Mówionej - Dom Spotkań z Historią/Ośrodek KARTA, 28 January 2018, https://www.facebook.com/archiwumhistoriimowionej/photos/a.14292 97617331335/1979020142359077/?type=3; Szymańska 2015, 12.
45. Warszawa w liczbach 1947, 4–5; Warszawa Feniksem XX Wieku, 69.
46. Maria Piechotka „Marianna", https://www.1944.pl/archiwum-historii-mowionej/maria-piechotka,354.html; Maria Piechotka – o okresie przedwojennym, o wojnie, o powrocie do Polski, Dom Spotkań z Historią, https://www.facebook.com/84072659617/videos/2886389184816493

Chapter 3. Go to the Forests, or Get to Work

1. Biegański 1984; Skalimowski 2018, Towarzysz odbudowy.
2. Piątek 2020, ch 5.
3. Piotr Biegański, 24 March 1985, O zachowanie historycznej tożsamości Warszawy, Stolica 12, 20–1; Skalimowski 2018, Warszawa 1945, epigraph.
4. Skalimowski 2018, Towarzysz odbudowy; Kończal 2017; Grzebałkowska 2015, Barachło.
5. Skalimowski 2018, Towarzysz odbudowy.
6. Khrushchev 2004, 622.
7. Piątek 2020, ch 6.
8. Ciborowski 1946, 64; Demokraci i „Demokraci", 3 March 1945, Życie Warszawy, 1.
9. Biegański 1984.
10. Skalimowski 2018, Towarzysz odbudowy.
11. Wapiński 2018; Michlic 2006, 114–15; Melzer 1997, ch. 5; Dr hab. Jolanta Żyndul: Głównym celem getta ławkowego było wypchnięcie Żydów z Polski, 10 October 2017, https://dzieje.pl/aktualnosci/dr-hab-jolanta-zyndul-glownym-celem-getta-lawkowego-bylo-wypchniecie-zydow-z-polski; Skalimowski 2018, Małe szczęście przedwojenne.
12. Melzer 1997, 72; Trębacz 2016; Konstantynów 2009; Rabinowicz 1964.
13. Komunikat SARP, 7–8–9, 1938, 8, 14.
14. Konstantynów 2009; Kohlrausch 2019, 241; Młoda Architektura Polska jest Narodowo-Radykalna, 1 October 1938, Falanga 46(126), 6.
15. Zasady Programu Narodowo–Radykalnego, 10 February 1937, Falanga 5(31), 1.
16. Kijek 2018.

17. T. Snyder 2005, 115–32; Morris 2004; Decision to commence investigation into Katyn Massacre, Institute of National Remembrance, 30 November 2004, https://ipn.gov.pl/en/news/77,dok.html
18. Hobsbawm 2004, 140.
19. Konstantynów 2009; *Komunikat SARP* 7–8–9, 1938, 5, 8. The official report did not name those who voted in favour of the proposal, but they represented a large majority of the assembly, so it is likely but not certain that Biegański was among them.
20. Do architektów polskich, *Rzeczpospolita* 30 January 1945, 2.
21. Nowożycki 2016; Grabski 2018, 466.
22. P. Majewski 2009, 40; Jankowski 1996 vol.2, 466–7, 590–2; Działalność wydziału legalizacji i techniki „AGATON I" i „AGATON II", 2006, *Zeszyty Historyczne* 4, 18–21.
23. Jankowski 1996 vol.2, 599–601.
24. Skalimowski 2018, Dyplom na budowę Trasy; Jankowski 1996 vol.2, 603–4; Maria Piechotka „Marianna", https://www.1944.pl/archiwum-historii-mowionej/maria-piechotka,354.html; Kazimierz Maciej Piechotka „Jacek", https://www.1944.pl/archiwum-historii-mowionej/kazimierz-maciej-piechotka,558.html
25. Konstantynów 2009; Maria Zakrzewska, Jan Poliński 1907–02–22 – 1977–09–30, https://www.ipsb.nina.gov.pl/a/biografia/jan-polinski; Jan Poliński, Oblicze architektoniczne miast … polskich, *Prosto z Mostu* 14–15, 2–9 April 1939, 22; Stanisław Jankowski, Architektura w młodych oczach, *Prosto z Mostu* 14–15, 2–9 April 1939, 15; Stanisław Jankowski, Polska wspólnota zawodowa, 1938, *Komunikat SARP* 11, 12–13.

Chapter 4. A Brigade of Goldsmiths

1. Krasiński 1953.
2. Wyporek 2015; Krzysztof Pilawski, Patrioci przy rajzbrecie – rozmowa z Bogdanem Wyporkiem, 12 February 2012, https://www.tygodnikprzeglad.pl/patrioci-przy-rajzbrecie/
3. Czapska 1989, 2006.
4. Karol Szpalski, 6 May 1945, O szabrownikach, *Przekrój* 4; Grzebałkowska 2015, Barachło.
5. Piątek 2020, ch 4.
6. Popiołek 2016, 63, 69, 101; Popiołek 2016, 101, 105; Mapy Warszawy, http://mapa.um.warszawa.pl/ - Zabytki – Materiały Biura Odbudowy Stolicy (BOS); Helena Kowalik, Pójdę na Stare Miasto…, 1 July 2002, https://www.tygodnikprzeglad.pl/pojde-na-stare-miasto/
7. Andrzej Fedorowicz, Jak warszawianki chowały powstańców, 16 July 2018, https://www.polityka.pl/tygodnikpolityka/klasykipolityki/1559551,1,jak-warszawianki-chowaly-powstancow.read; Kazimierz Wyka, Miecz Syreny, *Odrodzenie* 22, 29 April 1945, 8; Popiołek 2016, 113.
8. Jerzy Putrament, Warszawa w lutym, *Odrodzenie* 13, 25 February 1945, 4; Wśród gruzów Starego Miasta, 21 June 1945, *Życie Warszawy* 169(238), 3.
9. *Warszawa w liczbach 1947*, 97, 100; Ciborowski 1964, 64; Gawryszewski 2009, 85–6, quotes later estimates, including a figure of 685,000 (published in 1984) and one of 729,000 (2004).
10. E.g. Ciborowski 1964, 64; *Warsaw As It Was* 1985; Klekot 2015; Główna Komisja Badania Zbrodni Niemieckich w Polsce 1946, 65 (testimony) and plates (teletype from Warsaw governor). Teletype also reproduced in Ciborowski 1964, 58–9.
11. *Warszawa w liczbach 1947*, 20; Łagodziński 2013, 11.
12. Kazimierz Koźniewski, Zniszczone–odbudowane, *Przekrój* 19 July 1953, 8; Stanisław Herbst, Jan Kiliński 1760 – 1819–01–28, https://www.ipsb.nina.gov.pl/a/biografia/jan-kilinski-1760-1819-szewc-powstaniec-kosciuszkowski-pamietnikarz; Andrzej

Fedorowicz. Jak warszawianki chowały powstańców, 16 July 2018, https://www.polityka.pl/tygodnikpolityka/klasykipolityki/1559551,1,jak-warszawianki-chowaly-powstancow.read

13. Michał Gawałkiewicz, Wędrówka po Starym Mieście, *Życie Warszawy* 297, 28 October 1946, 3; Szymańska 2015, 25; Staromiejska gołębiarka, http://www.ekartkazwarszawy.pl/kartka/staromiejska-golebiarka/

14. Wanda Kragen, Obrazki dzisiejszej Warszawy, *Robotnik* 286, 17 October 1946, 8; Kazimierz Kożniewski, Zniszczone–odbudowane, *Przekrój* 19 July 1953, 10.

15. Znikają barykady bohaterskiej Starówki, *Życie Warszawy* 11 October 1946, 5; Tomasz Urzykowski, 60 lat warszawskiej Starówki. Dlaczego Bierut zgodził się na odbudowę? 20 July 2013, https://warszawa.wyborcza.pl/warszawa/1,54420,14300621,60_lat_warszawskiej_Starowki__Dlaczego_Bierut_zgodzil.html

16. Szymańska 2015, 37; Biogram Marianna Janowska, Archiwum Historii Mówionej, https://relacjebiograficzne.pl/demo/video/171-marianna-janowska; Przywara 2018.

17. Treber 2019; Jähner 2021, ch. 2.

18. *Ulica Brzozowa*, dir. Wojciech Jerzy Has, 1947, http://www.dokumentcyfrowo.pl/kategorie/miasto/ulica-brzozowa.html; Cieśliński 2020.

19. Tomasz Urzykowski, 60 lat warszawskiej Starówki. Dlaczego Bierut zgodził się na odbudowę? 20 July 2013, https://warszawa.wyborcza.pl/warszawa/1,54420,14300621,60_lat_warszawskiej_Starowki__Dlaczego_Bierut_zgodzil.html

20. Prezydent Bierut przy odgruzowywaniu rynku Starego Miasta, Polska Kronika Filmowa 37/47 http://www.repozytorium.fn.org.pl/?q=pl/node/6505

21. Borecka et al. 1982, 115; Tomasz Urzykowski, 60 lat warszawskiej Starówki. Dlaczego Bierut zgodził się na odbudowę? 20 July 2013, https://warszawa.wyborcza.pl/warszawa/1,54420,14300621,60_lat_warszawskiej_Starowki__Dlaczego_Bierut_zgodzil.html

22. Thum 2003, 197–8, 222–4.

23. Thum 2003, 197; Thum 2003, 191–209.

24. Thum 2003, 58.

25. Ciesielski 2008.

26. Zielinski 2009, 190–1; Cramsey and Wittenberg 2016; Zielinski 2009, 198; Prażmowska 2003, ch. 7; T. Snyder 1999, 2004 ch. 9; Dmowski 2014.

27. Polonsky 2013, 380, 381; The 75th anniversary of the tragic events of 4 July 1946 from the Western perspective, 7 July 2021, https://ipn.gov.pl/en/news/8426,The-75th-anniversary-of-the-tragic-events-of-4-July-1946-from-the-Western-perspe.html; Polonsky 2013, 382; Polonsky 2013, 383.

28. Zaremba 1997; Table 3.41 of Eberhardt 2015, page 141, gives estimated (not census) 1950 figure of 97.8% for proportion of ethnic Poles.

Chapter 5. The Whole Nation Is Building Its Capital City

1. Jozefacka 2011, 172–5; Piątek 2020, ch. 3.

2. Meng 2015, 77.

3. Jan Minorski, Po Krajowej Naradzie Partyjnej Architektów, *Stolica* 28, 10 July 1949, 4; Arnold Bartetzky in Rampley 2012, 105; Crowley 1994; Arnold Bartetzky in Rampley 2012, 105.

4. Crowley 1994; David I. Snyder in Pendlebury et al. 2015, 175; *Stolica* 17 July 1949, 3–7; Spałek 2005.

5. Bolesław Bierut, Zbudujemy Nową Warszawę – Stolicę Państwa Socjalistycznego, *Stolica* 29, 17 July 1949, 3–7; Crowley 1994; Polonsky 2013, 396–7; Zaremba 2001, 199–201; Bierut: 'pudełkatowych domów', *Stolica* 13 July 1947, 6, 7; Poliński: 'Pudełkowa żydowszczyzna', Oblicze architektoniczne miast . . . polskich, *Prosto z Mostu* 14–15, 2–9 April 1939, 22.

6. Motas 2010; Maria Zakrzewska, Jan Poliński 1907–02–22 – 1977–09–30, https://www.ipsb.nina.gov.pl/a/biografia/jan-polinski; Piątek 2020, ch. 16; Davis 2021, ch. 3.
7. Jan Zachwatowicz, Odbudowa Starego Miasta, *Stolica* 52, 25 December 1949, 4–5; Mordyński 2021, 165–6.
8. Popiołek 2016, 29; 120 lat temu urodził się Jan Zachwatowicz, rekonstruktor Zamku Królewskiego w Warszawie. 4 March 2020, https://dzieje.pl/aktualnosci/120-lat-temu-urodzil-sie-jan-zachwatowicz-rekonstruktor-zamku-krolewskiego-w-warszawie
9. Adam Wolmar, W trosce o rynek staromiejski, *Kurjer Warszawski* 152, 3 June 1928, 13–14.
10. Zachwatowicz 1938a.
11. Bruce and Creighton 2006; Creighton 2007; Bandarin and van Oers 2012, 7.
12. Ruskin 1849, 179–80; Ruskin 1849, 178.
13. Dehio 1905; Koshar 1998, 31–4; Riegl 1982; Ahmer 2020.
14. Cameron 2008; Historic Centre of Warsaw, http://whc.unesco.org/en/list/30
15. The Athens Charter for the Restoration of Historic Monuments – 1931, https://www.icomos.org/en/167-the-athens-charter-for-the-restoration-of-historic-monuments; Zachwatowicz 1938a, 1953b; Lorentz 1966.
16. Zachwatowicz 1946b.
17. Arnold Bartetzky in Rampley 2012, 95–7.
18. Jan Zachwatowicz, Odbudowa Starego Miasta, *Stolica* 52, 25 December 1949, 4–5; Bolesław Bierut, Zbudujemy nową Warszawę – stolicę państwa sojcalistycznego, *Stolica* 29, 17 July 1949, 3–7; J. Majewski 2017, 43.
19. Żuk 2017.
20. Tomasz Urzykowski, 60 lat warszawskiej Starówki. Dlaczego Bierut zgodził się na odbudowę? 20 July 2013, https://warszawa.wyborcza.pl/warszawa/1,54420,14300621,60_lat_warszawskiej_Starowki__Dlaczego_Bierut_zgodzil.html
21. Puget 1984.
22. Biegański 1937.
23. Zachwatowicz 1946b.
24. Stanisław Żaryn, Dzieje odbudowy Warszawskiego Starego Miasta, 22 July 1953, *Stolica* 30, 4–10; Józef Vogtman, https://www.1944.pl/powstancze-biogramy/jozef-vogtman,47122.html; Borecka et al., 1982, 112–13.
25. *Stolica* 13 July 1947, 7.
26. Skalimowski 2014; Polski Komitet Wyzwolenia Narodowego 1959 (1944).
27. Martyn 2001, 206; Knap 2013, 58.
28. Czapska 1989; P. Majewski 2009, 53–4.
29. Górski 1990, 401; P. Majewski 2009, 168.
30. Lorentz 1986, 36–7.
31. Sejm uchwalił odbudowę Zamku, *Stolica* 17 July 1949, 2; P. Majewski 2009, 162; Polska Kronika Filmowa 30 1949, *Czyn lipcowy Warszawy*, http://repozytorium.fn.org.pl/?q=pl/node/5375
32. Zachwatowicz 1938b; Martyn 2001, 208–11.
33. P. Majewski 2009, 58.

Chapter 6. The Stones Speak Polish

1. Polacy ze Stambułu odbudowują kamienice na Starym Mieście, *Stolica* 26, 27 June 1948, 5; Popiołek 2016, 137; Popiołek 2016, 160, 163.
2. Emil Kaliski, Wrocław wrócił do Polski – 'Wrocław has returned to Poland' – *Skarpa Warszawska* 9, 3 March 1946, 4–5; Thum 2003, 128–30.
3. Thum 2003, xii; Davies and Moorhouse 2003, 29, 36; Thum 2003, xxv.

4. Thum 2003, 94–5; Pietraszewski and Törnquist-Plewa 2016; Thum 2003, 94–5; Thum 2003, 98.
5. Thum 2003, 90; Davies and Moorhouse 2003, 409; Steinhaus 1992, 338; Tokarska-Bakir 2013b; Thum 2003, 123–4.
6. Thum 2003, 186–7; Demshuk 2012.
7. Emil Kaliski, Wrocław wrócił do Polski, *Skarpa Warszawska* 9, 3 March 1946, 4–5.
8. Thum 2003, 333, 335; Muszyński 2007 (transl. MK); Thum 2003, 203–4; Wrocław author Marek Krajewski, interviewed in Z Wrocławia do Breslau, 9 August 2014, https://www.rp.pl/artykul/1131742-Z-Wroclawia-do-Breslau.html
9. Thum 2003, 365; Thum 2003, 130; Tomasz Urzykowski, 60 lat warszawskiej Starówki. Dlaczego Bierut zgodził się na odbudowę? 20 July 2013, https://warszawa.wyborcza.pl/warszawa/1,54420,14300621,60_lat_warszawskiej_Starowki__Dlaczego_Bierut_zgodzil.html
10. Thum 2003, 326; Thum 2003, 373–4; Centralny Zarząd Muzeów i Ochrony Zabytków 1957; Thum 2003, 129–30.
11. Thum 2003, 355–6; Kozieł 2011; KUL po II wojnie światowej - Witold Kleiner - fragment relacji świadka historii, https://biblioteka.teatrnn.pl/dlibra/show-content/publication/edition/46058?id=46058&dirids=1; Chabiera 2020, 95–6.
12. Demshuk 2021; Thum 2003, 353–8; Czerner and Medeksza 2008.

Chapter 7. We Will Come to Believe in It Ourselves

1. Belotto in Warsaw, *Burlington Magazine* 80(470), 1942, 106–13.
2. Czapska 1989; Piotr Biegański, Stare Miasto. Pomnik kultury narodowej, 22 July 1953, *Stolica* 30, 2–3.
3. P. Majewski 2009, 196, 201; Borecka et al. 1982, 60, 119.
4. P. Majewski 2009, 195; Stefan Chwin in Kerski 2014, 24–5; Borecka et al. 1982, 42; P. Majewski 2009, 195.
5. P. Majewski 2009, 195.
6. Kronika odbudowy, *Stolica* 52, 25 December 1949, 3; J. Majewski 2017, 53; P. Majewski 2009, 197–8.
7. P. Majewski 2009, 199; Mieczysław Strzelecki in Borecka et al. 1982, 41.
8. Starówka – własność każdego z nas', Jacek Wołowski, 22 July 1953, *Życie Warszawy* 173, 8; Radośnie i dumnie odchodził cały naród polski, 23 July 1953, *Życie Warszawy* 174, 1.
9. Demshuk 2020.
10. Prof. Jan Zachwatowicz - audycja Jerzego Mikke z cyklu 'Wizerunki ludzi myślących', 14 January 1979, https://www.polskieradio.pl/39/156/Artykul/909950,Jan-Zachwatowicz-udaremnil-zamach-Niemcow-na-kulture-polska; P. Majewski 2009, 200; Braun and Hogenberg 2015, 698–9; St John's Cathedral and the Jesuits' Church in Warsaw, https://commons.wikimedia.org/wiki/File:John_Cathedral_Jesuits_Warsaw_1627.jpg; Górski 1990, 413.
11. Górski 1990, 413; P. Majewski 2009, 54.
12. J. Majewski 2017, 43.
13. Urszula Zielińska-Meissner, Czyli o barwach Starej Warszawy, December 2011, *Krajobraz Warszawski* 127, 1–12.
14. Goldsmid 1886, 23–7; Mike Dash, On the Trail of the Warsaw Basilisk, 23 July 2012, *Smithsonian Magazine*, https://www.smithsonianmag.com/history/on-the-trail-of-the-warsaw-basilisk-5691840/
15. Bazyliszek, 30 November 2016, https://varsisava.pl/bazyliszek/; Słomczyński 2007; Żeromska 1994, 204; Roman Padlewski, https://www.1944.pl/powstancze-biogramy/roman-padlewski,33148.html
16. D.K., Święto Odrodzenia w Warszawie, *Stolica* 31, 2 August 1953, 2; N.W., Kontrasty na Starym Mieście, *Stolica* 31, 2 August 1953, 10.

17. Lorentz 1966.
18. *Warszawa w liczbach 1939*, 16.
19. J. Majewski 2017, 43; Tomasz Urzykowski, 60 lat warszawskiej Starówki. Dlaczego Bierut zgodził się na odbudowę? 20 July 2013, https://warszawa.wyborcza.pl/warszawa/1,54420,14300621,60_lat_warszawskiej_Starowki__Dlaczego_Bierut_zgodzil.html; J. Majewski 2017, 43.
20. Borecka et al., 118–19.
21. Martyn 2001, 193 (quote translated by M. Kohn), 216 n38.

Würzburg

Chapter 8. Christmas Trees in Lent

1. Knell 2003, ch. 2.
2. Hansen 2020, ch. 6.
3. Karl-Georg Rötter, Neue Studie: 4000 statt 5000 Tote am 16. März 1945? 19 July 2016, https://www.mainpost.de/regional/wuerzburg/neue-studie-4000-statt-5000-tote-am-16-maerz-1945-art-9294563
4. Roland Flade, Ostern 1945: Der sinnlose Kampf um Würzburg, 16 December 2008, https://www.mainpost.de/regional/wuerzburg/ostern-1945-der-sinnlose-kampf-um-wuerzburg-art-4879909; Torsten Schleicher, Augenzeugenberichte: Wie die US-Army 1945 Würzburg eroberte, 28 March 2018, https://www.mainpost.de/regional/wuerzburg/
5. Roland Flade, 26 June 2020, Würzburg 1945: Als die Stadtteile eigene Bürgermeister bekamen, https://www.mainpost.de/regional/wuerzburg/wuerzburg-1945-als-die-stadtteile-eigene-buergermeister-bekamen-art-10463066; Jähner 2021, ch. 6; Friedhelm Ruf, 31 December 2016, Kohlenklau mit Gottes Segen, https://rp-online.de/kultur/kohlenklau-mit-gottes-segen_aid-21172981
6. Roland Flade, 2 March 2006, U-Boot-Stahl für Würzburgs Dom, https://www.mainpost.de/regional/wuerzburg/U-Boot-Stahl-fuer-Wuerzburgs-Dom-art-3455958
7. *The Bomber's Baedeker* 1944, 742–5; Hohn 1994; Johnson 1995, 237.
8. Hohn 1994.
9. Lambourne 2001, 147; Overy 2013, 328.
10. Harris 2005, 147.
11. Johnson 1995, 174.
12. Johnson 1995, 228–9, 242–7.
13. Johnson 1995, 247.
14. Johnson 1995, 248; Neue Publikation des Stadtarchivs: Das Massengrab vor dem Hauptfriedhof, 6 May 2020, https://www.wuerzburg.de/buerger/presse/aktuelle-pressemitteilungen/526152.Neue-Publikation-des-Stadtarchivs-Das-Massengrab-vor-dem-Hauptfriedhof.html
15. Johnson 1995, 248.
16. Overy 2013, 160.
17. Overy 2013, 328–9; Hohn 1994.
18. Harris 2005, 105; Lambourne 2001, 156; Webster and Frankland 1961 vol. 1, 391.
19. Jeiler et al. 2011; Hanseatic City of Lübeck, http://whc.unesco.org/en/list/272
20. Harris 2005, 105; Duwel and Gutschow 2013, 146–8.
21. Overy 2013, 118; Arthur Harris, Despatch on War Operations, pars 34, 33, in Mace and Grehan 2014.
22. *The Bomber's Baedeker* 1944, 446–8; Chernow 1995, 539; Glendinning 2013, 244–5. According to Chernow 1995, 524, Warburg contacted the President of the Red Cross (whom Chernow misidentifies) after failing to persuade Arthur Harris to call off the attack. See also Uwe Bahnsen, Der Mann, der Lübeck vor den Bomben bewahrte,

25 August 2013, https://www.welt.de/regionales/hamburg/article119322471/ Der-Mann-der-Luebeck-vor-den-Bomben-bewahrte.html for another version; Eric-Warburg-Brücke, https://www.luebeck.de/de/stadtleben/tourismus/luebeck/sehensw uerdigkeiten/bruecken-von-luebeck/eric-warburg-bruecke.html

23. Arthur Harris, Despatch on War Operations, par. 35, in Mace and Grehan 2014; Overy 2013, 327; Overy 2013, 334–5; Koshar 1998, 211.
24. Overy 2013, 309–10.
25. *The Bomber's Baedeker* 1944, 546.
26. Arthur Harris, Despatch on War Operations, par. 167, in Mace and Grehan 2014; Overy 2013, 396; Overy 2013, 476, discusses a range of estimates and arrives at a figure of 353,000.
27. Overy 2013, 396, 394; Biddle 2008; Overy 2013, 390.
28. Published in English as *On the Natural History of Destruction*, Sebald 2004. Peter Schneider, The Germans Are Breaking An Old Taboo, *New York Times* 18 January 2003, https://www.nytimes.com/2003/01/18/books/the-germans-are-breaking-an-old-taboo.html; Biddle 2008; Moeller 2006; Childers 2005; Nolan 2005; Jörg Arnold. Review of Friedrich, Jörg, *Der Brand. Deutschland im Bombenkrieg 1940-1945*. H-German, H-Net Reviews. November 2003, http://www.h-net.org/reviews/showrev. php?id=8358.
29. Jörg Arnold. Review of Friedrich, Jörg, *Der Brand. Deutschland im Bombenkrieg 1940-1945*. H-German, H-Net Reviews. November 2003, http://www.h-net.org/reviews/ showrev.php?id=8358; Terror from the sky, 13 December 2012 (originally published in *Exberliner* 20, October 2004), https://www.exberliner.com/features/people/terror-from-the-sky/
30. Würzburg vor 70 und 100 Jahren, https://www.facebook.com/Würzburg-vor-70-und-100-Jahren-155451194613156/; Interview, 26 September 2020.
31. Friedrich 2006, 272.
32. Friedrich 2006, 271.
33. Rafalski 1986, 16.
34. Jörg Arnold. Review of Friedrich, Jörg, *Der Brand. Deutschland im Bombenkrieg 1940-1945*. H-German, H-Net Reviews. November 2003, http://www.h-net.org/reviews/ showrev.php?id=8358

Chapter 9. The U-Boat Cathedral Roof

1. Hubert Gross, https://wuerzburgwiki.de/wiki/Hubert_Groß; Němec 2018.
2. Gerken 2004, 363.
3. Antonia Bieber in Skowronska et al. 2012, 59; Hubert Gross, https://wuerzburgwiki. de/wiki/Hubert_Groß
4. Gerken 2004, 259 n971; Atlas zum Wiederaufbau: Würzburg, https://www.bavaria-thek.bayern/wiederaufbau/orte/detail/wuerzburg/65; Hubert Gross, https://wuerz-burgwiki.de/wiki/Hubert_Groß
5. Roland Flade, Der Wiederaufbau des zerstörten Würzburg: Das Falkenhaus als „architektonische Lüge"? 15 November 2018, https://www.facebook.com/permalink. php?id=155451194613156&story_fbid=1124779174347015; Piątek 2020, ch. 2; P. Majewski 2009, 51; Antonia Bieber in Skowronska et al. 2012, 59; Jan Zachwatowicz, Odbudowa Starego Miasta, *Stolica* 52, 25 December 1949, 4–5.
6. Skilton 2008, 106.
7. Skilton 2008, 106–10.
8. Skilton 2008, 111–12.
9. Skilton 2008, 104; Würzburg Residence: Building history, https://www.residenz-wuerzburg.de/englisch/residenz/history.htm

10. Roland Flade, U-Boot-Stahl für Würzburgs Dom, 2 March 2006, https://www.main-post.de/regional/wuerzburg/u-boot-stahl-fuer-wuerzburgs-dom-art-3455958; Alice Natter, 20. Februar 1946: Die Katastrophe danach, 20 February 2016, https://www.mainpost.de/regional/wuerzburg/20-februar-1946-die-katastrophe-danach-art-9129166; Stippler 2012, 36–40.

11. Roland Flade, Der Wiederaufbau des zerstörten Würzburg: Das Falkenhaus als „architektonische Lüge"? 15 November 2018, https://www.facebook.com/permalink.php?id=155451194613156&story_fbid=1124779174347015; Das Pleicher Handwerkerhaus in Würzburg, https://www.verschoenerungsverein-wuerzburg.de/liegenschaften/liegenschaft-pleicher-handwerkerhaus/

Rothenburg ob der Tauber

Chapter 10. A Wall Round the Whole Place

1. Dwyer 2009, 118–30.
2. Hagen 2006, 233.
3. Dieter Balb, 31. März 1945: Eine Staffel von 16 amerikanischen Flugzeugen musste Rothenburg als Ausweichziel angreifen – Bomber-Pilot später: „Ich kannte die Stadt nicht", http://www.rothenburg-unterm-hakenkreuz.de/31-maerz-1945-eine-staffel-von-16-amerikanischen-flugzeugen-musste-ro%c2%adthenburg-als-ausweichziel-angreifen-bomber-pilot-spaeter-ich-kannte-die-stadt-nicht/; Combat Chronology of the US Army Air Forces, March 1945, https://media.defense.gov/2010/May/25/2001330283/-1/-1/0/AFD-100525-035.pdf
4. Maurer 1983, 10; MacDonald 1993, Map XV; Hans Wirsching, Die Bombardierung der Stadt am Karsamstag 1945 forderte 39 Tote. Wie die Feuerwehr die Brandherde bekämpfte und das Rathaus zu retten versuchte (originally written in 1950), http://www.rothenburg-unterm-hakenkreuz.de/die-bombardierung-der-stadt-am-karfreitag-1945-forderte-39-tote-wie-die-feuerwehr-die-brandherde-bekaempfte-und-das-rathaus-zu-retten-versuchte/
5. Rovere 1961.
6. Bird 2017, 233–4; Letter from McCloy quoted by Dwyer 2009, 120.
7. Chernow 1995, 576; Overy 2013, 467.
8. Rothenburg Wine Ceremony, *Information Bulletin* (Office of the US High Commissioner for Germany Office of Public Affairs) July 1950, 2.
9. Hagen 2005; Hagen 2006, 16; Hellmuth Möhring, personal communication.
10. Walker 1998, 7, 12; Hagen 2005; Hagen 2005.
11. Hagen 2006, 66–8; Charles W. Beck, Rothenburg, The City Time Forgot, *National Geographic* February 1926, 184–94.
12. Baedeker 1902, 148.
13. Möhring 2020, 63.
14. Unwin 1909, 89; Möhring 2020, 192–209; Temple Fortune House, 802–818 Finchley Road, London NW11.
15. Shackleton 1914, 8; Shackleton 1914 (3rd printing of 1913 edition), 10–11; Hagen 2006, 147.
16. Hagen 2004; The 'most German of towns': Hagen 2004, citing a late 1930s tourist brochure.
17. Wolf Stegemann, Zwischen NSDAP und Staat gab es einen von Hitler gewollten Kompetenzwirrwarr, doch die Partei war mächtiger. Struktur der Nazi-Partei, der 64 Prozent der Rothenburger angehörten, http://www.rothenburg-unterm-hakenkreuz.de/zwischen-nsdap-und-staat-gab-es-einen-von-hitler-gewollten-kompetenzwirrwarr-doch-die-partei-war-maechtiger-struktur-der-nazi-partei-der-64-prozent-der-rothenburger-angehoerten/
18. Hagen 2006, 285.

19. Rothenburg ob der Tauber, https://www.jewishvirtuallibrary.org/rothenburg-ob-der-tauber; Antisemitismus IV: Rothenburger Juden wurden noch vor dem Pogrom im November 1938 aus der Stadt getrieben. Spuren führen nach Auschwitz, Riga, Theresienstadt, http://www.rothenburg-unterm-hakenkreuz.de/antisemitismus-iv-rothenburger-juden-wurden-noch-vor-dem-pogrom-im-november-1938-aus-der-stadt-getrieben-spuren-fuehren-nach-auschwitz-riga-theresienstadt/
20. Barrier 1999, 259–66; Allan 1999, 78.
21. Conrad 2016.
22. L. Snyder 1996, ch. 2.

Chapter 11. Half-Timber Angst

1. Shackleton 1914, 189; Mace and Grehan 2014, 35, 56; Gregor 2000.
2. Berger and Lauterbach 2009.
3. Ullrich 2017.
4. Berger and Lauterbach 2009.
5. Hagen 2005; Hagen 2006, 238.
6. Wolf Stegemann, Adolf Hitlers überraschender Besuch 1935 – So wie er kam, war er nach einer Stunde wieder weg – nur gesättigt! http://www.rothenburg-unterm-hakenkreuz.de/adolf-hitlers-ueberraschender-besuch-1935-so-wie-er-kam-war-er-nach-einer-stunde-wieder-weg-nur-gesaettigt/
7. Hagen 2006, 234; Shackleton 1914, 189.
8. Confino 1993.
9. Hagen 2004; Rosenfeld 2000, 24; Arnold 2011.
10. Hagen 2005.
11. Hagen 2006, 239, 238.
12. Wolf Stegemann, Für den NS-Bürgermeister Friedrich Schmidt gab es 1945 kaum eine Zäsur. Er blieb seiner Gesinnung treu und saß 1952 wieder im Stadtrat – für die rechte „Deutsche Gemeinschaft", http://www.rothenburg-unterm-hakenkreuz.de/fuer-den-ns-buergermeister-friedrich-schmidt-gab-es-1945-kaum-eine-zaesur-er-blieb-seiner-gesinnung-treu-und-sass-1952-wieder-im-stadtrat-fuer-die-rechte-deutsche-gemein-schaft/; Profil: Deutsche Gemeinschaft (DG), https://www.apabiz.de/archiv/material/Profile/DG.htm; Hagen 2006, 253.
13. Ulrich Hertz, Ernst Unbehauen – Seine NS-Verstrickung und antisemitischen Hetz-Plakate wirkten sich für ihn nach 1945 nicht negativ aus. Doch ist er ein Stück umstrittener Rothenburger Kultur, http://www.rothenburg-unterm-hakenkreuz.de/ernst-unbehauen-seine-ns-verstrickung-und-antisemitischen-hetz-plakate-wirkten-sich-fuer-ihn-nach-1945-nicht-negativ-aus-doch-ist-er-ein-stueck-umstrittener-rothenburger-kultur/
14. Interview, 7 October 2020.
15. Berger, Hanns-Jürgen and Lauterbach, Tobias, 2009, Rothenburg ob der Tauber – der Wiederaufbau nach dem Zweiten Weltkrieg: eine städtebaulich-denkmalpflegerische Analyse, Verl. des Vereins Alt-Rothenburg; Interview, 25 January 2021.
16. In *Neuromancer* (1984).
17. Hagen 2006, 293–4.
18. Hagen 2006, 292, 288.

Vilnius

Chapter 12. What the Iron Wolf Meant

1. Venclova 2003, 13; Venclova 2003, 13; Vaitkevičius 2004; Bojtar 1999, 323–6; Kęstutis Gudmantas, 2 September 2016, Legend of Vilnius: facts and fiction, https://lithuaniatribune.com/fact-and-fiction-in-the-founding-legend-of-vilnius/

2. Dubonis 2000; Valionienė 2017; Rowell 2014, 134–7; Bojtar 1999, 323; Kęstutis Gudmantas, Legend of Vilnius: facts and fiction, 2 September 2016, https://lithuaniatribune.com/fact-and-fiction-in-the-founding-legend-of-vilnius/
3. Döblin 1991, 94.
4. Rindzevičiūtė 2010; Śledziewski and Bukowski 1938; Sigita Gasparavičienė, Katedros aikštė Vilniuje, https://www.archeonas.lt/index.php/lt/katedros-aikste-vilniuje; Briedis 2005, 322 n118.
5. Śledziewski and Bukowski 1938; Kieniewicz 1938; Antanavičiūtė 2012, 335–9.
6. Sigita Gasparavičienė, Katedros aikštė Vilniuje, https://www.archeonas.lt/index.php/lt/katedros-aikste-vilniuje
7. Antanavičiūtė 2012, 322; Wicher 2020; Eindetas et al. 2015, 221.
8. Lieven 1993, 66–8; Andreski 1981, 189.
9. Weeks 2008; Antanavičiūtė 2012, 324; Antanavičiūtė interview, 10 February 2021.
10. Antanavičiūtė 2012, 337.
11. Rindzevičiūtė 2010.
12. Karolis Kučiauskas, Karo Padarinių Vertinimas Vilniaus Senamiestyje 1944 m.: Ištakos, Schemos,Vertintojai,https://leidiniu.archfondas.lt/alf-05/karolis-kuciauskas-karo-padariniu-vertinimas-vilniaus-senamiestyje-1944-m
13. Rindzevičiūtė 2010; Rindzevičiūtė 2010; Vilniuje įmūryta pirmoji atstatomų Valdovų rūmų plyta, 16 March 2004, https://www.delfi.lt/kultura/naujienos/vilniuje-imuryta-pirmoji-atstatomu-valdovu-rumu-plyta.d?id=3932986; Symbolic opening of the Palace of the Grand Dukes of Lithuania, https://www.valdovurumai.lt/en/palace-history/historical-outline
14. Symbolic opening of the Palace of the Grand Dukes of Lithuania, https://www.valdovurumai.lt/en/palace-history/historical-outline
15. Briedis 2008, 60–1.
16. Srebrakowski 2020; Standl and Krupickaitė 2004; Weeks 2006; Miłosz 1981, 54.
17. In Venclova 2009, 224; Briedis 2008, 60–1; Venclova 2003, 7.
18. Interview, 10 February 2021.

Chapter 13. Wilno, Vilna, Vilne, Vilnius

1. Lazgi 2013. According to the 1931 census, the population was 50 per cent ethnically Polish and 33 per cent Jewish.
2. In Venclova 2009, 224.
3. Szívós 2015; Stravinskiene 2012.
4. Kvietkauskas 2021; Laučkaitė 2021.
5. Kuznitz 2017; Kłos 1937, 196; Kuznitz 2021.
6. Račiūnienė 2015; Eidintas et al. 2015, 237–40; T. Snyder 2004, 84–7; Weeks 2015, 197–202; Lipphardt 2008.
7. Sliesoriūnas 2009.
8. Borodziej 2006, 55-6; Piotr Niwiński, 2004, Przed Warszawą było Wilno, Biuletyn Instytutu Pamięci Narodowej 8–9(43–4); Ilona Lewandowska, Wileńskie ślady „OstrejBramy",15July2016,https://kurierwilenski.lt/2016/07/15/wilenskie-slady-ostrej-bramy/
9. Borodziej 2006, 56–7; Srebrakowski 2020.
10. Vitalija Stravinskienė in Antoni Radczenko, Skutki repatriacji są bolesne i długoterminowe, 21 December 2019, https://kurierwilenski.lt/2019/12/21/skutki-repatriacji-sa-bolesne-i-dlugoterminowe/; Weeks 2006.
11. Katarzyna Jarymowska, Ryszard Adamowicz: Nasza „patria" była w Wilnie, 15 January 2019, http://www.wilnoteka.lt/artykul/ryszard-adamowicz-nasza-patria-byla-w-wilnie; Roman Daszczyński, Paweł Adamowicz. Życie i los gdańszczanina, https://www.gdansk.pl/pawel-adamowicz; Kerski 2014, 210.

12. Weeks 2006, 2008.
13. Miłosz 1992, 40–1.
14. Davoliūtė 2014a.
15. Davoliūtė 2014a; Srebrakowski 2020.
16. Muth 2008.
17. Drėmaitė 2009, 36.
18. Drėmaitė 2009, 37; Weeks 2015, 192.
19. Davoliūtė 2014b, 3, 59; Davoliūtė 2014a.
20. Eidintas et al. 2015, 264; Drėmaitė 2019.
21. Drėmaitė 2019.
22. Drėmaitė 2019.
23. The story of Raeapteek, http://raeapteek.ee/en/our-story; The tale of Tallinn's most famous Christmas tree, https://www.visitestonia.com/en/why-estonia/the-tale-of-tallinns-most-famous-christmas-tree
24. Puustak 2012; Üprus 1972; Hansar 2012.
25. Hansar 2012.
26. Weeks 2008.
27. Rindzevičiūtė 2013; Memorial Museum of Holocaust in Lithuania and Vilna Ghetto, https://www.jmuseum.lt/en/about-the-museum-3/i/220/memorial-museum-of-holo-caust-in-lithuania-and-vilna-ghetto/; Sutzkever, Avrom, https://yivoencyclopedia.org/article.aspx/Sutzkever_Avrom; Kaczerginski, Shmerke, https://yivoencyclopedia.org/article.aspx/Kaczerginski_Shmerke
28. Memorial Museum of Holocaust in Lithuania and Vilna Ghetto, https://www.jmuseum.lt/en/about-the-museum-3/i/220/memorial-museum-of-holocaust-in-lithuania-and-vilna-ghetto/; Sutzkever, Avrom, https://yivoencyclopedia.org/article.aspx/Sutzkever_Avrom; Kaczerginski, Shmerke, https://yivoencyclopedia.org/article.aspx/Kaczerginski_Shmerke
29. Kerski 2014, 210–11.
30. Roman Daszczyński, Paweł Adamowicz. Życie i los gdańszczanina, https://www.gdansk.pl/pawel-adamowicz. This tribute page includes a family photo showing Paweł Adamowicz, his father and one of his daughters in front of the Gate of Dawn in Vilnius. Each is holding up a piece of paper stating their year and place of birth: '1928 Wilno', '1965 Gdańsk', '2003 Gdańsk'.
31. Adamowicz 2008, 9; Obracht-Prondzyński and Łuczeczko 2019.
32. Jacek Friedrich in Rampley 2012, 123; Bossak-Herbst 2011; Jacek Dominiczak in Kerski 2014, 276.
33. Interviewed in Z Wrocławia do Breslau, 9 August 2014, https://www.rp.pl/artykul/1131742-Z-Wroclawia-do-Breslau.html; Był Sobie Gdańsk, https://gdansk.gedanopedia.pl/gdansk/?title=BYŁ_SOBIE_GDAŃSK
34. Donald Tusk o swoim Gdańsku: Mam tu wszystko, co najświętsze, to, co się kocha, 27 November 2014, https://trojmiasto.wyborcza.pl/trojmiasto/1,35612,17035048, Donald_Tusk_o_swoim_Gdansku__Mam_tu_wszystko__co_najswietsze_.html; Adamowicz 2008; Kerski 2014.
35. Spod tynku patrzy Breslau, 5 September 2020, http://fundacja-karpowicz.org/spod-tynku-patrzy-breslau/. See also Blacker 2019, 'Reading the Walls' in chapter 1; Pietraszewski and Törnquist-Plewa 2016; Bossak-Herbst 2011; Jacek Friedrich in Rampley 2012, 127; Peter Oliver Loew in Kerski 2014, 128–41; Dymnicka and Szczepański 2016; Obracht-Prondzyński and Łuczeczko 2019; „Miłość może tylko łączyć". V Trójmiejski Marsz Równości z udziałem prezydent Dulkiewicz, 17 May 2019, https://www.gdansk.pl/wiadomosci/milosc-moze-tylko-laczyc-v-trojmiejski-marsz-rownosci-z-udzialem-magdaleny-adamowicz,a,145917

Middle Europe

Chapter 14. Stumbling Stones

1. Spenden. Profiteren. Erleben. https://www.kulturerbebayern.de/judengasse/spenden. html
2. Hagen 2006, 248. 'Virtual 3D tour' of Judengasse 10: https://www.kulturerbebayern.de/ blog/artikel/virtueller-rundgang.html
3. History, http://www.shalomeuropa.de/history.html; Klei 2020; Wurzburg, Germany, https://www.jewishvirtuallibrary.org/wuerzburg; Wurzburg, Germany, https://www. jewishvirtuallibrary.org/wuerzburg
4. Hagen 2006, 257.
5. Hagen 2006, 281.
6. Hagen 2006, 280–3.
7. Judengasse, https://www.alt-rothenburg.de/judengasse-10-2/; Judengasse 10, https:// www.alt-rothenburg.de/judengasse-10/; Judengasse 12, https://www.alt-rothenburg. de/judengasse-12/; Auch der Freistaat trägt seinen Teil zur Wiederbelebung der Judengasse 10 bei, https://www.kulturerbebayern.de/blog/artikel/auch-der-freistaat-traegt-seinen-teil-zur-wiederbelebung-der-judengasse-10-bei.html
8. Macdonald 2013, 193.
9. Bramy Nieba – promocja książki i spotkanie z Marią Piechotkową | Muzeum POLIN, 25 April 2016, https://www.youtube.com/watch?v=S6xeqMXxXeU
10. Pogrzeb architekt Marii Piechotki 16 grudnia w kościele św. Wincentego na Bródnie, 4 December 2020, https://dzieje.pl/wiadomosci/pogrzeb-architekt-marii-piechotki-16-grudnia-w-kosciele-sw-wincentego-na-brodnie; Bramy Nieba – promocja książki i spotkanie z Marią Piechotkową | Muzeum POLIN, 25 April 2016, https://www. youtube.com/watch?v=S6xeqMXxXeU; Filip Lech, Maria Piechotkowa: Dlaczego drewniane bóżnice powstały właśnie w Polsce? 13 October 2016, https://culture.pl/pl/ artykul/maria-piechotkowa-dlaczego-drewniane-boznice-powstaly-wlasnie-w-polsce
11. Piechotka and Piechotka 2004.
12. Maria Piechotkowa – commemoration, 11 December 2020, https://www.polin.pl/en/ maria-piechotkowa-commemoration; Our mission, https://www.handshouse.org/our-mission; In Honor of Maria and Kazimierz Piechotka, 21 January 2021, https://www. handshouse.org/blog/2021/o1/21maria-and-kaimierz-piechotka; Replicating the Gwozdziec wooden synagogue, https://www.handshouse.org/work#/gwozdziec/; Gwozdziec Re!construction – replica roof of the synagogue installed at the Museum! https://www.youtube.com/watch?v=MMlbhLlIqFg
13. Lachert 1949.
14. Lachert 1949; Meng 2011, 79–81; Świątek 2012; Klekot 2015; Matyjaszek 2016.
15. Klekot 2015; On the symbolism of bricks and ruins in Warsaw, see Elżanowski 2010; Konstanty Gebert in Lehrer and Meng 2015, 236–7; Biuro w kamienicy, 2 July 2013, https://sztuka-architektury.pl/article/4071/biuro-w-kamienicy. In Janiczka and Wilczyk 2013, the editors present and discuss their photographic study of the area of the former Jewish district, the 'Other City'.
16. Tytus Brzozowski, Jewish Warsaw, https://tytusbrzozowski.pl/en/murals/jewish-warsaw/; Tomasz Urzykowski, Nowy mural w centrum Warszawy. Przypomina o żydowskiej społeczności Dzielnicy Północnej, 9 October 2020, https://warszawa. wyborcza.pl/warszawa/7,54420,26383468,nowy-mural-w-centrum-warszawy-przypomina-o-zydowskiej-spolecznosci.html
17. The Camnitzer family lived at Breite Straße 41, https://www.stolpersteine-luebeck. de/n/en/main/location-addresses/breite-strasse-41-family-camnitzer.html
18. News, http://www.stolpersteine.eu/en/news/
19. FAQ, http://www.stolpersteine.eu/en/faq/

20. Sven Felix Kellerhoff, In München wachsen Stolpersteine jetzt in die Höhe, 31 July 2018, https://www.welt.de/geschichte/article180269598/Erinnerungspolitik-In-Muenchen-wachsen-Stolpersteine-jetzt-in-die-Hoehe.html
21. W odpowiedzi na informacje zawarte w artykule dotyczącym „kamieni pamięci o ofiarach Holocaustu", 30 October 2019, https://ipn.gov.pl/pl/dla-mediow/komu nikaty/80628,W-odpowiedzi-na-informacje-zawarte-w-artykule-dotyczacym-kamieni-pamieci-o-ofiar.html; Anna Gmiterek-Zabłocka, Nora Lerner z Tel Awiwu, której rodzina zginęła w Auschwitz, walczy o kamienie pamięci w Krakowie, 9 November 2019, https://www.tokfm.pl/Tokfm/7,103085,25393942,nora-lerner-z-tel-awiwu-ktorej-rodzina-zginela-w-auschwitz.html. On the issue of 'ethnicity/citizenship', see for example Poland's 2021 national census, which instructed respondents not to confuse nationality (narodowość) with citizenship: Lista pytań w NSP 2021, https://spis.gov.pl/lista-pytan-w-nsp-2021/.
22. Stola 2017; Kunicki 2005.
23. Obama angers Poles with 'death camp' remark, 30 May 2012, https://www.bbc.co.uk/news/world-europe-18264036
24. Dynner and Guesnet 2015, 14.

Lublin
Chapter 15. We Patiently Explain

1. Döblin 1991, 126.
2. Tomasz Pietrasiewicz, Idea projektu Dzieci żydowskie, https://teatrnn.pl/dzieci-zydowskie/idea-projektu-dzieci-zydowskie/; Pietrasiewicz 2017, 38–9.
3. Pietrasiewicz 2017, 40.
4. Jamiołkowska 1981; Adam Kopciowski in Zętar et al. 2006, 13.
5. Adam Kopciowski in Zętar et al. 2006, 15; Lublin: History, https://sztetl.org.pl/en/towns/l/264-lublin/99-history/137601-history-of-community; The Seer of Lublin – Yaakov Yitzhak haLevi Horowitz –Sternfeld, https://teatrnn.pl/lexicon/articles/the-seer-of-lublin-yaakov-yitzhak-halevi-horowitz-sternfeld/#the-seer-from-28-sze-roka-st
6. Piechotka and Piechotka 2004, 185–6.
7. The Displacement of the Jewish Inhabitants of German-Occupied Lublin Before the Creation of the Ghetto, https://teatrnn.pl/lexicon/articles/the-displacement-of-the-jewish-inhabitants-of-german-occupied-lublin-before-the-creation-of-the-ghetto-1/; Pietrasiewicz 2017, 5.
8. In the Bunkers during the Uprising, https://www.yadvashem.org/yv/en/exhibitions/warsaw_ghetto_testimonies/bunkers.asp; Wyburzanie dzielnicy żydowskiej na Podzamczu, https://teatrnn.pl/leksykon/artykuly/wyburzanie-dzielnicy-zydowskiej-na-podzamczu/
9. Lublin, Podzamcze i Czwartek (dwudziestolecie międzywojenne), https://teatrnn.pl/miejsca/mapa/lublin-podzamcze-czwartek-dwudziestolecie-miedzywojenne/; The Tragic City of Lublin, https://www.youtube.com/watch?v=tBgWznGxOe8
10. Wyburzanie dzielnicy żydowskiej na Podzamczu, https://teatrnn.pl/leksykon/artykuly/wyburzanie-dzielnicy-zydowskiej-na-podzamczu/
11. Lublin Castle, https://teatrnn.pl/lexicon/articles/lublin-castle/; Prison castle, https://zamek-lublin.pl/en/o-muzeum/prison-castle/; Więzienie na Zamku w Lublinie 1944-1954, https://teatrnn.pl/leksykon/artykuly/wiezienie-na-zamku-w-lublinie-1944-1954
12. Edward Hartwig – fotografie z odbudowy Lublina w 1954 roku, https://teatrnn.pl/leksykon/artykuly/edward-hartwig-fotografie-z-odbudowy-lublina-w-1954-roku/; Hartwig 1956, 7; Hartwig 1956, 8.
13. Hartwig 1956, 7; Zamkowy Square in Lublin, https://teatrnn.pl/lexicon/articles/zamkowy-square-in-lublin/

14. Narracje (nie)pamięci: Plac Zamkowy. Topografia palimpsestu (cz. 1) Joanna Zętar https://blog.teatrnn.pl/laboratorium-nn/narracje-niepamieci-1-plac-zamkowy-topografia-palimpsestu/; Panas 2004.
15. Ladd 2014.
16. Robert Kuwałek in Zętar et al. 2006, 69.
17. Zdrój na placu dworcowym PKS w Lublinie, https://teatrnn.pl/leksykon/artykuly/zdroj-na-placu-dworcowym-pks-w-lublinie/; Narracje (nie)pamięci: Plac Zamkowy. Topografia palimpsestu (cz. 1) Joanna Zętar https://blog.teatrnn.pl/laboratorium-nn/narracje-niepamieci-1-plac-zamkowy-topografia-palimpsestu/
18. *Lubelska Starówka*, dir. Bohdan Kosiński, 1956, https://www.youtube.com/watch?v=3N9tb-WgCyU
19. Szpulak 2019; Bohdan Kosiński, https://culture.pl/pl/tworca/bohdan-kosinski
20. Jamiołkowska 1981; *Warszawa w liczbach 1947*, 7; W 2020 roku w Lublinie ubyło ponad 2500 zameldowanych mieszkańców, https://gazeta.jawnylublin.pl/w-2020-roku-w-lublinie-ubylo-ponad-2500-zameldowanych-mieszkancow/; Jamiołkowska 1981.
21. Interview, 10 December 2020 (translated from Polish); see also photos in Jarzębowski 1981.
22. Interview, 10 December 2020 (translated from Polish).
23. Interview, 10 December 2020 (translated from Polish).
24. Pietrasiewicz 2019, 14–15. Teatr NN's story shares some of its historical and intercultural themes with that of Pogranicze (Borderland Foundation), which is based in a former synagogue in the town of Sejny, near the Lithuanian border, and was set up around the same time by people also involved in theatre: Ośrodek 'Pogranicze - sztuk, kultur, narodów', https://www.pogranicze.sejny.pl/; Czyżewski 2022; Pietrasiewicz 2017, 115.
25. Pietrasiewicz 2017, 153–95.
26. Pietrasiewicz 2017, 199; Pietrasiewicz 2017, 208.
27. Kubiszyn 2015; Döblin 1991, xiii. Aschheim 2008 discusses German Jews' perceptions of 'Eastern Jews'; see also Polonsky 2008.
28. Dylewski 2003; Tumulty i procesy o mord rytualny w Lublinie w XVII w., https://teatrnn.pl/leksykon/artykuly/tumulty-i-procesy-o-mord-rytualny-w-lublinie-w-xvii-w/
29. Tokarska-Bakir 2013a; Tokarska-Bakir 2019, 248; Pogrom kielecki, http://muzhp.pl/pl/e/1694/pogrom-kielecki; Michlic and Polonsky 2005; Tokarska-Bakir 2008, 40; Tokarska-Bakir 2019, 215.
30. Daniel Tilles, Jewish museum condemns Catholic university for not disciplining professor over ritual murder claims, 6 April 2021, https://notesfrompoland.com/2021/04/06/jewish-museum-condemns-catholic-university-for-not-disciplining-professor-over-ritual-murder-claims/; Adam Leszczyński, Ks. prof. Guz bredził o mordzie rytualnym. Dla KUL „nierozstrzygnięta dyskusja naukowa", 3 April 2021, https://oko.press/ks-prof-guz-bredzil-o-mordzie-rytualnym/. Joanna Tokarska-Bakir made her 2008 book freely available online as a response to the disciplinary commission's statement, at https://www.academia.edu/45646438/Legendy_o_krwi_Antropologia_przes%25C4%2585du. Her English-language 2019 book is also openly accessible, at https://library.oapen.org/bitstream/handle/20.500.12657/42402/978363 1789445.pdf.
31. Daniel Tilles, The "compelling need for truth": reflections on Sandomierz's blood-libel plaque, 25 February 2015, https://notesfrompoland.com/2015/02/25/the-compelling-need-for-truth-reflections-on-sandomierzs-blood-libel-plaque/
32. Tokarska-Bakir 2006. See also Marek Kohn, Against the Grain, 19 November 2012, https://marekkohn.info/zm.html
33. Tokarska-Bakir 2008, 454, translated by M. Kohn; alternative English translations given in Tokarska-Bakir 2006. Age and gender of second individual: Tokarska-Bakir 2008, 35.

34. Tokarska-Bakir 2008, 426, translated by M. Kohn; alternative English translation in Tokarska-Bakir 2006.
35. Dzielnica żydowska na Podzamczu – Romuald Dylewski – fragment relacji świadka historii, https://biblioteka.teatrnn.pl/dlibra/dlibra/doccontent?id=33533&dirids=1; Kubiszyn 2015.
36. Briedis 2005, 386; Giustino 2021.
37. Dylewski 2003; Dzielnica żydowska na Podzamczu – Romuald Dylewski – fragment relacji świadka historii, https://biblioteka.teatrnn.pl/dlibra/dlibra/doccontent?id=33533 &dirids=1
38. Sztop-Rutkowska 2011.
39. Interview, 10 December 2020 (translated from Polish).
40. Interview, 10 December 2020 (translated from Polish).
41. Polska Marka [Polish Brand], https://sklep.polskamarka.pl/
42. Prawdziwy Kebab u Prawdziwego Polaka, https://www.facebook.com/Prawdziwy-Kebab-u-Prawdziwego-Polaka-551853598339408/; To chyba jest prawdziwa praca marzeń. Żeby ją dostać musisz mieć . . . prawicowe poglądy, 9 June 2018, https://wiado-mosci.radiozet.pl/Polska/Prawdziwy-Kebab-u-Prawdziwego-Polaka-rekrutuje-pracownikow.-Zeby-dostac-prace-konieczne-prawicowe-poglady
43. Bluza patriotyczna Bóg Honor Ojczyzna, https://sklep.polskamarka.pl/product-pol-604--Bluza-patriotyczna-Bog-Honor-Ojczyzna.html; About Restaurant, https://mandragora.lublin.pl/en/restauracja-2/
44. Interview, 26 May 2021 (translated from Polish).
45. Interview, 26 May 2021 (translated from Polish).
46. *Koleżanki*, by Julia Hartwig. The murals in the Podzamcze ghetto area / 2. 3 Kowalska Street, https://teatrnn.pl/pamiec/en/1/#3-kowalska-st
47. Gruber 2009, 2002.
48. Rynek 10 w Lublinie, https://teatrnn.pl/leksykon/artykuly/rynek-10-w-lublinie/; Rynek 10, https://biblioteka.teatrnn.pl/Content/27205/Rynek%2010_.pdf
49. Kugelmass and Orla-Bukowska 1998.
50. Zubrzycki 2016.
51. Lehrer and Meng 2015, 9; Siddi and Gaweda 2019; Stanley Bill, Poles and the Holocaust: new research, old controversies, 29 June 2018, https://notesfrompoland.com/2018/06/29/poles-and-the-holocaust-new-research-old-controversies/
52. About Restaurant, https://mandragora.lublin.pl/en/restauracja-2/; Interview, 26 May 2021 (translated from Polish).
53. Lehrer 2007.
54. Personal communication (translated from Polish); Pietrasiewicz 2019, 104.

Prague
Chapter 16. If the Twentieth Century Had Not Happened

1. Gold 1998.
2. Le Corbusier 1973, 86–9 (Articles 65–70).
3. Eliot 2013, 40–1; Hamáčková and Justa 2011.
4. Toman 2012; Demetz 1997, 318.
5. Prague, https://yivoencyclopedia.org/article.aspx/prague; Giustino 2021.
6. Giustino 2010, 2005; Pařík 2009, 185.
7. Pařík 2009, 192; Pařík 2009, 193.
8. Sitte 1965; Ladd 2014; Sitte 1965, 60, 67, 86; Švácha 1995, 22.
9. Giustino 2005.
10. In Bernstein 1921, 33. The chapter is reproduced in Bernstein 1921, 22–41.

11. Bernstein 1921, 54; Segel 1995, 95–6; Stephen Whitfield, Why the 'Protocols of the Elders of Zion' is still pushed by anti-Semites more than a century after hoax first circulated, 2 September 2020, https://theconversation.com/why-the-protocols-of-the-elders-of-zion-is-still-pushed-by-anti-semites-more-than-a-century-after-hoax-first-circulated-145220
12. Ripellino 1994, 124–5; Giustino 2010.
13. Giustino 2021; Klub Za starou Prahu, https://www.zastarouprahu.cz/; Ripellino 1994, 125; Breton et al. 1972, 255.
14. Golem, https://www.jewishencyclopedia.com/articles/6777-golem#1137
15. Švácha 1995, 149–50.
16. Old Town Hall, http://sudekproject.cz/en/old-town-hall

Frankfurt am Main
Chapter 17. The New Old Town

1. Ed Simon, Is Frankenstein's Monster the Golem's Son? https://www.tabletmag.com/sections/arts-letters/articles/is-frankensteins-monster-the-golems-son; Lessing 2018, part 2, https://www.projekt-gutenberg.org/lessingt/haarmann/chap003.html
2. Paul Zalewski in Enss and Vinken 2016, 116; Lessing 2018, part 1, https://www.projekt-gutenberg.org/lessingt/haarmann/chap002.html
3. Ballhof und 'Altstadtgesundung', https://zukunft-heisst-erinnern.de/orte-der-verfolgung/ballhof-lang/
4. Zalewski 2012; Stadtbaurat Rudolf Hillebrecht: Über den Wandel des Stadtbildes, https://stadthistorie.info/geschichte/hillebrecht.htm; Rote Reihe Haarmann, https://stadthistorie.info/vergleich/69/Rote%20Reihe%20Haarmann; Rote Reihe, https://stadthistorie.info/vergleich/70/Rote%20Reihe
5. Hohn 1994; Arnold 2011; Bombennacht am 22. Oktober 1943, https://www.kassel.de/buerger/stadtgeschichte/erinnerungskultur/zerstoerung-kassels.php
6. Arnold 2011; Altmarkt – Die Freiheit, https://www.kassel.de/buerger/stadtgeschichte/erinnerungskultur/altmarkt-die-freiheit.php
7. Druselturm, https://www.kassel.de/buerger/kunst_und_kultur/sehenswertes/druselturm.php
8. Arnold 2011.
9. Demshuk 2021; Die Altstadt, https://www.freunde-frankfurts.de/projekte/altstadt.html; Beutlers Vorahnung, https://frankfurter-goethe-haus.de/von-der-zerstoerung-zum-wiederaufbau-des-frankfurter-goethe-hauses-1944-1951/beutlers-vorahnung/; Geschichte des Vereins, https://www.freunde-frankfurts.de/verein/geschichte.html
10. Koshar 2000, 156–7.
11. Diefendorf 1993, 73; Koshar 2000, 156–7.
12. Die Entscheidung, https://frankfurter-goethe-haus.de/von-der-zerstoerung-zum-wiederaufbau-des-frankfurter-goethe-hauses-1944-1951/die-entscheidung/
13. Robert P. Ball, Goethe House Restored, *Information Bulletin* (Office of the US High Commissioner for Germany Office of Public Affairs) June 1951, 3–6.
14. Sturm and Cachola Schmal 2018, 20.
15. Joy Gantevoort, Wie die Frankfurter Oper fast gesprengt wurde: 'Nur ein bisschen Dynamit', 22 January 2918, https://www.fnp.de/frankfurt/frankfurter-oper-fast-gesprengt-wurde-nur-bisschen-dynamit-10416691.html; Demshuk 2020, 2021; Kęsik 2015; Bukal and Samól 2017.
16. Demshuk 2020.
17. Rainer Schulze, Teures Fachwerk am Römerberg, 4 July 2021, https://www.faz.net/aktuell/rhein-main/frankfurt/teures-fachwerk-am-roemerberg-in-frankfurt-17417690.html; Enrico Santifaller, 1 June 2018, Die Frankfurter Altstadt hat viele

Mütter und Väter, https://www.db-bauzeitung.de/diskurs/die-frankfurter-altstadt-hat-viele-muetter-und-vaeter/; Neue Altstadt: KSP gewinnen Wettbewerb für Zentrum von Frankfurt, 19 September 2005, https://www.baunetz.de/meldungen/Meldungen-KSP_gewinnen_Wettbewerb_fuer_Zentrum_von_Frankfurt_21347.html

18. Gerhard Vinken in Enss and Vinken 2016, 16; Bertram and Fischer 2014, 212–14; Freddie Langer, Die Sehnsucht nach dem Gestern, 4 October 2019, https://www.faz.net/aktuell/reise/neue-frankfurter-altstadt-sehnsucht-nach-dem-gestern-16411196.html; Sophie Jung, Die immer neue Altstadt, 13 September 2018, BauNetzWoche #519, 7–20; Spektakuläre Drohnenshow mit 110 Drohnen über Frankfurt, https://www.youtube.com/watch?v=GiaJNt2AcIs; Drone show 'Constellations' celebrates the NewOldTownofFrankfurt,https://www.markgraph.de/projects/drone-show-constellations-frankfurt

19. DomRömer, https://www.domroemer.de; Peter Cachola Schmal in Sturm and Cachola Schmal 2018, 243; Enrico Santifaller, 1 June 2018, Die Frankfurter Altstadt hat viele Mütter und Väter, https://www.db-bauzeitung.de/diskurs/die-frankfurter-alt-stadt-hat-viele-muetter-und-vaeter/; Christian Riethmüller, Dom-Römer-Areal: Teures Altstadtprojekt, 28 January 2014, https://www.op-online.de/region/frankfurt/dom-roemer-areal-frankfurt-teures-altstadtprojekt-3336221.html; Mirjam Schmidt in Sturm and Cachola Schmal 2018, 333; Sophie Jung, Einkaufszentrum ohne Dach, 13 September 2018, BauNetzWoche #519, 21–8.

20. Stephan Trüby, Wir haben das Haus am rechten Fleck, 16 April 2018, https://www.faz.net/aktuell/feuilleton/neue-frankfurter-altstadt-durch-rechtsradikalen-initiiert-15531133.html

21. Claus Wolfschlag, Frankfurts Neue Altstadt – Das Herz am rechten Fleck. Eine Antwort, 9 April 2018, https://clauswolfschlag.wordpress.com/2018/04/09/frankfurts-neue-altstadt-das-herz-am-rechten-fleck-eine-antwort/; 'Schwarz-Grün hat in der Integration schwere Fehler gemacht', https://www.bff-frankfurt.de/artikel/index.php?id=733; Unser Beitrag zur Neuen Altstadt, http://www.pro-altstadt-frankfurt.de/index.php/wiederherstellung; Der Verein Pro Altstadt E.V., http://www.pro-altstadt-frankfurt.de/index.php/ueber-uns

22. Bertram and Fischer 2014, 218; 54.1 per cent, comprising 30 per cent 'foreign' and 24.1 per cent 'German with migration background'. *Statistisches Jahrbuch 2020 Frankfurt am Main*, Statistical Office of Frankfurt, V; Freddy Langer, Neue Frankfurter Altstadt: Sehnsucht nach dem Gestern, 4 October 2019, https://www.faz.net/aktuell/reise/neue-frankfurter-altstadt-sehnsucht-nach-dem-gestern-16411196.html

23. Bertram and Fischer 2014, 209, 216; Interviewed in Museumsdirektor über Fake-Altstadt:, Authentisch ist nicht wichtig', 1 April 2018, https://taz.de/Museumsdirektor-ueber-Fake-Altstadt/!5473829

24. Campus Galli, https://www.campus-galli.de/; Campus Galli - Karolingische Klosterstadt e.V. (DE), https://exarc.net/members/venues/campus-galli-de

Middle Europe
Chapter 18. What Stories They Could Tell

1. DenkOrt Deportationen, https://denkort-deportationen.de/; Haugerring 2. Liste der Stolpersteine in Würzburg, https://de.wikipedia.org/wiki/Liste_der_Stolpersteine_in_Würzburg#Altstadt

2. Beata Chomątowska, Mały Powstaniec. Budzi wzruszenie, przerażenie, niesmak, 8 August 2017, https://warszawa.wyborcza.pl/warszawa/7,54420,22204556,maly-powstaniec-budzi-wzruszenie-przerazenie-niesmak-felieton.html; Stańczyk 2015.

3. The Miracle of the Holy Cross Wood Relics in 1649, https://teatrnn.pl/lexicon/articles/the-miracle-of-the-holy-cross-wood-relics-in-1649/; Widoki Lublina – „Pożar

miasta Lublina" (około 1740), https://teatrnn.pl/leksykon/artykuly/widoki-lublina-pozar-miasta-lublina-okolo-1740/; Lublin Legends, https://lublin.eu/en/lublin/about-the-city/lublin-legends/#id_4

4. Lubelska trasa podziemna, https://teatrnn.pl/podziemia/; "Teatrzyk" pożar miasta 1719 r., https://teatrnn.pl/podziemia/teatrzyk-pozar-miasta-1719/

5. European Heritage Label Sites, https://culture.ec.europa.eu/cultural-heritage/initiatives-and-success-stories/european-heritage-label-sites; Decision No 1194/2011/EU of the European Parliament and of the Council of 16 November 2011 establishing a European Union action for the European Heritage Label, https://eur-lex.europa.eu/eli/dec/2011/1194/oj; European Heritage Label 2014 Panel Report, Directorate General Education and Culture, European Commission; European Heritage Label [leaflet], 2017, Municipal Conservator's Office, Lublin Municipal Office; Znak Dziedzictwa Europejskiego 2015. Unia Lubelska 1569, https://www.youtube.com/watch?v=n7Gp5k5-kvQ [English subtitles available].

6. Sławomir Sierakowski, Timothy Snyder: If Ukrainians hadn't fought back, the world would've been a much darker place, 31 March 2022, https://euromaidanpress.com/2022/03/31/if-ukrainians-hadnt-fought-back-the-world-wouldve-been-a-much-darker-place/; Daniel Tilles, Poland sees mass tourist cancellations amid war in neighbouring Ukraine, 24 March 2022, https://notesfrompoland.com/2022/03/24/poland-sees-mass-tourist-cancellations-amid-war-in-neighbouring-ukraine/; Julia Buckley, How the Ukraine invasion flattened Eastern European tourism, 6 August 2022, https://edition.cnn.com/travel/article/ukraine-invasion-tourism-eastern-europe/index.html

Bibliography

Adamowicz, Paweł. 2008. *Gdańsk jako wyzwanie*. Gdańsk: słowo/obraz terytoria.

Ahmer, Carolyn. 2020. 'Riegl's "Modern Cult of Monuments" As a Theory Underpinning Practical Conservation and Restoration Work'. *Journal of Architectural Conservation* 26 (2):150–65.

Allan, Robin. 1999. *Walt Disney and Europe: European Influences on the Animated Feature Films of Walt Disney*. London: John Libbey.

Andreski, Stanisław. 1981. Chapter 8: Poland. In *Fascism in Europe*, ed. S.J. Woolf. London: Methuen.

Antanavičiūtė, Rasa. 2012. 'Urban Development in Vilnius during the Second World War'. In *Art and Artistic Life during the Two World Wars*, eds G. Jankevičiūtė and L. Laučkaitė, 319–50. Vilnius: Lithuanian Culture Research Institute.

Arnold, Jörg. 2011. '"Once upon a Time There Was a Lovely Town . . .": The Allied Air War, Urban Reconstruction and Nostalgia in Kassel (1943–2000)'. *German History* 29 (3):445–69.

Aschheim, Steven E. 2008. 'Reflection, Projection, Distortion: The "Eastern Jew" in German-Jewish Culture'. *Osteuropa* 58 (8–10):61–74.

Ashworth, G.J. and Larkham, P.J. 1994. *Building A New Heritage: Tourism, Culture and Identity in the New Europe*. London: Routledge.

Assmann, Jan and Czaplicka, John. 1995. 'Collective Memory and Cultural Identity'. *New German Critique* 65:125–33.

Baedeker, Karl. 1902. *Southern Germany: Handbook for Travellers*. Leipzig: Karl Baedeker.

Bandarin, Francesco and Oers, Ron van. 2012. *The Historic Urban Landscape: Managing Heritage in an Urban Century*. Chichester: Wiley-Blackwell.

Barański, Marek. 2003. 'Koncepcje odbudowy Starego Miasta'. *Almanach Muzealny* 4:153–66.

Barrier, J. Michael. 1999. *Hollywood Cartoons: American Animation in Its Golden Age*. Oxford University Press.

Bartetzky, Arnold. 2015. 'Architecture Makes History: Reconstruction and Nation-Building in East Central Europe'. In *Architecture RePerformed: The Politics of Reconstruction*, ed. T. Mager, 19–34. London: Routledge.

Behrends, Jan C. 2009. 'Nation and Empire: Dilemmas of Legitimacy during Stalinism in Poland (1941–1956)'. *Nationalities Papers* 37 (4):443–66.

Berger, Hanns-Jürgen, and Lauterbach, Tobias. 2009. 'Der Wiederaufbau der Stadt Rothenburg ob der Tauber'. In *Wiederaufbau und Wirtschaftswunder. Aufsätze zur Bayerischen Landesausstellung 2009*, eds. C. Daxelmüller et al., 8–19. Augsburg: Haus der Bayerischen Geschichte.

Bernstein, Herman. 1921. *The History of a Lie: 'The Protocols of the Wise Men of Zion'*. New York: J.S. Ogilvie.

Bertram, Grischa F. and Fischer, Friedhelm. 2014. 'Post-Postwar Re-Construction of a Destroyed Heimat: Perspectives on German Discourse and Practice'. In *Transnationalism and the German City*, eds. J.M. Diefendorf and J. Ward, 207–21. New York: Palgrave Macmillan.

Biddle, Tami Davis. 2008. 'Dresden 1945: Reality, History, and Memory'. *Journal of Military History* 72:413–49.

Biegański, Piotr. 1937. 'Architektura Włoch Mussoliniego'. *Architektura i Budownictwo* 10:367–77.

Biegański, Piotr. 1953. 'Odbudowa Starego Miasta w Warszawie jako dzielnicy mieszkaniowej'. *Ochrona Zabytków* 3:78–85.

Biegański, Piotr. 1983. 'Jan Zachwatowicz'. *Ochrona Zabytków* 36/3-4 (142–3):159–61.

Biegański, Piotr. 1984. 'Działo się to 40 lat temu'. *Ochrona Zabytków* 37/2 (145):84–5.

Bieńkowski, Jan. 1953. 'Blok, kamienice i mieszkania na Starym Mieście w Warszawie'. *Ochrona Zabytków* 6/2–3 (21–2):86–92.

Bird, Kai. 2017. *The Chairman: John J. McCloy & The Making of the American Establishment*. New York: Simon & Schuster.

Blacker, Uilleam. 2016. 'The Return of the Jew in Polish Culture'. In *Reverberations of Nazi Violence in Germany and Beyond: Disturbing Pasts*, eds. S. Bird et al. London: Bloomsbury.

Blacker, Uilleam. 2019. *Memory, the City and the Legacy of World War II in East Central Europe: The Ghosts of Others*. Abingdon: Routledge.

Błoński, Jan. 8 October 1987. 'Biedni Polacy patrzą na getto'. *Tygodnik Powszechny* 2, 1.

Bojtár, Endre. 1999. *Foreword to the Past: A Cultural History of the Baltic People*. Budapest: Central European University Press.

Borecka, Emilia. 1975. *Warszawa 1945*. Warsaw: Państwowe Wydawnictwo Naukowe.

Borecka, Emilia et al., ed. 1982. *Warszawskie Stare Miasto z dziejów odbudowy*. Warsaw: Państwowe Wydawnictwo Naukowe.

Borodziej, Włodzimierz, transl. Harshav, Barbara. 2006. *The Warsaw Uprising of 1944*. Madison: University of Wisconsin Press.

Bossak-Herbst, Barbara. 2011. 'The Changing Image of Gdańsk, Poland: From Regained Homeland to Multicultural City'. In *Cities Full of Symbols: A Theory of Urban Space and Culture*, ed. P.J.M. Nas, 107–26. Leiden University Press.

Braun, Georg and Hogenberg, Franz. 2015. *Cities of the World: 230 Colour Engravings Which Transformed Urban Cartography 1572–1617*, ed. S. Füssel. Cologne: Taschen.

Breton, André et al. 1972. *Manifestoes of Surrealism*. Ann Arbor: University of Michigan Press.

Briedis, Laimonas. 2005. 'European Crossings: Vilnius Encounters'. Vancouver: University of British Columbia.

Briedis, Laimonas. 2008. *Vilnius, City of Strangers*. Vilnius: Baltos Lankos.

Bruce, David and Creighton, Oliver. 2006. 'Contested Identities: The Dissonant Heritage of European Town Walls and Walled Towns'. *International Journal of Heritage Studies* 12 (3):234–54.

Bukal, Grzegorz and Samól, Piotr. 2017. 'Authenticity of Architectural Heritage in a Rebuilt City. Comments to Vaclav Havel's Impression after His Visit in Gdansk in 2005'. *IOP Conference Series: Materials Science and Engineering* 245 (5).

Cameron, Christina. 2008. 'From Warsaw to Mostar: The World Heritage Committee and Authenticity'. *APT Bulletin: Journal of Preservation Technology* 39 (2):19–24.

Cammy, Justin D. 2001. 'Tsevorfene Bleter: The Emergence of Yung Vilne'. *Polin* 14: 170–91.

Centralny Zarząd Muzeów i Ochrony Zabytków. 1957. 'W sprawie ochrony zabytków w Polsce'. *Ochrona Zabytków* 10/1 (36):6–17.

Cervinkova, Hana and Golden, Juliet. 2017. 'The Containment of Memory in the "Meeting Place": City Marketing and Contemporary Memory Politics in Central Europe'. In *Diversity and Local Contexts: Urban Space, Borders, and Migration*, eds. J. Krase and Z. Uherek, 55–70. Cham: Palgrave Macmillan.

Chabiera, Piotr. 2020. 'Marian Morelowski (1884–1963) – Historyk sztuki, kolekcjoner, ekspert Komisji Rewindykacyjnych'. Uniwersytet Kardynała Stefana Wyszyńskiego w Warszawie.

Chernow, Ron. 1995. *The Warburgs*. London: Pimlico.

Childers, Thomas. 2005. '"Facilis Descensus Averni Est": The Allied Bombing of Germany and the Issue of German Suffering'. *Central European History* 38 (1):75–105.

Ciborowski, Adolf. 1964. *Warszawa – o zniszczeniu i odbudowie miasta*. Warsaw: Wydawnictwo Polonia.

Ciesielski, Stanisław. 2008. 'EXIT. Kresy wschodnie – ziemie zachodnie'. *Pamięć i Przyszłość* 1:8–16.

Cieśliński, Marek Kosma. 2020. 'Destrukcja jako tworzywo. Ikonografia ruin Warszawy w polskim kinie dokumentalnym po II wojnie światowej'. *Images* 27 (36):169–81.

Confino, Alon. 1993. 'The Nation as a Local Metaphor: Heimat, National Memory and the German Empire'. *History and Memory* 5 (1):42–86.

Conrad, JoAnn. 2016. 'Fantasy Imaginaries and Landscapes of Desire: Gustaf Tenggren's Forgotten Decades'. *Barnboken* 39:1–27.

Cramsey, Sarah A. and Wittenberg, Jason. 2016. 'Timing Is Everything: Changing Norms of Minority Rights and the Making of a Polish Nation-State'. *Comparative Political Studies* 49 (11):1480–1512.

Creighton, Oliver. 2007. 'Contested Townscapes: The Walled City as World Heritage'. *World Archaeology* 39 (3):339–54.

Crowley, David. 1994. 'Building the World Anew: Design in Stalinist and Post-Stalinist Poland'. *Journal of Design History* 7 (3):187–203.

Crowley, David. 1997. 'People's Warsaw / Popular Warsaw'. *Journal of Design History* 10 (2):203–23.

Crowley, David. 2003. *Warsaw*. London: Reaktion.

Czapska, Anna. 1988. 'Moje wspomnienie o profesorze Piotrze Biegańskim'. *Ochrona Zabytków* 41/1 (160):62–5.

Czapska, Anna. 1989. 'Wydział Zabytkowy BOS'. *Kronika Warszawy* 20 (1):29–43.

Czapska, Anna. 2006. 'Wywiad z Anną Czapską'. *Kronika Warszawy* 33 (3):21–32.

Czerner, Olgierd and Medeksza, Łukasz. 2008. 'Mury do góry'. *Pamięć i Przyszłość* 1:18–24.

Czyżewski, Krzysztof. 2022. *Towards Xenopolis: Visions from the Borderland*. Rochester, NY: University of Rochester Press.

Davies, Norman and Moorhouse, Roger. 2003. *Microcosm: Portrait of a Central European City*. London: Pimlico.

Davis, Cayce. 2021. 'Continuous Extremes: Architecture of Uncertainty in Poland, 1945 –'. Yale School of Architecture.

Davoliūtė, Violeta. 2014a. 'Postwar Reconstruction and the Imperial Sublime in Vilnius during Late Stalinism'. *Ab Imperio* 2014 (1):176–203.

Davoliūtė, Violeta. 2014b. *The Making and Breaking of Soviet Lithuania: Memory and Modernity in the Wake of War*. London: Routledge.

Dawidowicz, Lucy S. 1991. *From That Place and Time: A Memoir, 1938–1947*. New York: Bantam.

Dehio, Georg, transl. Blower, Jonathan. 1905. 'Monument Protection and Monument Preservation in the Nineteenth Century'. In *Denkmalschutz und Denkmalpflege im Neunzehnten Jahrhundert. Rede zur Feier des Geburtstages Sr. Majestät des Kaisers, Gehalten in der Aula der Kaiser-Wilhelms-Universität Strassburg am 27. Januar 1905*. Strasbourg: Heitz & Mündel.

Dembowska, Maria. 1995. 'Akcja Pruszkowska – ratowanie zbiorów bibliotecznych po Powstaniu Warszawskim. Fakty i ludzie'. *Przegląd Biblioteczny* 1:5–14.

Demetz, Peter. 1997. *Prague in Black and Gold: Scenes from the Life of a European City*. New York: Hill & Wang.

Demshuk, Andrew. 2012. 'Reinscribing Schlesien as Śląsk: Memory and Mythology in a Postwar German-Polish Borderland'. *History and Memory* 24 (1):39–86.

Demshuk, Andrew. 2020. 'A Polish Approach for German Cities? Cement Old Towns and the Search for Rootedness in Postwar Leipzig and Frankfurt/Main'. *European History Quarterly* 50(1):88–127.

Demshuk, Andrew. 2021. *Three Cities After Hitler: Redemptive Reconstruction Across Cold War Borders*. University of Pittsburgh Press.

Dickinson, Robert E. 1945. 'The Morphology of the Medieval German Town'. *Geographical Review* 35 (1):74–97.

Diefendorf, Jeffry M. 1993. *In the Wake of War: The Reconstruction of German Cities after World War II*. Oxford University Press.

Diefendorf, Jeffry M. 1997. 'The New City: German Urban Planning and the Zero Hour'. In *Stunde Null: The End and the Beginning Fifty Years Ago*, ed. G.J. Giles, 89–103. Washington, D.C.: German Historical Institute.

Dmowski, Roman. 2014. 'Thoughts of a Modern Pole'. Translated excerpts from 1902 original in *Discourses of Collective Identity in Central and Southeast Europe 1770–1945: Anti-Modernism: Radical Revisions of Collective Identity*, vol. IV, eds D. Mishkova et al., 61–9. Budapest: Central European University Press.

Döblin, Alfred, transl. Neugroschel, Joachim. 1991. *Journey to Poland*. New York: Paragon House.

Dolińska, Kamilla and Makaro, Julita. 2015. 'Wrocław Residents about the Multicultural Character of Their City – "crawling Germanisation", or Restoration of the German Heritage?' *Forum Socjologiczne* 6:69–86.

Drėmaitė, Marija. 2009. 'Lost in 1944? Vilnius: The City That Was Destroyed and Rebuilt'. In *Vilnius 1944: Jano ir Janušo Bulhakų fotografijų archyvas*, ed. M. Matulytė, 35–42. Vilnius: Lietuvos dailės muziejus.

Drėmaitė, Marija. 2019. '"Vilnius. A Baroque City": Changing Perceptions of Baroque Heritage during the Twentieth Century'. *RIHA Journal* 0212.

Dubonis, Artūras. 2000. 'The Case of the Chronicle of Rivius'. *Lithuanian Historical Studies* 5:7–20.

Duwel, Jorn and Gutschow, Niels. 2013. *A Blessing in Disguise: War and Town Planning in Europe 1940–1945*. Berlin: DOM.

Dwyer, William M. 2009. *So Long for Now: A World War II Memoir*. Lawrenceville, New Jersey: Xlibris.

Dylewski, Romuald. 2003. 'Lubelski Orient'. *Scriptores* 28 (2):110–16.

Dymnicka, Małgorzata and Szczepański, Jakub. 2016. 'Polityki pamięci i tożsamości wobec (nie)chcianego dziedzictwa. Od Gdańska do Gdańzigu'. *Przegląd Socjologiczny* 65 (1):81–100.

Dynner, Glenn and Guesnet, François. 2015. 'Introduction'. In *Warsaw. The Jewish Metropolis: Essays in Honor of the 75th Birthday of Professor Antony Polonsky*, eds. G. Dynner and F. Guesnet, 1–16. Leiden: Koninklijke Brill NV.

Eberhardt, Piotr, transl. Owsinski, Jan. 2003. *Ethnic Groups and Population Changes in Twentieth-Century Eastern Europe: History, Data and Analysis*. Armonk: M.E. Sharpe.

Eidintas, Alfonsas et al., transl. Kondratas, Skirma and Kondratas, Ramūna. 2015. *The History of Lithuania*. Vilnius: Eugrimas.

Eliot, George. 2013. *George Eliot's Life, as Related in Her Letters and Journals*, vol. II, ed. J.W. Cross. Project Gutenberg, from New York: Harper and Brothers, 1885.

Elżanowski, Jerzy. 2010. 'Manufacturing Ruins: Architecture and Representation in Post-Catastrophic Warsaw'. *Journal of Architecture* 15 (1):71–86.

Enss, Carmen M. and Vinken, Gerhard. 2016. *Produkt Altstadt: Historische Stadtzentren in Städtebau und Denkmalpflege*. Bielefeld: transcript.

Fałkowski, Wojciech, et al. 2004. 'Raport o stratach wojennych Warszawy'. Warsaw: Miasto Stołeczne Warszawa.

Foreign Office and Ministry of Economic Warfare. 1944. *The Bomber's Baedeker (Guide to the Economic Importance of German Towns and Cities)*. London: Foreign Office and Ministry of Economic Warfare.

Friedrich, Jörg, transl. Brown, Allison. 2006. *The Fire: The Bombing of Germany 1940–1945*. New York: Columbia University Press.

Gantner, Eszter B. 2014. 'Interpreting the Jewish Quarter'. *Anthropological Journal of European Cultures* 23 (2):26–42.

Gawryszewski, Andrzej. 2009. *Ludność Warszawy w XX wieku*. Warsaw: Polska Akademia Nauk.

Gawryszewski, Andrzej. 2010. 'Rozwój demograficzno-społeczny Warszawy w XX Wieku'. *Mazowsze. Studia Regionalne* 5:11–28.

Gerken, Daniel. 2004. 'Die Selbstverwaltung der Stadt Würzburg in der Weimarer Republik und im Dritten Reich'. Julius-Maximilians-Universität Würzburg.

Gieysztor, Aleksander et al. 1979. *History of Poland*. Warsaw: Państwowe Wydawnictwo Naukowe.

Giustino, Cathleen M. 2003. *Tearing Down Prague's Jewish Town: Ghetto Clearance and the Legacy of Middle-Class Ethnic Politics around 1900*. New York: Columbia University Press.

Giustino, Cathleen M. 2005. 'Persistent Anti-Jewish Hostility and Modern Technologies: The Entanglement of Old and New and the Radicalization of Politics in Prague around 1900'. *Historical Reflections / Réflexions Historiques* 31(3):351–72.

Giustino, Cathleen M. 2010. 'Prague'. In *Capital Cities in the Aftermath of Empires: Planning in Central and Southeastern Europe*, eds E.G. Makas and T.D. Conley, 157–73. New York: Routledge.

Giustino, Cathleen M. 2021. 'The Ghetto and the Castle: Modern Urban Design and Knowledge Transfer in Historic Prague before and after 1918'. In *Interurban Knowledge Exchange in Southern and Eastern Europe, 1870–1950*, eds E. Gantner et al., 25–49. New York: Routledge.

Glendinning, Miles. 2013. *The Conservation Movement: A History of Architectural Preservation: Antiquity to Modernity*. London: Routledge.

Główna Komisja Badania Zbrodni Niemieckich w Polsce. 1946. *Zburzenie Warszawy. Zeznania generałów niemieckich przed polskim prokuratorem członkiem Polskiej Delegacji przy Międzynarodowym Trybunale Wojennym w Norymberdze*. Katowice.

Gold, John R. 1998. 'Creating the Charter of Athens: CIAM and the Functional City, 1933–43'. *Town Planning Review* 69 (3):225–47.

Goldsmid, Edmund (ed.). 1886. *Un-Natural History, Or Myths of Ancient Science*, vol. 1. Edinburgh.

Górski, Jan. 1972. *Pamięć Warszawskiej odbudowy, 1945–1949. Antologia*. Warsaw: Państwowy Instytut Wydawniczy.

Górski, Jan. 1990. *Warszawa w latach 1944–1949. Odbudowa*. Warsaw: Państwowe Wydawnictwo Naukowe.

Grabski, August. 2018. 'The Jews and the "Disavowed Soldiers"'. In *New Directions in the History of the Jews in the Polish Lands*, eds A. Polonsky et al., 452–71. Boston: Academic Studies Press.

Gregor, Neil. 2000. 'A Schicksalsgemeinschaft? Allied Bombing, Civilian Morale, and Social Dissolution in Nuremberg, 1942–1945'. *Historical Journal* 43 (4):1051–70.

Gruber, Ruth Ellen. 2002. *Virtually Jewish: Reinventing Jewish Culture in Europe*. Berkeley: University of California Press.

Gruber, Ruth Ellen. 2009. 'Beyond Virtually Jewish: New Authenticities and Real Imaginary Spaces in Europe'. *Jewish Quarterly Review* 99 (4):487–504.

Grudzińska-Gross, Irena. 2012. 'Muranów czyli karczowanie', *Studia Litteraria et Historica* 1:1–6.

Grzebałkowska, Magdalena. 2015. *1945: Wojna i pokój*. Warsaw: Agora.

Guerquin, Anna. 1984. 'Wspomnienia o Profesorze Janie Zachwatowiczu'. *Ochrona Zabytków* 37 (2):87–9.

Hagen, Joshua. 2004. 'The Most German of Towns: Creating an Ideal Nazi Community in Rothenburg ob der Tauber'. *Annals of the Association of American Geographers* 94 (1):207–27.

Hagen, Joshua. 2005. 'Rebuilding the Middle Ages after the Second World War: The Cultural Politics of Reconstruction in Rothenburg ob der Tauber, Germany'. *Journal of Historical Geography* 31 (1):94–112.

Hagen, Joshua. 2006. *Preservation, Tourism and Nationalism: The Jewel of the German Past.* Aldershot: Ashgate.

Halbwachs, Maurice, transl. Ditter, Francis J. and Ditter, Vida Yazdi. 1980. *The Collective Memory*. New York: Harper & Row.

Hamáčková, Vlastimila and Justa, Petr. 2011. 'The World Heritage City of Prague and Its Jewish Cemeteries: Values and Conservation Strategies'. *ICOMOS – Hefte Des Deutschen Nationalkomitees* 53:152–7.

Hansar, Lilian. 2011. 'Helmi Üprus and the Old Town of Tallinn'. *Baltic Journal of Art History* 3:57–76.

Hansen, Randall. 2020. *Fire and Fury: The Allied Bombing of Germany, 1942–45*. London: Faber & Faber.

Hanson, Joanna K.M. 2004. *The Civilian Population and the Warsaw Uprising of 1944.* Cambridge University Press.

Harris, Arthur. 2005. *Bomber Offensive*. Barnsley: Pen & Sword.

Hartwig, Julia. 1956. *Lublin: fotografie i opracowanie Edward Hartwig*. Warsaw: Sport i Turystyka.

Hillmann, Roman. 2001. 'Wie Phönix aus der Asche . . . Prof. Jan Zachwatowicz zum 100. Geburtstag'. *kunsttexte.de (Journal für Kunst- und Bildgeschichte)* 1:1–5.

Hobsbawm, Eric. 2003. *Interesting Times: A Twentieth-Century Life*. London: Abacus.

Hohn, Uta. 1994. 'The Bomber's Baedeker – Target Book for Strategic Bombing in the Economic Warfare against German Towns 1943–45'. *GeoJournal* 34 (2):213–30.

Holtorf, Cornelius. 2007. 'What Does Not Move Any Hearts – Why Should It Be Saved? The Denkmalpflegediskussion in Germany'. *International Journal of Cultural Property* 14 (1):33–55.

Jähner, Harald, transl. Whiteside, Shaun. 2021. *Aftermath: Life in the Fallout of the Third Reich 1945–1955*. London: Penguin.

Jamiołkowska, Jadwiga. 1982. 'Projekt rewaloryzacji i adaptacji kamienic przy ulicy Grodzkiej w Lublinie'. *Ochrona Zabytków* 35 (1–2):58–70.

Jamiołkowska, Jadwiga. 1981. 'Stare Miasto w Lublinie – plan rewaloryzacji'. *Ochrona Zabytków* 34 (3–4):142–54.

Janicka, Elżbieta and Wilczyk, Wojciech. 2013. *Janicka & Wilczyk: Inne Miasto / Other City.* Warsaw: Zachęta – Narodowa Galeria Sztuki.

Jankowski, Stanisław. 1996. *Z fałszywym ausweisem w prawdziwej Warszawie. Wspomnienia 1939–1946* [2 vols]. Warsaw: Państwowy Instytut Wydawniczy.

Jarzębowski, Jerzy. 1981. 'Rewaloryzacja Starego Miasta w Lublinie z perspektywy dziesięciu lat'. *Ochrona Zabytków* 34(3–4):155–61.

Jeiler, Antonius et al. 2011. 'Management Plan "Hanseatic City of Lübeck"'. Hansestadt Lübeck.

Johnson, Peter. 1995. *The Withered Garland: Reflections and Doubts of a Bomber*. London: New European Publications.

Jozefacka, Anna. 2011. 'Rebuilding Warsaw: Conflicting Visions of a Capital City, 1916-1956'. New York University.

Kerski, Basil (ed.). 2014. *Gdańskie tożsamości. Eseje o mieście*. Gdańsk: Instytut Kultury Miejskiej.

Kęsik, Grzegorz. 2015. 'The Policy towards Historical Urban Spaces in Poland and Germany'. In *Memory and Politics of Cultural Heritage in Poland and Germany*, ed. K. Ziemer, 94–116. Warsaw: Uniwersytet Kardynała Stefana Wyszyńskiego.

Khrushchev, Nikita Sergeevich, transl. Shriver, George. 2004. *Memoirs of Nikita Khrushchev: Commissar, 1918–1945*, vol. 1. Pennsylvania State University Press.

Kieniewicz, Kazimierz. 1938. 'Problem Placu Katedralnego w Wilnie'. *Architektura i Budownictwo* (11–12):373–5.

Kijek, Kamil. 2018. 'Between a Love of Poland, Symbolic Violence, and Antisemitism: The Idiosyncratic Effects of the State Education System on Young Jews in Interwar Poland'. *Polin* 30:237–64.

Klei, Alexandra. 2020. '"Jewish Building" in the Federal Republic of Germany and the German Democratic Republic after the Holocaust. Possibilities, Limits, Spaces'. *Arts* 9 (38).

Klekot, Ewa. 2012. 'Constructing a "Monument of National History and Culture" in Poland: The Case of the Royal Castle in Warsaw'. *International Journal of Heritage Studies* 18 (5):459–78.

Klekot, Ewa. 2015. 'Memory and Oblivion in the Cityscape: Commemorations in the Warsaw Districts of Muranów and Mirów'. *Ethnologia Europaea* 45 (1):58–79.

Klíma, Ivan, transl. Wilson, Paul. 1994. 'The Spirit of Prague'. In *The Spirit of Prague and Other Essays*, 39–47. London: Granta.

Kłos, Juljusz. 1937. *Wilno. Przewodnik krajoznawczy*. Wilno: Wydawnictwo Wileńskiego Oddziału Polskiego Towarzystwa Turystyczno-Krajoznawczego.

Knap, Paweł (ed.). 2013. *Pod dyktando ideologii. Studia z dziejów architektury i urbanistyki w Polsce Ludowej*. Szczecin: Instytutu Pamięci Narodowej.

Knell, Hermann. 2003. *To Destroy a City: Strategic Bombing and Its Human Consequences in World War 2*. Cambridge, MA: Da Capo Press.

Koczorowska-Pielińska, Ewa. 1958. 'Struktura gospodarczo-społeczna Nowej Warszawy w XV wieku'. *Przegląd Historyczny* 49 (2):296–310.

Kohlrausch, Martin. 2019. *Brokers of Modernity: East Central Europe and the Rise of Modernist Architects, 1910–1950*. Louvain University Press.

Kołodziejczyk, Arkadiusz. 1995. '"Mały Londyn". Milanówek w ostatnich miesiącach okupacji niemieckiej: październik 1944 – styczeń 1945 roku'. *Niepodległość i Pamięć* 2/3 (4):113–30.

Kończal, Kornelia. 2017. 'The Quest for German Property in East Central Europe after 1945: The Semantics of Plunder and the Sense of Reconstruction'. In *Imaginations and Configurations of Polish Society: From the Middle Ages through the Twentieth Century*, eds Y. Kleinmann et al., 291–312. Göttingen: Wallstein Verlag.

Konstantynów, Dariusz. 2009. 'Żydzi i architektura (z perspektywy polskiego nacjonalizmu lat trzydziestych XX wieku)'. *Kwartalnik Historii Żydów* 4:411–25.

Koshar, Rudy. 1998. *Germany's Transient Pasts: Preservation and National Memory in the Twentieth Century*. Chapel Hill: University of North Carolina Press.

Koshar, Rudy. 2000. *From Monuments to Traces: Artifacts of German Memory, 1870–1990*. Berkeley: University of California Press.

Kozieł, Andrzej. 2011. 'Marian Morelowski (1884–1963)'. *Rocznik Historii Sztuki* 36:47–56.

Krasiński, Stanisław. 1953. 'Kronika odbudowy Starego Miasta'. *Ochrona Zabytków* 3 (2–3):157–61.

Kubiszyn, Marta. 2015. 'Miejsce rzeczywiste – miejsce wyobrażone: nieistniejąca dzielnica żydowska w Lublinie we wspomnieniach mieszkańców'. *Wrocławski Rocznik Historii Mówionej* V:5–33.

Kucia, Marek et al. 2014. 'Anti-Semitism in Poland: Survey Results and a Qualitative Study of Catholic Communities'. *Nationalities Papers* 42 (1):8–36.

Kugelmass, Jack, and Orla-Bukowska, Annamaria. 1998. '"If You Build It They Will Come": Recreating an Historic Jewish District in Post-Communist Krakow'. *City & Society* 10 (1):315–53.

Kunicki, Mikołaj. 2005. 'The Red and the Brown: Bolesław Piasecki, the Polish Communists, and the Anti-Zionist Campaign in Poland, 1967–68'. *East European Politics and Societies* 19 (2):185–225.

Kuznitz, Cecile E. 2017. 'The Capital of Yiddishland: Yiddish Culture in Vilna between the Two World Wars'. In *Yiddishism and Creation of the Yiddish Nation*, eds Y. Nishimura and M. Nomura, 101–16. Tokyo: Kanazawa University.

Kuznitz, Cecile E. 2021. 'Touring Vilna: Images of the City and Its Jews in Guidebooks and Travelogues, 1856–1939'. *Colloquia* 48:56–73.

Kvietkauskas, Mindaugas. 2021. 'From Shulhoyf to Montparnasse: Cultural Collage in Moshé Vorobeichic's Photography Book *The Ghetto Lane in Wilna* (1931)'. *Colloquia* 48:170–93.

Lachert, Bohdan. 1949. 'Muranów – dzielnica mieszkaniowa'. *Architektura* 5(19):129–37.

Ladd, Brian. 2014. 'The Closed Versus the Open Cityscape: Rival Traditions from Nineteenth-Century Europe'. *Change Over Time* 4 (1):58–74.

Lagzi, Gábor. 2013. 'Multicultural Past and Present in the Cities of Central Europe: The Cases of Wrocław/Breslau and L'viv/Lemberg/Lwów'. *Darbai Ir Dienos* (60):191–204.

Lähdesmäki, Tuuli et al. 2019. *Dissonant Heritages and Memories in Contemporary Europe*. Cham: Palgrave Macmillan.

Lambourne, Nicola. 2001. *War Damage in Western Europe: The Destruction of Historic Monuments during the Second World War*. Edinburgh University Press.

Laučkaitė, Laima. 2021. 'The Iconography of Jewish Vilna during the First World War'. *Colloquia* 48:113–37.

Le Corbusier, transl. Eardley, Anthony. 1973. *The Athens Charter*. New York: Grossman.

Lehrer, Erica. 2007. 'Bearing False Witness? "Vicarious" Jewish Identity and the Politics of Affinity'. In *Imaginary Neighbors: Mediating Polish-Jewish Relations after the Holocaust*, eds D. Glowacka and J. Żylinska, 84–109. Lincoln: University of Nebraska Press.

Lehrer, Erica. 2010. 'Can There Be a Conciliatory Heritage?' *International Journal of Heritage Studies* 16 (4–5):269–88.

Lehrer, Erica. 2014. 'Virtual, Virtuous, Vicarious, Vacuous? Towards a Vigilant Use of Labels'. *Jewish Cultural Studies* 4:383–95.

Lehrer, Erica and Meng, Michael (eds). 2015. *Jewish Space in Contemporary Poland*. Bloomington: Indiana University Press.

Lessing, Theodor. 2018. *Haarmann. Die Geschichte eines Werwolfs*. Projekt Gutenberg-DE; first published 1925. Berlin: Verlag Die Schmiede.

Lieven, Anatol. 1993. *The Baltic Revolution: Estonia, Latvia, Lithuania and the Path to Independence*. New Haven: Yale University Press.

Lipphardt, Anna, transl. Belcher, Mark. 2008. 'Forgotten Memory: The Jews of Vilne in the Diaspora'. *Osteuropa* 58 (8–10):187–98.

Lorentz, Stanisław. 1951. 'Zygmunt Miechowski'. *Biuletyn Historii Sztuki*, no. 13:206.

Lorentz, Stanisław. 1966. 'Reconstruction of the Old Town Centers of Poland'. In *Historic Preservation Today: Essays Presented to the Seminar on Preservation and Restoration, Williamsburg, Virginia, September 8–11, 1963*, eds W.M. Whitehill et al., 43–72. Charlottesville: University of Virginia Press.

Lorentz, Stanisław (ed.). 1970. *Walka o dobra kultury. Warszawa 1939–1945* [2 vols]. Warsaw: Państwowy Instytut Wydawniczy.

Lorentz, Stanisław. 1986. *Walka o Zamek, 1939–1980*. Warsaw: Zamek Królewski w Warszawie.

Łagodziński, Władysław Wiesław. 2013. 'Dokumenty i informacje dot. odbudowy Warszawy'. Warsaw: Oddział Warszawski Polskiego Towarzystwa Statystycznego.

MacDonald, Charles B. 1993. *The Last Offensive*. Washington, D.C.: Center of Military History, United States Army.

Macdonald, Sharon. 2013. *Memorylands: Heritage and Identity in Europe Today*. London: Routledge.

Mace, Martin and Grehan, John. 2014. *Bomber Harris: Sir Arthur Harris' Despatch on War Operations 1942–1945*. Barnsley: Pen and Sword.

Majewski, Jerzy S. 2017. *A Phoenix City: Warsaw 1945–50 through the Lens of Karol Pęcherski*. Warsaw Rising Museum.

Majewski, Piotr. 2009. *Ideologia i konserwacja. Architektura zabytkowa w Polsce w czasach socrealizmu*. Warsaw: Trio.

Majewski, Piotr. 2017. 'What Was Ours Was Invaluable to Us … Preserving Cultural Heritage as Part of the Polish Underground State's (PPP) Operations (1939–1945)'. *Muzealnictwo* 58:14–18.

Markowski, Marcin. 2014. 'Lublin w roku 1954 w świetle prasy: Centralna Wystawa Rolnicza'. *Rocznik Lubelski* 40:168–97.

Martyn, Peter. 2001. 'The Brave New-Old Capital City: Questions Relating to the Rebuilding and Remodelling of Warsaw's Architectural Profile from the Late 1940s until 1956'. In *Falsifications in Polish Collections and Abroad*, eds J. Miziołek and P. Martyn, 193–233. Warsaw: Instytut Archeologii UW.

Matyjaszek, Konrad. 2016. 'Wall and Window: The Rubble of the Warsaw Ghetto as the Narrative Space of the POLIN Museum of the History of Polish Jews'. *Studia Litteraria et Historica* 20 (5):59–97.

Maurer, Maurer. 1983. *Air Force Combat Units of World War II*. Washington, D.C.: Office of Air Force History.

Melzer, Emanuel. 1997. *No Way Out: The Politics of Polish Jewry 1935-1939*. Cincinnati: Hebrew Union College Press.

Meng, Michael. 2011. *Shattered Spaces: Encountering Jewish Ruins in Postwar Germany and Poland*. Cambridge, MA: Harvard University Press.

Michlic, Joanna B. 2006. *Poland's Threatening Other: The Image of the Jew from 1880 to the Present*. Lincoln: University of Nebraska Press.

Michlic, Joanna and Polonsky, Antony. 2005. 'Catholicism and the Jews in Post-Communist Poland'. *Studies in Contemporary Jewry* XXI:35–65.

Miłosz, Czesław, transl. Leach, Catherine S. 1981. *Native Realm: A Search for Self-Definition*. Berkeley: University of California Press.

Miłosz, Czesław, transl. Levine, Madeline G. 1992. *Beginning with My Streets: Essays and Recollections*. New York: Farrar, Straus and Giroux.

Ministry of Culture and Art and Ministry of Reconstruction of the Country. 1945. *Warsaw Accuses: Guide-Book to the Exhibition Arranged by the Office of Reconstruction of the Capital Together with the National Museum in Warsaw*. Warsaw: Ministry of Culture and Art and Ministry of Reconstruction of the Country.

Moeller, Robert G. 2006. 'On the History of Man-Made Destruction: Loss, Death, Memory, and Germany in the Bombing War'. *History Workshop Journal* 61 (1):103–34.

Möhring, Hellmuth. 2020. *PITTORESK! Selbstbild - Fremdbild - Wiederaneignung / PICTURESQUE! Self Image – Extrinsic Image – Re-Appropriation*. Rothenburg Museum.

Mordyński, Krzysztof. 2021. *Sny o Warszawie. Wizje Przebudowy Miasta 1945–1952*. Warsaw: Prószyński i S-ka.

Morris, James. 2004. 'The Polish Terror: Spy Mania and Ethnic Cleansing in the Great Terror'. *Europe – Asia Studies* 56 (5):751–66.

Motas, Maciej. 2010. 'Działalność Komitetu Zagranicznego Obozu Narodowego (1942–1943), jako próba integracji środowisk narodowych na emigracji w czasie drugiej wojny światowej'. *Niepodległość i Pamięć* 31:163–84.

Murawski, Michał. 2009. '(A)Political Buildings: Ideology, Memory and Warsaw's "Old" Town', *Docomomo E-Proceedings* 2:13–20.

Murzyn-Kupisz, Monika and Purchla, Jacek. 2009 (eds). *Reclaiming Memory: Urban Regeneration in the Historic Jewish Quarters of Central European Cities.* Kraków: International Cultural Centre.

Muszyński, Henryk J. 2007. 'Prymasowskie Gniezno w nauczaniu i życiu Stefana Kardynała Wyszyńskiego'. *Studia Prymasowskie* 1:199–213.

Muth, Sebastian. 2008. 'Multiethnic but Multilingual as Well? The Linguistic Landscapes of Vilnius'. In *Norddeutsches Linguistisches Kolloquium 2008*, eds S. Sahel and R. Vogel, 121–46. Universität Bielefeld.

Němec, Richard. 2018. 'Planowanie i przebudowa, Nowego Niemieckiego Wschodu'. Generalne Gubernatorstwo: Warszawa (1939–1945)'. *Rocznik Historii Sztuki* 43:155–84.

Nolan, Mary. 2005. 'Air Wars, Memory Wars'. *Central European History* 38 (1):7–40.

Nora, Pierre, et al., transl. Goldhammer, Arthur. 1996. *Realms of Memory: Rethinking the French Past* [3 vols]. New York: Columbia University Press.

Nowożycki, Bartosz. 2016. 'Soldiers of the Home Army Group "Radosław" After the Fall of the Warsaw Uprising and the End of World War II'. *Polish Review* 61 (2):45.

Obracht-Prondzyński, Cezary and Łuczeczko, Paweł. 2019. 'Wielokulturowość Gdańska – problem, szansa czy ryzyko?' *Miscellanea Anthropologica et Sociologica* 20 (4):107–21.

Oppmann, Artur. 1931. *Pieśń o Rynku i zaułkach. Nowy cykl o Starem Mieście.* Warsaw: Jakób Mortkowicz.

Overy, Richard. 2013. *The Bombing War: Europe 1939–1945.* London: Allen Lane.

Panas, Władysław. 2004. *Oko Cadyka.* Lublin: Wydawnictwo Uniwersytetu Marii Curie-Skłodowskiej.

Pendlebury, John, et al. (eds). 2015. *Alternative Visions of Post-War Reconstruction: Creating the Modern Townscape.* London: Routledge.

Piątek, Grzegorz. 2020. *Najlepsze miasto świata. Warszawa w odbudowie 1944–1949.* Warsaw: WAB.

Piechotka, Maria and Piechotka, Kazimierz. 2004. *Oppidum Judaeorum: Żydzi w przestrzeni miejskiej dawnej Rzeczypospolitej.* Warsaw: Wydawnictwo Krupski i S-ka.

Pietrasiewicz, Tomasz, transl. Metlerska-Colerick, Monika. 2017. *Theatre of Memory by the NN Theatre: Lublin 1997–2017.* Lublin: 'Grodzka Gate – NN Theatre' Centre.

Pietrasiewicz, Tomasz, transl. Metlerska-Colerick, Monika. 2019. *Theatre of Memory by the NN Theatre: Guidebook.* Lublin: 'Grodzka Gate – NN Theatre' Centre.

Pietraszewski, Igor and Törnquist-Plewa, Barbara. 2016. 'Wrocław: Changes in Memory Narratives'. In *Whose Memory? Which Future? Remembering Ethnic Cleansing and Lost Cultural Diversity in Eastern, Central and Southeastern Europe*, ed. B. Törnquist-Plewa, 17–48. New York: Berghahn.

Polonsky, Antony. 2004. 'Poles, Jews and the Problems of a Divided Memory'. *Ab Imperio* 2:125–47.

Polonsky, Antony. 2008. 'Fragile Coexistence, Tragic Acceptance: The Politics and History of the East European Jews'. *Osteuropa* 58 (8–10):7–24.

Polonsky, Antony. 2013. 'From the End of the Second World War to the Collapse of the Communist System'. In *The Jews in Poland and Russia: A Short History*, 380–423. Liverpool University Press.

Polski Komitet Wyzwolenia Narodowego. 1959. 'Manifest Polskiego Komitetu Wyzwolenia Narodowego'. *Rocznik Lubelski*, 7–14.

Popiołek, Małgorzata, transl. Mićinska, Anna. 2016. *Od kamienicy do muzeum / From a tenement house to a museum.* Warsaw: Muzeum Warszawy.

Prażmowska, Anita J. 2003. *Civil War in Poland, 1942–1948.* Basingstoke: Palgrave Macmillan.

Pruszak, Tomasz A. 2014. 'Zabezpieczanie i ratowanie dzieł sztuki w Warszawie wobec zagrożeń w okresie II wojny światowej'. *Almanach Muzealny* 8:191–219.

Przywara, Adam. 2018. 'Rubble Warsaw, 1945–1946: Urban Landscaping and Architectural Remains'. *Ikonotheka* 28:121–38.

Puget, Wanda. 1984. 'Redaktorem był wytrawnym'. *Ochrona Zabytków* 37 (2):117–18.

Puustak, Ülo. 2012. 'The Development of Heritage Protection in Estonia'. *Estonian Cultural Heritage: Preservation and Conservation* 1:5–8.

Rabinowicz, H. 1964. 'The Battle of the Ghetto Benches'. *Jewish Quarterly Review* 55 (2):151–9.

Račiūnienė, Aistė Niunkaitė. 2015. 'The Plastic Plan of Vilnius from the Vilnius Ghetto. Circumstances, Testimonies and Creators'. Vilna Gaon Museum of Jewish History.

Rafalski, Piotr, transl. Jakubowicz, Karol. 1986. *Warsaw*. Warsaw: Interpress.

Rampley, Matthew. 2012. *Heritage, Ideology, and Identity in Central and Eastern Europe: Contested Pasts, Contested Presents*. Woodbridge: Boydell Press.

Richie, Alexandra. 2013. *Warsaw 1944: Hitler, Himmler and the Crushing of a City*. New York: Farrar, Straus and Giroux.

Riegl, Alois, transl. Forster, Kurt W. and Ghirardo, Diane. 1982. 'The Modern Cult of Monuments: Its Character and Its Origin'. *Oppositions* 25:21–51.

Rindzevičiūtė, Eglė. 2010. 'Imagining the Grand Duchy of Lithuania: The Politics and Economics of the Rebuilding of Trakai Castle and the "Palace of Sovereigns" in Vilnius'. *Central Europe* 8(2):181–203.

Rindzevičiūtė, Eglė. 2013. 'Institutional Entrepreneurs of a Difficult Past: The Organisation of Knowledge Regimes in Post-Soviet Lithuanian Museums'. *European Studies* 30:63–95.

Ripellino, Angelo M., transl. Marinelli, David N. 1994. *Magic Prague*. Berkeley: University of California Press.

Rosenfeld, Gavriel D. 2000. *Munich and Memory: Architecture, Monuments, and the Legacy of the Third Reich*. Berkeley: University of California Press.

Rothschild, Joseph. 1974. *East Central Europe between the Two World Wars*. Seattle: University of Washington Press.

Rovere, Richard H. 1961. 'Notes on the Establishment in America'. *American Scholar* 30 (4):489–95.

Rowell, Stephen C. 2014. *Lithuania Ascending: A Pagan Empire within East-Central Europe, 1295–1345*. Cambridge University Press.

Ruskin, John. 1849. *The Seven Lamps of Architecture*. London: Smith, Elder and Co.

Sebald, Winfried Georg, transl. Bell, Anthea. 2004. *On the Natural History of Destruction: With Essays on Alfred Andersch, Jean Améry and Peter Weiss*. London: Penguin.

Segel, Binjamin W., transl. Levy, Richard S. 1995. *A Lie and a Libel: The History of the Protocols of the Elders of Zion*. Lincoln: University of Nebraska Press.

Shackleton, Robert. 1914. *Unvisited Places of Old Europe*. Philadelphia: Penn.

Siddi, Marco and Gaweda, Barbara. 2019. 'The National Agents of Transnational Memory and Their Limits: The Case of the Museum of the Second World War in Gdańsk'. *Journal of Contemporary European Studies* 27 (2):258–71.

Sitte, Camillo, transl. Collins, George R. and Collins, Christiane Crasemann. 1965. *City Planning According to Artistic Principles*. Mineola: Random House.

Skalimowski, Andrzej. 2011. 'Partyjny kolektyw i jego eksponenci. Bezpośrednia ingerencja kierownictwa PZPR w organizację odbudowy Warszawy w latach 1949–1956'. *Letnia Szkoła Historii Najnowszej* 2011, 42–56.

Skalimowski, Andrzej. 2014. '"Budowniczy Stolicy". Warszawski mecenat Bolesława Bieruta w latach 1945–1955'. *Pamięć i Sprawiedliwość* 2(24):75–94.

Skalimowski, Andrzej. 2018. *Sigalin. Towarzysz odbudowy*. Wołowiec: Wydawnictwo Czarne.

Skilton, John Davis. 2008. *Memoirs of a Monuments Officer: Protecting European Artworks*. Portland, OR: Inkwater Press.

Skowronska, Renata et al. (eds). 2012. *Vielerlei Wiederaufbau - Różne drogi odbudowy. Erfahrungen und Wahrnehmungen in Städten Polens und Frankens nach 1945 – Doświadczenia i spostrzeżenia w odnawianiu miast Polski i Frankonii po 1945 roku*. Stadtarchivs Würzburg.

Sliesoriūnas, Gintautas. 2009. 'The First Occupation of Vilnius during the Great Northern War (April–May 1702)'. *Lithuanian Historical Studies* 14:71–104.

Słomczyński, Adam. 2007. 'Muzeum m. st. Warszawy 1946-1950. Fragmenty wspomnień'. *Almanach Muzealny* 5:241–72.

Smith, Laurajane. 2006. *Uses of Heritage*. London: Routledge.

Snyder, Louis L. 1996. *Roots of German Nationalism*. New York: Barnes & Noble.

Snyder, Timothy. 1999. ' "To Resolve the Ukrainian Problem Once and for All": The Ethnic Cleansing of Ukrainians in Poland, 1943–1947'. *Journal of Cold War Studies* 1 (2):86–120.

Snyder, Timothy. 2004. *The Reconstruction of Nations: Poland, Ukraine, Lithuania, Belarus, 1569–1999*. New Haven: Yale University Press.

Snyder, Timothy. 2005. *Sketches from a Secret War: A Polish Artist's Mission to Liberate Soviet Ukraine*. New Haven: Yale University Press.

Sosnowski, Oskar. 1930. *Powstanie, układ i cechy charakterystyczne sieci ulicznej na obszarze Wielkiej Warszawy*. Warsaw: Wydawnictwo Zakładu Architektury Polskiej Politechniki Warszawskiej.

Spałek, Robert. 2005. 'Światło na Spychalskiego'. *Biuletyn Instytutu Pamięci Narodowej* 01–02:83–90.

Srebrakowski, Aleksander. 2020. 'The Nationality Panorama of Vilnius'. *Studia z Dziejów Rosji i Europy Środkowo-Wschodniej* 55 (3):33.

Stańczyk, Ewa. 2015. 'Heroes, Victims, Role Models: Representing the Child Soldiers of the Warsaw Uprising'. *Slavic Review* 74 (4):738–59.

Standl, Harald and Krupickaitė, Dovilė. 2004. 'Gentrification in Vilnius (Lithuania): The Example of Užupis'. *Europa Regional* 12 (1):42–51.

Statystycznego Prezydium Rady Narodowej. *Warszawa w liczbach 1947*. Warsaw: Wydziału w m. st. Warszawie.

Statystycznego Zarząd Miejskiego w m. st. Warszawie. *Warszawa w liczbach 1939*. Warsaw Wydawnictwo Wydziału Statystycznego Zarząd Miejskiego w m. st. Warszawie.

Steinbacher, Sybille, transl. Whiteside, Shaun. 2005. *Auschwitz: A History*. London: Penguin.

Steinhaus, Hugo. 1992. *Wspomnienia i zapiski*. London: Aneks.

Stippler, Georg. 2012. 'Der Würzburger Sankt Kiliansdom – Der Wiederaufbau von der Zerstörung 1945 bis zur Wiedereinweihung 1967'. Julius-Maximilians-Universität Würzburg.

Stola, Dariusz. 2017. 'Jewish Emigration from Communist Poland: The Decline of Polish Jewry in the Aftermath of the Holocaust'. *East European Jewish Affairs* 47 (2–3):169–88.

Stravinskienė, Vitalija. 2012. 'Ethnic-Demographic Changes in the Data of the Statistical Sources of the City of Vilnius (1920–1939)'. *Lithuanian Historical Studies* 17:125–46.

Sturm, Philipp and Cachola Schmal, Peter (eds). 2018. *Die Immer Neue Aldstadt: Bauen zwischen Dom und Römer Seit 1900 / Forever New: Frankfurt's New Old Town: Building between Dom and Römer since 1900*. Berlin: Jovis.

Szívós, Erika. 2015. 'Introduction: Historic Jewish Spaces in Central and Eastern European Cities'. *East Central Europe* 42 (2–3):139–62.

Szpulak, Andrzej. 2019. 'View from the inside. The Images of the City in the "Black Series" Documentary Films in Poland in the 1950s'. *Images* 22 (31):113–22.

Sztop-Rutkowska, Katarzyna. 2011. 'Niepamiętane historie miasta. Żydowska przeszłość Białegostoku i Lublina w (nie)pamięci obecnych mieszkańców'. *Pogranicze. Studia Społeczne* XVIII:68–83.

Szymańska, Magda. 2015. *Powroty. Warszawa 1945–46*. Warsaw: Dom Spotkań z Historią.

Śledziewski, Krzysztof. 2014. 'Postępowanie z przebudową zabytkowych obiektów komunikacyjnych na przykładzie ulicy Zamkowej w Lublinie'. *Budownictwo i Architektura* 13 (1):277–94.

Śledziewski, Piotr and Bukowski, Stanisław. 1938. 'O projekcie regulacji Placu Katedralnego w Wilnie w związku z zamierzoną budową Pomnika Pierwszego Marszałka Polski Józefa Piłsudskiego'. *Architektura i Budownictwo* 11–12:366–72.

Świątek, Paulina. 2012. 'Building on the Ruins: The Muranów District in Warsaw'. *Biuletyn Polskiej Misji Historycznej* 7:41–63.

Švácha, Rostislav, transl. Büchler, Alexandra. 1995. *The Architecture of New Prague 1895– 1945.* Cambridge, MA: MIT Press.

Thum, Gregor, transl. Lampert, Tom and Brown, Allison. 2003. *Uprooted: How Breslau Became Wrocław during the Century of Expulsions.* Princeton University Press.

Tokarska-Bakir, Joannna. 2006. 'Sandomierz Blood-Libel Myths. Final Report 2006'.

Tokarska-Bakir, Joanna. 2008. *Legendy o krwi. Antropologia przesądu.* Warsaw: WAB.

Tokarska-Bakir, Joanna. 2013a. 'The Figure of the Bloodsucker in Polish Religious, National and Left-Wing Discourse, 1945–1946: A Study in Historical Anthropology'. *Dapim: Studies on the Holocaust* 27 (2):75–106.

Tokarska-Bakir, Joanna. 2013b. 'Communitas of Violence: The Kielce Pogrom as a Social Drama'. *Yad Vashem Studies* 41 (1):1–39.

Tokarska-Bakir, Joanna, transl. Zahorjanova, Blanka et al. 2019. *Pogrom Cries – Essays on Polish-Jewish History, 1939–1946.* Berlin: Peter Lang.

Toman, Jindřich. 2012. 'Making Sense of a Ruin: Nineteenth-Century Gentile Images of the Old Jewish Cemetery in Prague'. *Bohemia* 52 (1):108–22.

Trębacz, Zofia. 2016. '"Ghetto Benches" at Polish Universities: Ideology and Practice.' In *Alma Mater Antisemitica. Akademisches Milieu, Juden und Antisemitismus an den Universitäten Europas zwischen 1918 und 1939,* eds. R. Fritz et al., 113–35. Vienna: New Academic Press.

Treber, Leonie. 2019. 'The Big Cleanup: Men, Women, and Rubble Clearance in Postwar East and West Germany'. In *Gendering Post-1945 German History: Entanglements,* eds. K. Hagemann et al., 93–114. New York: Berghahn.

Tunbridge, J.E. and Ashworth, G.J. 1996. *Dissonant Heritage: The Management of the Past as a Resource in Conflict.* Chichester: Wiley.

Ullrich, Jan. 2017. 'Übermorgen und Geschichte: Am Beispiel von Rothenburg ob der Tauber und Warschau'. *Raum und Resilienz: Zukunft von Stadtregionen* 2:28–31.

Unwin, Raymond. 1909. *Town Planning in Practice: An Introduction to the Art of Designing Cities and Suburbs.* Chichester: T. Fisher Unwin.

Üprus, Helmi. 1972. 'The Old Town of Tallinn and Its Future'. *Monumentum* 8 (4):71–97.

Urry, John. 1990. *The Tourist Gaze: Leisure and Travel in Contemporary Societies.* London: Sage.

Urząd Statystyczny w Warszawie. 2012. *Warszawa feniksem XX wieku.* Warsaw: Urząd Statystyczny w Warszawie.

Vaitkevičius, Vykintas. 2004. 'The Main Features of the State Religion in Thirteenth-Century Lithuania'. *Balto-Slavic Studies* 16:289–356.

Valionienė, Oksana. 2017. 'Pirmosios Vilniaus šventyklos tyrimų problema'. *Lietuvos Istorijos Metraštis* 1:5–21. (Summary in English)

Venclova, Tomas, transl. Simanavičiūtė, Aušra. 2003. *Vilnius City Guide.* R. Paknys.

Venclova, Tomas, transl. Bettauer Dembo, Margot. 2009. *Vilnius: A Personal History.* Riverdale-on-Hudson: Sheep Meadow Press.

Volavková, Hana. 2004. *The Lost Jewish Town of Prague.* Prague: Paseka.

Walker, Mack. 1998. *German Home Towns: Community, State, and General Estate, 1648– 1871.* Ithaca: Cornell University Press.

Wapiński, Roman. 1999. 'The Endecja and the Jewish Question'. *Polin: Studies in Polish Jewry* 12:271–83.

Warsaw As It Was: Original City Maps before 1939 and in 1945. [text by Jerzy Kasprzycki]. 1985. Warsaw: Wydawnictwa ALFA.

Webster, Charles Kingsley and Frankland, Noble. 1961. *The Strategic Air Offensive against Germany, 1939–1945*. London: Her Majesty's Stationery Office.

Weeks, Theodore R. 2006. 'A Multi-Ethnic City in Transition: Vilnius's Stormy Decade, 1939–1949'. *Eurasian Geography and Economics* 47 (2):153–75.

Weeks, Theodore R. 2008. 'Remembering and Forgetting: Creating a Soviet Lithuanian Capital. Vilnius 1944–1949'. *Journal of Baltic Studies* 39 (4):517–33.

Weeks, Theodore R. 2015. *Vilnius between Nations, 1795–2000*. DeKalb: Northern Illinois University Press.

Wicher, Sebastian. 2009. 'The Architectural Legacy of Stanisław Bukowski in Vilnius – a Contribution to Further Research'. *Acta Academiae Artium Vilnensis* 98:140–79.

Wółkowski, Wojciech. 2021. 'Architecture in Warsaw, 1939–1944'. *Zeitschrift für Ostmitteleuropa-Forschung / Journal of East Central European Studies* 70 (4):689–708.

Wyporek, Bogdan. 2015. 'Warszawa 1945 i BOS'. Towarzystwo Urbanistów Polskich, Posted 14 February 2020 on https://www.tup.org.pl/

Zachwatowicz, Jan. 1938a. 'Odsłonięcie murów obronnych Starej Warszawy'. *Kronika Warszawy* 2–3:81–8.

Zachwatowicz, Jan. 1938b. 'O zabudowie Powiśla'. *Architektura i Budownictwo* 2:62–3.

Zachwatowicz, Jan. 1946a. 'Oskar Sosnowski'. *Biuletyn Historii Sztuki i Kultury* 1/2:6–11.

Zachwatowicz, Jan. 1946b. 'Program i zasady konserwacji zabytków'. *Biuletyn Historii Sztuki i Kultury* 8:48–52.

Zachwatowicz, Jan. 1953a. 'Stare Miasto Warszawa wraca do życia'. *Ochrona Zabytków* 6 (2–3):73–7.

Zachwatowicz, Jan. 1953b. 'Mury i barbakan Starej Warszawy'. *Ochrona Zabytków* 6 (2–3):93–106.

Zachwatowicz, Jan. 1981. 'O polskiej szkole odbudowy i konserwacji zabytków'. *Ochrona Zabytków* 34 (1–2):4–10.

Zachwatowicz et al. 1956. *Stare Miasto Warszawy w odbudowie*. Warsaw: Ministerstwo Kultury i Sztuki.

Zalewski, Paul. 2012. 'Zur ‚Konstruktion der Heimat' im funktionalistischen Aufbau Hannovers nach 1945'. *Biuletyn Polskiej Misji Historycznej* 7:293–338.

Zaremba, Marcin. 1997. 'Próba legitymizacji władzy komunistycznej w latach 1944–1947 poprzez odwołanie się do treści narodowych'. *Polska 1944/45–1989. Studia i Materiały* 2:35–61.

Zaremba, Marcin. 2001. *Komunizm, legitymacja, nacjonalizm. Nacjonalistyczna legitymacja władzy komunistycznej w Polsce*. Warsaw: Trio.

Zętar, Joanna et al. (eds). 2006. *The Jews in Lublin – The Jews in Lviv: Places – Memory – Present*. Lublin: John Paul II Catholic University of Lublin.

Zielinski, Konrad. 2009. 'To Pacify, Populate and Polonise: Territorial Transformations and the Displacement of Ethnic Minorities in Communist Poland, 1944–49'. In *Warlands: Population Resettlement and State Reconstruction in the Soviet Borderlands, 1945–50*, eds. P. Gatrell and N. Baron, 188–209. Basingstoke: Palgrave Macmillan.

Zubrzycki, Geneviève. 2011. 'History and the National Sensorium: Making Sense of Polish Mythology'. *Qualitative Sociology* 34 (1):21–57.

Zubrzycki, Geneviève. 2016. 'Nationalism, "Philosemitism", and Symbolic Boundary-Making in Contemporary Poland'. *Comparative Studies in Society and History* 58 (1): 66–98.

Zwierz, Krzysztof. 2014. 'Zapomnienie i uznanie. Zmienne losy Rynku i dzielnicy staromiejskiej w Warszawie na tle procesów modernizacyjnych do 1939 roku.' *Almanach Muzeum Warszawy* 8:117–50.

Zyblikiewicz, Lidia A. (ed.). 2022. *The Report on the Losses Sustained by Poland as a Result of German Aggression and Occupation during the Second World War, 1939–1945*. Vol. 1. Warsaw: Instytut Strat Wojennych im. Jana Karskiego.

Żeromska, Monika. 1994. *Wspomnień ciąg dalszy*. Warsaw: Czytelnik.

Żuk, Piotr. 2017. 'Inequalities, Social Exclusion and Radical Political Struggle – Some Historical and Social Thoughts on the Interwar Period in Poland (1918–1939)'. *European History Quarterly* 47 (3):509–17.

Index